MORE ADVANCE PRAISE FOR

Newspapers: A Complete Guide to the Industry

"The authors of this book explore the rapidly changing newspaper landscape through both the practiced eye of newsroom experience and focused lens of academic scholarship. The combination provides clear, fresh insights into the digital evolution of print news, without losing sight of the immutable principles of a free press. Readers are sure to enjoy this enlightening look at an industry in flux and the authors' convincing forecasts for the future."

J. Patrick Moynahan, Vice Provost, Northern Kentucky University,
Former city editor, The Kentucky Post

newspapers

Media Industries

David Sumner
General Editor

Vol. 6

PETER LANG
New York • Washington, D.C./Baltimore • Bern
Frankfurt • Berlin • Brussels • Vienna • Oxford

Mike Farrell and Mary Carmen Cupito

newspapers

A Complete Guide to the Industry

PETER LANG
New York • Washington, D.C./Baltimore • Bern
Frankfurt • Berlin • Brussels • Vienna • Oxford

Library of Congress Cataloging-in-Publication Data

Farrell, Mike.
Newspapers: a complete guide to the industry /
Mike Farrell, Mary Carmen Cupito.
p. cm. — (Media industries; vol. 6)
Includes bibliographical references and index.
1. Press—United States. 2. American newspapers.
I. Cupito, Mary Carmen. II. Title.
PN4855.F37   071'.3—dc22   2010001846
ISBN 978-0-8204-9509-5 (hardcover)
ISBN 978-0-8204-8153-1 (paperback)
ISSN 1550-1043

Bibliographic information published by **Die Deutsche Nationalbibliothek**.
Die Deutsche Nationalbibliothek lists this publication in the "Deutsche
Nationalbibliografie"; detailed bibliographic data is available
on the Internet at http://dnb.d-nb.de/.

Cover design by Clear Point Designs

The paper in this book meets the guidelines for permanence and durability
of the Committee on Production Guidelines for Book Longevity
of the Council of Library Resources.

© 2010 Peter Lang Publishing, Inc., New York
29 Broadway, 18th floor, New York, NY 10006
www.peterlang.com

Printed in the United States of America

Contents

Acknowledgments

We are passionate about newspapers and journalism. We both remember that when we were children, we loved to read the newspaper, to find out what the Cincinnati Reds had done, to learn what was going on in the world or just to enjoy an interesting story.

Newspapers have shaped our lives. One of us followed a traditional route, working on them in high school and in college, while the other came to journalism after other fields proved unfulfilling. We worked for them professionally after college, and now we both have spent years in classrooms trying to impart our knowledge—but especially our passion—for newspapers to another generation. We came to understand that newspapers and journalism are vitally important to a healthy democracy, and we make that point class after class, semester after semester, trusting that most of our students will see the light.

We learned journalism from our classroom teachers, but we also learned it from our newsroom colleagues. Some of the greatest teachers who shaped our skills were other reporters, assistant city editors, city editors, and editors.

In many ways, this book reflects the ideas and the impact of all those teachers who taught us how to write, our colleagues who taught us from their own experiences, and our editors who taught us from their knowledge. We stand on the shoulders of those who were willing to help us hone our skills. And it would be a huge oversight if we failed to mention that we have learned from our journalism students, who brought to the classroom that questioning spirit that forced us to rethink and re-examine what we teach.

The list of people to thank is endless. But special thanks are due to our editor David Sumner, who patiently encouraged us through this process. Mary Savigar at Peter Lang has been a steady guide throughout.

Deborah Chung, assistant professor at the University of Kentucky, wrote the chapter on newspapers and new media based on her research program. Al Cross, director of the Institute for Rural Journalism and Community Issues at the University of Kentucky, made large contributions to the chapter on rural newspapers. Richard Labunski, professor of journalism at the University of Kentucky, reviewed the chapter on newspapers and the law and made important suggestions.

And most importantly, we thank our spouses, who allowed us to write day after day, week after week and kept us from losing our minds when it didn't go well and it seemed like it would never end.

—Mike Farrell and Mary Carmen Cupito

Just What Is
News Anyway?

Even those who were children on November 22, 1963, remember the moment they heard the rumor that John F. Kennedy, the charismatic president, hero of PT 109 from World War II, had been shot in Dallas, Texas. The unthinkable, the unbelievable, struck on a Friday afternoon just before school ended in the Eastern Time Zone.

It was news that stopped a nation and plunged Americans into sorrow.

Almost six years later, astronaut Neil Armstrong set foot on the Moon on a sticky summer night, and Americans young and old held their breath until he uttered those famous words, "One small step for man, one giant leap for mankind." One estimate is that some 600 million people watched around the world.[1]

It was news that thrilled a nation and inspired a generation who learned it was possible to conquer new worlds.

The phone rang at the *Star-News* in Wilmington, North Carolina. The caller said, "I have a century plant my grandfather bought long ago and it's going to bloom Tuesday night and I thought the paper would like to know about it." The stringer who answered that call, a young reporter paid by the story, learned that a century plant blooms at intervals between five and one hundred years, hence its name. The *Star-News* ran a one-inch item quoting the plant owner. That night in 1938, the street was choked with traffic. The fire truck showed up to focus a floodlight on the street. Vendors sold grape and orange

Popsicles, and people knocked on neighbors' doors begging to use the bathroom. The reluctant plant, growing in a ceramic pot on the woman's porch, drew a crowd but didn't offer a bloom.

It was news that captivated a community and produced absolutely nothing. The stringer's story about the non-event landed him a job and launched a career.[2]

News is the reason 42.8 million people in the United States buy a newspaper every day.[3] That number has fallen from 61 million in 1968, but today's audience is still a large one, people looking to learn what is happening in their community, their state, their nation and the world.[4] They're paying for news.

Identifying the News

One of the first questions new journalism students are asked is "What is news?" Those who are going to report on it and write about it need to be able to recognize it. Surprisingly, no common answer exists to this most basic question about a practice, reporting, that is vital to the life of a democracy.

One dictionary defines news as "information about recent events or happenings, especially as reported by newspapers, periodicals, radio, or television."[5] A journalism history text defines news as "new information about a subject of some public interest that is shared with some portion of the public." In essence, news is what is on a society's mind.[6] Arthur McEwen, an editor of the *San Francisco Chronicle* declared, "News is anything that makes a reader say 'Gee Whiz!'"[7]

The most quoted definition of news is commonly attributed to John Bogart, city editor of the *New York Sun* in the late nineteenth century: "When a dog bites a man, that isn't news. It often happens. But if a man bites a dog, that's news."[8] Bogart's editor, Charles Dana, developed his own definition: News is "anything that interests a large part of the community and has never been brought to its attention before."[9] David Brinkley, the newspaper and wire service reporter who wrote about that century plant in Wilmington, North Carolina, before he became one of the most successful pioneers of television news, said news is "What I say it is."[10]

Perhaps most telling is a statement published in a journalism textbook more than a half-century ago: "It is easier to recognize news than to define it."[11]

Sociologist Stuart Hall wrote, "news is a slippery concept, with journalists defining newsworthiness as those things that get into the news media."[12] Most journalists approach their daily work without a strong theoretical understanding of what it is that separates what is news from what is not news. They claim to know news when they see it. The practice is circular; something becomes news because reporters and editors recognize it as news.

By definition, events that affect people are news. When the president announces a plan to raise taxes, the news media will cover it. When a member of the Supreme Court of the United States announces plans to retire, that is news. When a jet crashes into the ocean, that is news. When the automakers announce they are closing 25 percent of their dealerships, that is news. News outlets will cover these events.

But news is not only events that people want to know about and talk about with others. Journalists report and develop stories about less obvious items of interest and importance. They write stories about the city's budget, the most dangerous traffic intersections and the latest development in the fight to cure cancer.

Journalists don't make most decisions about whether something is newsworthy in a vacuum. They are bombarded by messages from political figures, corporations, issue advocates and civic organizations that aim to persuade journalists to publicize an event, an idea, or an accomplishment.[13] For example, one study found that most national news in the leading newspapers originated in routine channels in government institutions.[14] Another study showed that nearly half of local beat story ideas came from institutional sources.[15] In a study of statehouse news, the researcher discovered legislators were using reporters who could help them advance policy or institutional goals.[16]

Another element in the definition of news is the need or desire of the audience. Before the Internet, scholars argued that reporters and editors had a sense of what readers wanted to know and what readers needed to know, interesting or not, because it was important to their lives. But without effective feedback methods, reporters and editors were forced to predict what readers were looking for in newspaper content.[17] Sociologists argue that reporters' "sense of news," as it is commonly called, is learned from editors and colleagues in the newsrooms where they work and from their competitors on beats they cover.[18]

Some journalists have always marched to their own drummer, investigating stories that other reporters ignore until those who have ignored them are forced to play catch-up with the competition. The Internet has brought news sites and Web blogs where anyone with a keyboard can report and publish news.

News from the Beginning

"News" is an old word and an even older concept. By about 1500, people had begun using the word "tydings" to describe their exchanges of information. The word "newes" was coined to describe "tydings" of a more systematic sort: a deliberate method of gathering and sharing information that others might want to know.[19] "Newes" was the plural of "newe,"[20] meaning "new things," and so news was originally considered a plural

("There are news today from Washington").[21]

News, however, has a longer story. Ancient civilizations had alphabets and writing. Some Old Testament manuscripts, containing accounts of wars and the daily life of a people, are thousands of years old, for example. A new level of sophistication began during the Roman Empire, which became a power in about the sixth century B.C.

Rome's upper classes were highly literate and vitally interested in public affairs. An early attempt to systematically collect and distribute information was the *Acta Diurna Populi Romani*, a type of gazette recording the daily acts or occurrences of the Roman people, which was begun by Julius Caesar. The "news" usually consisted of official government actions, decrees and votes by the Roman Senate. It also contained general information about goings-on in Rome and other parts of the Roman Empire, and news of famous people, fires, executions and even the weather.

The *Acta Diurna* was hand-lettered and carved on stone or metal and posted regularly in the forum and other popular public places, such as the baths, in Rome. According to the Roman historian Suetonius, these records began appearing about 59 B.C., and the *Historia Augusta* refers to them as late as A.D. 222.[22] Those who could not read sometimes stood around listening while someone read the news aloud. The wealthy sometimes sent a literate slave to make a copy for sharing at a dinner party or for mailing to friends abroad. At the end of the first century A.D., the *Acta Diurna* departed from its official tradition and began reporting crime, divorces, marriages, gossip and bizarre events. Since the later "editions" were written on perishable papyrus, copies have not survived.[23]

Journalists never have agreed upon a definition of "news," which is central to their business. What constitutes news in American newspapers—and other forms of mass media—has evolved and continues to evolve in the Internet age. While in one way it has changed so radically that the country's earliest editors would probably neither recognize nor approve of the tidings in newspapers of today, in another way the roots of what makes the news *newsworthy* can be traced back to the newspapers that started when the country did.

Deciding what is news is the most important element of the journalistic process. It determines how reporters and editors work. It determines the nature of the information the public has to work with.[24] A 2001 study of one hundred newspaper markets concluded newspapers are remarkably consistent both in what is considered news and in how it's covered.[25]

Deciding What Is Newsworthy: News Judgment

If journalists have a hard time defining news, they have a formula for deciding what is newsworthy. Most college textbooks on reporting detail a list of journalism values to help students identify the news. Those lists vary. One textbook written by a veteran newspaper and wire service reporter suggested news could be identified by the significance of the event, the impact on readers, the timeliness of that event, the proximity to the audience, the unusualness of the event and the inclusion of prominent people, conflict, human interest and humor.[26]

Another textbook identifies impact, weight (or seriousness), controversy, emotion, unusualness, involvement of prominent people, proximity, timeliness, currency (what people are talking about) and information that is useful and has educational value.[27] One textbook includes entertainment (stories that make readers laugh), helpfulness (how-to and consumer information), inspiration (stories about people who have overcome difficulties), trends (shifts in issues that affect people's lives such as crime, the price of gasoline, vacation plans), community problems and special interests (such as business, religion, news for women).[28]

One of the standard reporting textbooks—the eleventh edition was published in 2008—lists eight values to determine the "newsworthiness of events, personalities and ideas": timeliness, impact, prominence, proximity, conflict, the unusual, currency and necessity (defined as something a journalist has learned that he or she believes must be disclosed to readers).[29] Another standard text reduces the list to six characteristics: timeliness, impact, prominence, proximity, singularity (unusualness) and conflict or controversy.[30]

Just as journalists don't agree on a definition of news, so scholars who write textbooks for journalism students don't agree on what values in stories make them newsworthy. The lists vary to some degree, and some textbooks appear to combine categories with broader definitions. In any event, journalism students are taught that news can be defined by a formula that is broad enough to include many events.

The Missouri Group text, in its ninth edition, lists these six news values:[31]

Impact

News makes a difference. Whether they affect a lot of people slightly or a few people deeply, events that are relevant to the lives of readers are news. If an abandoned barn five miles out of town was blown over in the storm last night, the news value ranges from minimal to nil, even in the smallest news market. But if the wind tore shingles off of one-third of the homes on the city's south side, the news value is high. Reporters will seek construction "experts" to assess the damage, weather "experts" to explain why such wind developed and eyewitnesses to tell their experience, explain their loss and, if they are displaced, say where they are headed. News impacts people.

Journalists have to make sure they answer questions readers will ask: Why should I care about this story? What does this story mean to me?

Journalists must translate their stories into personal terms. For example, it is not enough to tell readers the city council is considering a proposal to raise property taxes by 1 percent. Journalists must tell readers that this means the owner of a home valued at $100,000 will pay $250 more per year if the increase is approved. It is not enough to tell readers the hurricane contaminated the water supply; journalists must tell them where they can get safe water and how long this crisis will last.

Conflict

This is a central issue in life; people struggle to overcome obstacles and health issues; politicians debate ideas and policy agendas; countries go to war over resources, territory and ideologies. Strife has been an element in storytelling since the beginning of the human race.

Much of the news involves conflict. Candidate Smith is running to unseat Congresswoman Jones. Mayor Brown disagrees with Police Chief Green's latest policy concerning police department overtime, and they debate their positions during a city meeting. The state Senate wants to spend $250 million on improving water treatment facilities, while the governor is asking for twice that. The school board has voted to close three elementary schools, and parents are upset their children will no longer be able to attend classes right in their own neighborhood. The accused in a murder trial has maintained his innocence since the day he was interviewed by police. Professor Williams is suing the university, claiming he was fired because his views are not the views of the president.

Conflict involves drama, usually has something at stake for both sides and allows readers to identify with one side or the other. Conflict is also somewhat comfortable for reporters to cover; giving both sides an opportunity to explain their positions fits into the reporting practices of journalists seeking to be fair.

Novelty

Something that happens rarely or is virtually unthinkable is news. The first child born in the century, the first patient in a new hospital or the first time a Hispanic judge is elevated to the Supreme Court—all are news. Anything happening for the first time or the last time is a pretty sure bet as a news choice. The unusual—a swarm of insects pestering a pitcher during the World Series or a cat running across the football field while a tailback sets sail for the end zone—is also a strong news candidate.

Some of the most famous sports stories involve events that were never supposed to happen or the underdog that pulled off an unthinkable upset. The 1986 movie *Hoosiers* thrilled audiences with the story of a high school basketball team from Milan, Indiana, enrollment 161, that won the 1954 state basketball championship on a last-second shot by Bobby Plump. In the 1980 Winter Olympics, the U.S. team upset the favored team from the Soviet Union and went to the championship game, where it won the gold medal. The unexpected is news.

Prominence

Names are news. The death of a star such as Michael Jackson is a huge news event. Stars are news when they marry, divorce, have children, win an award or hold a concert, or when someone thinks they have married or divorced. The public's appetite for celebrity news seems insatiable. If one car backs into another car on Broadway in Lexington, Kentucky, reporters will not rush to the scene. But if the president of the University of Kentucky was driving one car and the men's basketball coach was driving the other, it is a major human-interest story, even though no one was injured and the damage was minimal. Names are news.

Proximity

The closer an event is to home, the more likely readers are to be interested. If two men are killed in Seoul, South Korea, the story is likely to get little notice in the *Columbus Dispatch* in Ohio. If two Ohio State University students are killed in an apartment fire in Columbus, readers will look for that story. But it is also news in Columbus if a Columbus family vacationing in California has to be rescued from a forest fire.

Another kind of proximity is related to connections. Editors in Lexington, Kentucky., will look at using stories from anywhere about horses because of the state's many horse farms. Editors in Illinois and Iowa will review any story about new uses for corn. Newspapers near military bases will pay special attention to news relating to military actions, policies, deployments and budgets.

Timeliness

By its very label, news is something new, something that just happened: Breaking news is the election results just announced, the violence that just broke out, the football game that just ended, the prisoners who just escaped, the tornado that just touched down. News is the update on the search for the escapees, the death toll from the tornado, the pre-inauguration plans for a new administration.

Historical events are not news unless something has been learned for the first time or something related has just happened: the death of the last survivor of the *Titanic*, the diary of a soldier found in an attic. Historical events are news again on anniversaries of the original event. November 22 never goes by without some remembrance of the assassination in Dallas of the president in 1963. September 11 will be marked with ceremonies for decades to come.

Timeliness is a relatively recent addition to the definition of news. Early newspapers published "news" that was months old. The invention of the telegraph in 1844 changed that. The invention of the radio, and later of the television, gave timeliness even more immediacy. Newspapers for decades trailed radio and then television in the ability to be first with a story. Now, utilizing their websites, newspapers can continue to update an ongoing story even after the newspaper has gone to press.

One added element of timeliness is its importance in a democracy. Reporting that the city council has approved a proposal to tear down five blocks in downtown to make way for a hotel/shopping complex is relatively useless to those who disagree with the decision; a story published before the vote would have allowed opponents to learn more about the proposal and build a case against it.

No list of factors could unmask the mystery of news judgment, and no formula could explain all the factors that are involved in story selection. Anyone who has ever participated in a meeting to plan the front-page layout for the next edition—except on those occasions when blockbuster stories are breaking—knows that if five editors meet, more than one opinion will develop as to how the next day's front page should look. A study of news meetings found that editors relied on four factors—potential audience, type of impact, area and conflict—to choose front-page stories.[32]

The news values journalists look for are affected by other factors as well. The newspaper's audience, the environmental factors of the community and the newspaper's traditional role in that community all influence how journalists identify news for publication. Media scholar George Gerbner observed more than four decades ago, "There is no fundamentally non-ideological apolitical, non-partisan news gathering and reporting system."[33] News selection is not always an impersonal decision, either. A journalist's relationships, memberships and interests can factor into the formula. It is easier to tell a stranger that your newspaper doesn't write stories about the birth of twins than it is to tell that to your sister who just delivered them. It is easier to tell the public relations officer of a large company that his event isn't newsworthy than to tell that to someone who interned at the newspaper last summer.[34]

Despite the subjective nature of news selection by use of an indefinite list of news values, the differences in newspaper coverage areas and the differences among various media, it is no stretch to declare that the news is the news. A comparative study of news published in two Chicago newspapers and broadcast on six nightly newscasts, half of them local to Chicago, during a fifty-day period in the fall of 2000 found that the same kind of stories were reported across all media. Graber called the media in this study "rivals in conformity."[35]

A forty-year-old study offers some interesting insights into the interplay of media. The study found that the news media actually complement each other: (1) To some degree, they convey the same information to different people. (2) They display different aspects of the identical information to different people. (3) They also display different aspects of the identical information to the same people. (4) Finally they arouse and reinforce interests which other media help to satisfy. (Television has stimulated interest in spectator sports, but this only increased the readership of newspaper sports pages.)[36]

Newspaper Content

Staff organization helps drive newspaper content. Newspaper reporters have traditionally been assigned to coverage beats, either a topic, such as business or education, or a geographic area, such as the inner city or the near suburbs. Once assigned to such a beat, the reporter must know what is going on in terms of that topic or coverage area and must produce stories from the beat. As part of that assignment, reporters will develop sources who are likely to tip them to news events and provide them more details of a story, and they will develop expertise, understanding of the geographic or topic area, that will allow them to do a better job of putting events in context for readers. On the other hand, content areas that are not assigned to a regular reporter will produce fewer news stories and will be covered by a general assignment reporter, who will likely have little background and fewer sources to rely on for a news story.

The average newspaper, according to a study of fifty-two newspapers conducted in October 2003 by the Readership Institute, consisted of roughly one-half editorial content, one-quarter paid ads and one-quarter classified ads.[37]

Those figures may have changed as a result of an economic recession and a declining readership. During the first quarter of 2009, for example, the National Newspaper Association reported that newspaper advertising nationwide had declined 28 percent over the first quarter in 2008.[38] Over the same period, circulation declined 7 percent,[39] and to save money, newspapers have been shrinking the size of their daily products.

The Readership Institute analysis also found:

- Two topics dominated news content: politics/government and sports. Together they accounted for nearly half of all stories in newspapers.
- Almost half (45 percent) of the stories on the front page were about government and politics, and nearly one-third of them were produced by wire or news services.
- Overall, wire stories accounted for almost half (about 45 percent) of all stories in newspapers during the study period.
- Stories about ordinary people, obituaries and community announcements made up less than 5 percent of the content.
- Visual aids—photos, graphics or emphasized text—accompanied less than half of stories, although more visuals appeared in Sunday editions. Front-page stories on average were more likely to have photos and graphic elements.

A 2001 Readership Institute study of one hundred newspaper markets in the United States found that the typical weekday U.S. newspaper offered its readers a mix of news that emphasized (1) sports; (2) politics, government and war; (3) police and crime; (4) health, home, food, fashion and travel and

(5) business stories. These five categories added up to nearly 75 percent of the content. A mix of entertainment, science, arts, disasters and other subjects accounted for the remainder.[40]

Because of the seasonal nature of sports—for example, professional sports dominate during the summer months, when college sports are idle—the results will be swayed by the season and the proximity to teams. The study found sports coverage to be divided into 40 percent professional sports, 38 percent college (inflated because of the National Collegiate Athletic Association basketball tournament, which fell during the study period), 13 percent high school and 10 percent women's sports (at all levels).

The second major category, politics, divided into 38 percent stories about elections, 22 percent stories about the impact of government on business, 11 percent crime (for example, stories about official corruption) and 8 percent war; the balance was spread out over a range of other topics.[41]

Smaller newspapers put more locally written stories on their front pages than did larger papers, 58 percent to 43 percent. Perhaps this fact is explained by the finding that larger newspapers devoted more front-page space to national and international stories.

But that is the front page. Overall, the Readership Institute found that newspapers covered local news in the same proportion regardless of size. On average, newspapers filled 34 percent of space with local news, 16 percent with state and regional news, 40 percent with national news and 10 percent with international news.[42]

Other findings:

- Larger newspapers used more photographs, one for every two stories, compared with one photograph for every three stories in smaller newspapers.
- Larger newspapers published slightly more graphics.
- Larger newspapers produced more long stories. Smaller newspapers ran 10 percent long stories, compared with 13 percent in the largest newspapers. In Sunday editions, the difference was 15 percent to 23 percent for large papers.
- Large newspapers printed 54 percent "straight news" stories on Sunday, versus 65 percent for smaller papers. Weekday figures were almost identical: 71 percent straight news.[43]

A study of media content in ten countries, predominately newspapers but also including television and radio news, found that the most prevalent news stories concerned sports and internal politics.[44] Sports stories were most frequent in Australia, South Africa and the United States and least frequent in China. Internal politics was the most frequent topic in Chile, China, India and Russia. Business and commerce news was found more frequently in the United States than in the other countries and more frequently than internal politics.

The study also found that the topics of newspaper coverage differed from the coverage of television. In the United States, newspaper coverage was 17 percent about sports, 15 percent about business, 12 percent about internal politics and 10.5 percent about cultural events. Television news, in contrast, was 29 percent about sports, 11 percent about business, 11 percent about internal politics and 2 percent about cultural events.[45]

The authors of the study concluded that despite the many differences relating to language, economy, geography, culture, political systems, population and area, they found "remarkable agreement across the countries on what kinds of events, ideas and people should constitute news."[46]

The content analysis of 2008 newspapers conducted for the annual *The State of the News Media* prepared by the Project for Excellence in Journalism found that the leading news story was the presidential campaign and election (23 percent); that was followed by news of the U.S. economy, including the financial crisis, economic issues, gas/oil prices, the failing U.S. auto industry, and the economic failure of Freddie Mac/Fannie Mae (19 percent); and then by the Iraq War (6 percent). These three topics filled almost half of the space newspapers devoted to news in 2008.

Other topics in 2008 that received 2 percent or 1 percent (in descending order) were domestic terrorism, immigration, the Olympics, health care, Pakistan, Afghanistan and the conflict between the nations of Georgia and Russia.[47]

Breaking down those numbers uncovers what the report called "some notable differences in the news agenda." Newspapers with circulations of less than 100,000 covered the economic downturn more extensively than the 2008 election. The smaller newspapers' coverage of the war in Iraq focused on how it was affecting the home front, even more than events unfolding inside Iraq. The report concluded, "These findings suggest that the more community-oriented dailies were well positioned to report on national or even international issues by covering the local angle to a bigger story."[48]

Media scholar Walter Lippmann suggested that a key role of the press is to signal important developments as soon as possible.[49] In fulfilling that role, newspapers convey to their readers a sense of what the community is like. But their content choices can actually distort the pictures newspapers create.

Crime reporting is the most frequently cited example of this. Murder and sexual assault are obviously among the most serious crimes. A study of crime reporting in the *Chicago Tribune* in 2000 found that murder accounted for 31 percent of the crime stories reported in the newspaper and sexual assault accounted for 12 percent. However, the two crimes together represented just about 1 percent of the crimes reported in Chicago that year. Robbery, theft, burglary and arson represented 86 percent of the crimes in Chicago, and 43 percent of the crimes reported. If Lippmann's argument is correct, Chicagoans had a distorted view of their safety.[50]

Reporting from Washington

Arguably, only New York City, the financial and publishing capital of the United States, rivals Washington as a source for news in this country. The White House, the Congress and the Supreme Court of the United States are institutions that dominate the political news, all located in the nation's capital.

To cover this news, organizations and newspapers have long had bureaus in Washington. In 1985, more than 600 newspapers had bureaus covering the capital. A Pew Center special report updated in mid-2009 found the number was down more than half, to just about 300. The report asserted that this "transformation will markedly alter what Americans know and (do) not know about the new government (elected in 2008), as well as who will know it and who will not."[51]

For example, Newhouse, which once had twenty-six reporters in a Washington bureau, now has no bureau. Copley Newspapers and Copley News Service, which once had nine reporters, now has no bureau. *BusinessWeek*, which once had twenty reporters, now has three. The Pew report found that only the *New York Times* and the *Wall Street Journal* have managed to maintain their Washington bureau staffing levels.

The report's findings suggest:[52]

- The reporting power of mainstream newspapers has declined significantly. The number of newspaper reporters accredited to cover Congress has fallen by 30 percent, according to *Congressional Directories*.
- The retreat of the mainstream press has made room for niche publications, specialty newspapers, magazines and newsletters. The number of staff accredited to cover Congress for these outlets grew nearly 50 percent from 1997 to 2009, according to *Congressional Directories*.
- The number of representatives of foreign media covering Washington has grown from 160 in 1968 to about 1,600 in 2008. The Pew report suggested that their presence has changed the way the world learns about American news and that it affects America's image.

Health Coverage

A recurring story since the early 1990s has been the high cost of health care in this country, the lack of health insurance for a sizeable portion of the population and the effort to make it more affordable and more available. Health care was heavily debated during the 2008 presidential election campaign. A study of newspaper content as early as 1981 found that news about health issues was of moderate interest to readers. ("Moderate interest" was the middle of three categories used in that study.)[53]

According to the News Coverage Index produced by the Pew Research Center's Project for Excellence in Journalism, during the eighteen months from January 2007 though June 2008 health was the eighth most covered subject in the national news. The study, which included small, medium and large newspaper markets and network television news, found that health news constituted 3.6 percent of all coverage. One limitation is that the study measured only front-page stories.[54]

Of greater value is the contrast. The amount of health news the study found was more than three times the amount of coverage for education or transportation, but much less than coverage for foreign affairs, crime or natural disasters.

The health topic that received the most coverage, 16 percent of the total, was the debate over health care policies in the United States. The disease that received the most media attention was cancer, perhaps driven around the diagnoses of Elizabeth Edwards, wife of presidential candidate John Edwards, and Tony Snow, a former journalist and talk radio host who was then White House press secretary. The Pew study found cancer received 10 percent of the coverage, diabetes and obesity received 5 percent, heart disease was third at 4 percent and HIV/AIDS and autism each received 2 percent.[55]

But the future looks less bright as newspapers reduce staff and the space for news content. In a survey of members of the Association of Health Care Journalists, 40 percent said fewer reporters were covering the health beat since they began working at their media outlet, while 16 percent said there were more. More than one third of the respondents believed their position could be eliminated in the next few years.[56]

One result of the decimation of reporting staff is the loss of experience. One veteran reporter, interviewed for a report on the state of health care journalism, said, "It takes time to develop expertise to cover health care with authority. When you downsize something has to give. What gives is both quality and quantity."[57] While the number of jobs lost could be measured, what cannot be measured is the impact the loss of health care expertise will have on the debate over President Obama's push for health care reform.

But researchers long have raised questions about the quality of health-related information newspapers and other media provide. An Annenberg Public Policy Center study found that even though the media devoted considerable coverage to the 1993 health care reform debate, the coverage proved less than useful to much of the public. Problems the report cited included the use of jargon the public could not understand, focus on only some of the reform alternatives introduced in Congress and stories that discussed political strategy for passage of the bill rather than accurate information and analysis of competing policy positions.[58]

Sports Coverage

James Michener, the Pulitzer Prize-winning novelist, once observed that the best-written stories in a newspaper are often found on the sports pages, perhaps one of the reasons newspapers devote so much space to sports' many topics.[59]

The first sports story appeared in 1733, a story in the *Boston Gazette* about a boxing match between John Faulconer and Bob Russel.[60] The *Spirit of the Times*, the first weekly sports newspaper in the United States, began providing information about horse racing, hunting and fishing in 1831.[61] After Joseph Pulitzer purchased the *New York World* in 1883, he formed what is considered the first newspaper sports department.[62] His reporters covered boxing, baseball, football and racing of all sorts—horse racing, roller-skating and bicycling.[63] William Randolph Hearst is credited with publishing the nation's first sports section in 1895 in the *New York Journal*, and by the 1920s, sports sections were pervasive across the country because editors learned what Hearst learned: They increased circulation.[64] One of the last daily newspapers to establish a sports section was *The New York Times*. Former managing editor Arthur Gelb wrote, "From its inception, *The Times* had looked upon sports as an uncouth country cousin, acknowledging its existence but treating it as though it didn't quite belong at the same table as 'the real news.'"[65]

In the 1920s, sports represented between 12 and 20 percent of a newspaper's editorial content. That percentage remained through the 1970s and then began to expand because readers wanted it and because covering sports was not expensive and generated little controversy. When *USA Today* debuted, it devoted almost 25 percent of its content to sports. Sportswriter Frank Deford described the national newspaper as "a daily *Sporting News* wrapped in color weather maps."[66]

Television's embrace of sports changed the way newspapers covered sporting events. It was no longer necessary to offer a play-by-play account of an event that millions had watched. This opened the door to more analysis and background information about the sport, the games and the players. Newspapers also placed a greater emphasis on statistics. Reporters tried to improve their stories with post-game interviews in the locker room.[67]

Sports pages remain among the best-read sections of the newspaper. Male readers are likely to turn to the sports section after reading the front page and the local news section. The sports section is read by 76 percent of men and 34 percent of women. Sports attracts readers of all ages—from 55 percent for those aged eighteen to twenty-four to 56 percent for those over sixty-five.[68]

Studies have consistently shown that despite women making up 40 percent of the athletes in high school, college and the Olympics, sports coverage continues to emphasize male athletes in both quantity and quality.[69] One topic that has become increasingly important over the years is the business of sports: franchises worth millions, athletes seeking contracts far in excess of what average Americans earn, efforts to build new stadiums with taxpayer support, salary caps and a host of other issues.[70]

The Times (and All Newspapers) Are *A-Changing*

Newspapers in the United States have changed dramatically in the past few years, faced with declining ad revenue, competition from other media and a severe economic recession. Today most newspapers have fewer pages, fewer features and smaller pages, and most of them have far fewer reporters. Some newspapers no longer even exist. Those that do usually have a website where readers can check for updated news or get their news for free. Most of these sites are interactive. This means, for the first time, editors don't have to commission surveys or form focus groups to find out what readers want to read in newspapers because the interactive features give them a better idea than they have ever had.

All of these changes mean, of course, that the content has been affected. A Project for Excellence in Journalism report in 2008, even before some of the worst economic news intensified newspaper cuts, found, on the basis of a survey of 250 senior newsroom executives, that over the three previous years:[71]

- Newspapers large and small had begun investing a larger percentage of their shrinking resources and their front-page display in covering local news rather than national and international news. A whopping 97 percent of the executives surveyed labeled local news as "very essential" to their news product. Even among the largest newspapers, the percentage was 94. Almost two-thirds of the executives said their newspaper was devoting more of its space to community and neighborhood news.
- The amount of foreign coverage had decreased, even at a time when U.S. military forces were engaged in Afghanistan and Iraq, Iran and Korea were drawing world attention for their aspirations for nuclear weapons, the world economy was staggering along with the American stock market and China was continuing to make major inroads in world trade. Almost two-thirds (64 percent) of editors interviewed for the survey said the amount of space dedicated to foreign news had declined during the previous three years, and only 10 percent deemed foreign coverage as "very essential."
- The amount of space for national news had been reduced by 57 percent of the newsroom executives over the past three years; 18 percent said they considered national news "very essential." These cuts were made and these opinions expressed in the middle of a

presidential election during a year in which the incumbent could not seek re-election.

The newspapers also reported that over the three-year period they had reduced the amount of space and resources for coverage of science, the arts, lifestyles and business. Thirty-four percent of the executives said their newspapers were devoting less space to business, even though the country was in the middle of the worst economic downturn since the Great Depression.

Topics that the Pew Center report found were getting more reporting resources than three years earlier included education, police and crime, local government and politics, investigative reporting, sports, the environment and obituaries. Twenty percent of executives said their newspapers were devoting more space to courts, while 20 percent said their newspapers were reducing court coverage.[72]

One of the factors driving all of this change, of course, is the Internet. The Pew Center report found that 57 percent of the executives interviewed believed the Internet was a newspaper's ally, agreeing "web technology offers the potential for greater-than-ever journalism and will be the savior of what we once thought of as newspaper newsrooms."[73]

Since the early 1990s, the proportion of Americans saying they read a newspaper on a typical day has declined by about 40 percent; the proportion that regularly watches nightly network news has fallen by half. The 2008 news consumption survey by the Pew Research Center for the People & the Press found that the percentage of news consumers who said they had read a newspaper the day before had fallen from 58 percent in 1994 to 34 percent, and from 40 percent to 34 percent in the past two years alone. But factored into those figures are newspaper websites. Most of the loss in readership since 2006 has come among those who read the print newspaper; those who read only the print version fell from 34 percent in 2006 to 27 percent in 2008.[74]

Newspapers are changing dramatically and quickly. The content is different, the size of the newspaper is smaller, the staff is smaller and the urgency of publishing the news to compete with the electronic media is greater. And it is very possible that this is still an early phase of change and not the last phase.

Notes

1. Guinness World Records, www.guinnessworldrecords.com/news/2008/02/080228.aspx
2. David Brinkley, *Brinkley's Beat* (New York: Knopf, 2003), x.
3. Ryan Chittum, "Newspaper Readers Buy Papers for the Content," *Columbia Journalism Review*, posted on July 23, 2009, available at http://www.cjr.org/the_audit/newspaper_readers_buy_papers_f.php.

4. Leo Bogart, "Changing News Interests and the News Industry," *Public Opinion Quarterly*, (Winter 1968–69, Volume 32:4), 560–574.

5. *The American Heritage Dictionary of the English Language* (Boston, Mass.: Houghton Mifflin, 2000, 4th ed.), 1185.

6. Mitchell Stephens, *A History of News* (Fort Worth, Tex.: Harcourt & Brace, 1997), 4.

7. James Fallows, "The President and the Press," *Washington Monthly*, October 1979, 9–17, cited in Everette E. Dennis and Arnold H. Ismach, *Reporting Processes and Practices: Newswriting for Today's Readers* (Belmont, Calif.: Wadsworth, 1981), 30.

8. "John B. Bogart Dies, Veteran Journalist: City Editor of The Sun From 1873 to 1890 and a Master Teacher of His Day Was 75," *New York Times*, September 18, 1921.

9. Quoted in Melvin Mencher, *News Reporting and Writing* (Boston, Mass.: McGraw-Hill, 2008, 11th ed.), 61.

10. Quoted in John R. Bender et al., *Reporting for the Media* (New York: Oxford University Press, 2009, 9th ed.), 127.

11. Stanley Johnson and Julian Harris, *The Complete Reporter: A General Text in News Writing and Editing, Complete with Exercises* (New York: Macmillan, 1942), 19, cited in Barbie Zelizer, "Definitions of Journalism," in Geneva Overholser and Kathleen Hall Jamieson, eds., *The Press* (New York: Oxford University Press, 2005), 67.

12. Stuart Hall, "The Determination of News Photographs," in Stanley Cohen and Jock Young, eds., *The Manufacture of News: A Reader* (Beverly Hills, Calif.: Sage, 1973), 226–243.

13. Judy VanSlyke Turk, "Public Relations' Influence on the News," *Newspaper Research Journal* (Summer 1986, Volume 7:4), 15–27.

14. Leon V. Sigal, *Reporters and Officials* (Lexington, Mass.: D.C. Heath, 1973), cited in Frederick Fico and Stan Soffin, "Covering Local Conflict: Fairness in Reporting a Public Policy Issue," *Newspaper Research Journal* (Fall 1994, Volume 15:4), 66.

15. Stephen Lacy and David Matustik, "Dependence on Organization and Beat Sources for Story Ideas," *Newspaper Research Journal* (Winter 1984), 9–16, cited in Fico and Soffin, *supra* note 14.

16. Frederick Fico, "How Lawmakers Use Reporters," *Journalism Quarterly* (Winter 1984), 793–800, cited in Fico and Soffin, *supra* note 14.

17. Pamela J. Shoemaker and Stephen D. Reese, *Mediating the Message* (White Plains, N.Y.: Longman, 1991), 91.

18. Doris Graber, *Mass Media and American Politics* (Washington, D.C.: CQ Press, 2002), 95–98. See also Warren Breed, "Social Control in the Newsroom," in Wilbur Schramm, ed., *Mass Communication* (Urbana, Ill.: University of Illinois Press, 1960), 178–194.

19. Michael Emery, Edwin Emery and Nancy L. Roberts, *The Press and America: An Interpretive History of the Mass Media* (Boston, Mass.: Allyn & Bacon, 2000, 9th ed.), 8.

20. *The American Heritage Dictionary of the English Language*, *supra* note 5, at 1185.

21. Bergen Evans and Cornelia Evans, *A Dictionary of Contemporary American Usage* (New York: Random House, 1957), 317.

22. Stephens, *supra* note 6.

23. William David Sloan, ed., *The Media in America: A History* (Northport, Ala.: Vision Press, 2008, 7th ed.), 7.

24. Dennis and Ismach, *supra* note 7, at 28.

25. "Newspaper Content: What Makes Readers More Satisfied," Readership Institute, posted June 2001, available at http://www.readership.org/new_readers/data/content_analysis.pdf.

26. Maria Braden and Richard L. Roth, *Getting the Message Across: Writing for the Mass Media* (Boston, Mass.: Houghton Mifflin, 1997), 82–86.

27. Jerry Lanson and Mitchell Stephens, *Writing and Reporting the News* (New York: Oxford University Press, 2000, 3rd ed.), 7–14.

28. Carol Rich, *Writing and Reporting News: A Coaching Method* (Belmont, Calif.: Wadsworth, 2000, 3rd ed.), 20–25.

29. Mencher, *supra* note 9, at 63–67.

30. Bender et al., *supra* note 10, at 128–132.

31. Brian Brooks et al., *News Reporting and Writing* (Boston, Mass.: Bedford/St. Martin's, 2008, 9th ed.), 6.

32. George Sylvie and J. Sonia Huang, "Value Systems and Decision-Making Styles of Front-Line Editors," *Journalism and Mass Communication Quarterly* (Spring 2008, Volume 85:1), 61–82.

33. George Gerbner, "Ideological Perspective and Political Tendencies in News Reporting," *Journalism Quarterly* (August 1964), 495–508, cited in Graber, *supra* note 18, at 104.

34. Minabere Ibelema, "Becoming More Critical When Teaching about News Values," *Journalism and Mass Communication Educator* (Summer 2000, Volume 55:2), 73–77.

35. Graber, *supra* note 18, at 112. She attributed the term to Stanley K. Bigman, "Rivals in Conformity: A Study of Two Competing Dailies," *Journalism Quarterly* (August 1949), 127–131.

36. Bogart, *supra* note 4, at 562.

37. "An Analysis of Content in 52 U.S. Daily Newspapers," Readership Institute, posted June 2001, available at http://www.readership.org/new_readers/data/content_analysis.pdf

38. "Community Papers Report First Quarter 2009 Results," National Newspaper Association, posted on June 3, 2009, available at http://www.nna.org/eweb/Dynamicpage.aspx?webcode=NewsTemplate&wps_key=f3c86c1b-0a6e-42ea-8ef1-39133809803e.

39. Shira Ovide and Russell Adams, "Circulation Drops at Most Big Newspapers," *Wall Street Journal*, April 28, 2009.

40. "Newspaper Content: What Makes Readers More Satisfied," *supra* note 25.

41. Ibid.

42. Ibid.

43. Ibid.

44. Pamela J. Shoemaker and Akiba A. Cohen, *News around the World* (New York: Routledge, 2006), 37.

45. Ibid., 40–45.

46. Ibid., 45.

47. "The State of the News Media 2009," Pew Project for Excellence in Journalism, available at *http://www.stateofthemedia.org/2009/index.htm*. Accessed Nov. 19, 2009.

48. Ibid.

49. Walter Lippmann, *Public Opinion* (New York: Simon & Schuster, 1927, 1997 ed.).

50. Graber, *supra* note 18, at 107.

51. "The New Washington Press Corps: A Special Report," Pew Research Center's Project for Excellence in Journalism, updated on July 16, 2009, available at http://www.journalism.org/node/14678.

52. Ibid.
53. Michael Burgoon, Judee K. Burgoon and Miriam Wilkinson, "Dimensions and Readership of Newspaper Content," *Newspaper Research Journal* (October 1981, Volume 3:1), 74–93.
54. "Health News Coverage in the U.S. Media," Pew Research Center's Project for Excellence in Journalism, posted on November 24, 2008, available at http://www.journalism.org/node/13770.
55. Ibid.
56. Kaiser Family Foundation/Association of Health Care Journalists, "Survey of AHCJ Members," in Gary Schwitzer, *The State of the Health Journalism in the U.S.: A Report to the Kaiser Family Foundation* (March 2009), 2, available at http://www.kff.org/entmedia/upload/7858.pdf.
57. Ibid.
58. Kathleen Hall Jamieson and Joseph N. Cappella, "Media in the Middle: Fairness and Accuracy in the 1994 Health Care Reform Debate," a report by the Annenberg Public Policy Center of the University of Pennsylvania, 1995.
59. Wayne Wanta, "The Coverage of Sports in Print Media," in Arthur A. Raney and Jennings Bryant, eds., *Handbook of Sports and Media* (Mahwah, N.J.: Erlbaum, 2006), 105.
60. Daniel Beck and Louis Bosshart, "Sports and the Press," *Communication Research Trends* (2003, Volume 22:4), 6.
61. Frederic Hudson, *Journalism in the United States from 1690 to 1872* (New York: Harper and Brothers, 1873), 341.
62. Wanta, *supra* note 59, at 106.
63. Paul M. Pederson, Kimberly S. Moloch and Pamela C. Laucella, *Strategic Sports Communication* (Champaign, Ill.: Human Kinetics, 2007), 155.
64. Ibid.
65. Arthur Gelb, *City Room* (New York: Putnam, 2003), cited in Pederson et al., *supra* note 63, at 156.
66. Robert McChesney, "Media Made Sport: A History of Sports in the United States," in Lawrence A. Wenner, ed., *Media Sports and Society* (Thousand Oaks, Calif.: Sage, 1989), 66.
67. Ibid., 67.
68. "2008 Readership Report," Newspaper Association of America, 2008, available at *http://www.naa.org/TrendsandNumbers/Readership.aspx*. Accessed November 19, 2009.
69. Ibid.
70. Ibid., 109.
71. "The Changing Newsroom," Pew Research Center's Project for Excellence in Journalism, posted on July 21, 2008, available at http://www.journalism.org/node/11961.
72. Ibid., available at http://www.journalism.org/node/11963.
73. Ibid., available at http://www.journalism.org/node/11966.
74. "Key News Audiences Now Blend Online and Traditional Sources," Pew Research Center for the People & the Press, August 17, 2008, available at http://people-press.org/report/444/news-media.

2

The History of Newspapers

Newspapers have always offered their writers a pulpit. Journalists recognize the extraordinary power of words, words that tell entertaining stories or recount horrific tales, words that applaud the way things are or cry for change. Because words can rouse the populace, governments have always wanted to control the press, even in America. The stories of the people who produced this country's newspapers reflect their struggles for power and autonomy as well their hardships and joys.

When the colonists printed their first newspapers, the news wasn't even likely to be new. Editors of newspapers in colonial America, who were usually also the postmasters, often did little, if any, original reporting. Most simply reprinted information from newspapers that had been shipped over the Atlantic Ocean, whenever those papers happened to arrive.[1]

The country's second newspaper, Postmaster John E. Campbell's *Boston News-Letter*, began in 1704 and published official announcements from the Massachusetts governor as well as items, sometimes months old, from European papers in chronological order,[2] in a kind of trans-Atlantic echo chamber. "News" of the day also may have been stale because colonial newspapers were usually weeklies. The paper had to be made by hand, and it took a long time to print a typical four-page edition—about sixteen hours.[3]

The Start of the American Press

Even before this country *was* a country, newspapers got into trouble with authorities. The Massachusetts governor shut down what many consider to be the first American newspaper, *Publick Occurrences Both Forreign and Domestick*, after its only issue, published September 25, 1690. *Publick Occurrences* was to have been a monthly newspaper—"furnished once a month (or if any Glut of Occurrences happen, oftener)"—but the governor of Massachusetts closed it because of "sundry doubtful and uncertain Reports."[4] Despite being the first newspaper in the New World, *Publick Occurrences* displayed a much more modern news sense than newspapers would for the next fifty years.[5] The paper's feisty and energetic editor, Benjamin Harris, was not content to reprint only other people's words; he had his own voice. He wrote much about local events in his only edition: Thanksgiving being celebrated by "Christianized Indians in some parts of Plimouth," a different band of "barbarous Indians" being suspected of abducting local children, the fewer number of deaths resulting from small-pox, fires devastating Boston. The paper also reported scandal, a consistent characteristic of news throughout the ages: "[The King of] France is in much trouble (and fear) not only with us but also with his Son, who has revolted against him lately, and has great reason, if reports be true, that the *Father used to lie with the Son's Wife*."[6] Harris inserted the italics.

While that last bit of gossip might have offended government censors and contributed to the paper's demise, Harris had also neglected to get the proper permit from the governor before publication, which was required in the colony at the time. Such attempts by government to control the press rankled many American editors from the start. James Franklin, Benjamin's older brother, was one. Although Massachusetts did not require permits prior to publication by the time Franklin published in 1721, in the first issue of his *New England Courant*, his paper criticized powerful Puritan leaders Increase Mather and his son Cotton for supporting smallpox vaccination. A week later, a broadside called the *Anti-Courant* appeared with the Mathers' response (it too was published by Franklin, who apparently not only enjoyed but also prospered from a good fight). Franklin's *Courant* also printed reports about crime and scandal, and it published biting essays on Boston life by Silence Dogood, the pen name for his apprentice and brother, Benjamin Franklin.[7] One of Silence Dogood's essays, for example, satirized the "dunces and blockheads" at the local college, Harvard.[8] James Franklin riled the authorities again when he printed an anonymous letter attacking the governor's anti-piracy efforts. The authorities called him in, Franklin refused to reveal its author, and he was imprisoned for a month.[9] While he was incarcerated, Ben Franklin kept the paper going, reprinting, among other things, an essay from abroad that argued that the government was merely a trustee of ordinary people and that only guilty officials feared free-dom of speech.[10] Even though James had apologized for his actions while in jail, once freed, he again printed criticism of officialdom, and the government ordered him to stop publishing the newspaper. Instead, he installed Ben as the nominal editor and publisher. The true editor remained James, who continued publishing until 1723, even after Ben had run away from his apprenticeship.[11] After these first tests of the limits of freedom of the press, James Franklin moved his press to Rhode Island in 1726 to print that colony's first newspaper, the *Rhode Island Gazette*.[12]

Perhaps the most well-known early newspaper publisher who got into trouble with authorities was John Peter Zenger, who had started his business mainly as a printer of Dutch religious material. In 1733, the Popular Party hired him to be publisher of the *New York Weekly Journal*, a political newspaper in opposition to the governor. Among the items Zenger printed were sarcastic comments, including one about "a Monkey of the larger sort," which people in the know took to refer to Governor William Cosby, and a letter to the editor claiming the governor was incompetent. As a result, Zenger was charged with seditious libel and imprisoned for eight months. He, too, never revealed who wrote the offending words, and the newspaper continued publishing under the supervision of Zenger's wife and the probable author of the letter, lawyer James Alexander. Eventually, Zenger was acquitted. His lawyer had argued a critical point for the American press: the jury should decide not only that the words were published but also that they truly constituted libel, and, importantly, that publishing the truth absolutely protected against a libel charge. Slowly, over the next one hundred years, states adopted these principles into their libel laws.[13]

Printing newspapers has always been expensive. In the early 1700s, editors were often printers who earned cash from political parties, government printing contracts, postmasterships and other printing jobs,[14] beginning the classic tension in news reporting that continues to this day: how to publish news of important public controversies while not driving away those who pay the salaries of editors and reporters.

From the beginning of American newspaper publishing, editors recognized that a newspaper's role was not merely to inform but also to entertain. Early newspapers routinely printed literary fiction, often lengthy stories that ran in installments. The 1719 best seller *Robinson Crusoe* "was printed serially in many colonial papers as fast as installments could be pirated from abroad."[15] Remaining objective—an assumed goal of many modern news reporters—would never have occurred to many early American editors. As Ben Franklin wrote, "The Business of Printing has chiefly to do with Men's Opinions."[16] Through much of the 1700s and the early 1800s, political parties owned their own newspapers with editors taking partisan positions.[17] In the "news" pages of colonial days, editors wrote their opinions, sometimes under false names, and citizens wrote letters to the editors slinging dirt on politicians and British overlords:

Early American newspapers tend to look like one long and uninterrupted invective, a ragged fleet of dung barges. In a way, they were. Plenty of that nose thumbing was mere gimmickry and gamboling. Some of it was capricious, and much of it was just plain malicious. But much of it was more. All that invective, taken together, really does add up to a long and revolutionary argument against tyranny, against arbitrary authority—against, that is, the rule of men above law.[18]

The Press and the Revolution

Printers before and during the Revolutionary War became news editors, or, by modern standards, they became purveyors of propaganda. In Boston, the *Gazette* printed letters promoting revolutionary action from the likes of John Adams, John Hancock and Sam Adams, all writing under pen names. To madden the masses, the front page of the paper ran an engraving by Paul Revere of four coffins with skulls over them, each with the initial of one of the colonists killed during the Boston Massacre in 1770. Isaiah Thomas' *Massachusetts Spy* printed such revolutionary diatribes that when the British army moved into Boston in 1775, he felt it best to leave the city. But from Worcester, Massachusetts, he started the *Worcester Spy*, publishing this news of the Battle of Lexington: "Americans! Forever bear in mind the Battle of Lexington! Where British Troops, unmolested and unprovoked, wantonly and in a most cruel manner fired upon and killed a number of our countrymen, then robbed them of their provisions, ransacked, plundered and burnt their houses!" William Goddard's *Pennsylvania Gazette* published John Dickinson's *Letters of a Pennsylvania Farmer,* letters that argued against British taxation and that were reprinted in many other colonial papers. Interestingly, the independent Goddard also set up his own private postal system because he did not approve of how Ben Franklin was running the British postal network in the colonies at the time. The Continental Congress, however, later made Franklin the first postmaster general.[19]

Scholar Bernard A. Weisberger wrote that the Tory press, which favored the British cause, was "generally unable to match the output or quality of the Patriot press, although this was partly due to the fact that the risks were considerable." In 1767 John Mein, who had tried to start a royalist paper in Boston, was hanged in effigy, then beaten and had to move to England, even though he contended he was actually neutral. James Rivington, an upper-crust Britisher who had lost a fortune gambling before moving to the colonies, published the *New York Gazette*, where he criticized the Patriots. He outraged many colonists, and the New Jersey governor said that if Rivington were captured during the war, "he wanted one of his ears, the governor of New York should have another, and Washington, 'if he pleases, may take his head.'" Rivington, too, fled to England, claiming that Americans' professed love of a free press extended only to newspapers they agreed with. Rivington returned when the British took over New York and called his paper the *Royal Gazette*. After the war, incredibly, he stayed in the city, where he operated a thriving bookstore.[20]

Benjamin Russell was only a boy when the battles of Lexington and Concord signaled the start of the Revolutionary War. He happily ran errands for soldiers near his home in Massachusetts until his father found out, whipped him and sent him off to apprentice with Isaiah Thomas' *Massachusetts Spy*.[21] Russell became a lifelong newspaperman but also served in the Army, witnessing the battles of Bunker Hill and Saratoga. In 1784, he started the *Columbian Centinel*, which, under his patriotic pen, lasted forty-two years. Russell also had correspondents who would send him letters with news that he would publish, such as the death of George Washington. His little paper was financially successful because of advertising revenue. The paper's motto was "Uninfluenced by Party; we aim only to be JUST."[22] Yet the *Columbian Centinel* had a strong point of view—that of Russell. He practiced a kind of personal journalism that would be right at home with a number of bloggers of the twenty-first century. Here is a snippet of news from a letter to the captain of a slave ship he published in 1789:

> If the Printer thinks the following extract of a letter, wrote to an old Sea Captain in an adjoining town, will be the means of any way preventing that horrid inhuman trade of kidnapping an unfortunate race of human begins [*sic*], he is desired to publish it…
>
> Yes, Sir, you stand accused before that God who is father of all, and who have made of one flesh all nations that dwell on earth for your conduct herein…the Ghosts of these innocent blacks—which you have consigned while here on earth to slavery and misfortune shall await around your expiring soul…persecute no longer the children of men![23]

Newspaper editors would for many decades practice this form of personal journalism, mixing viewpoint with factual reporting. Editors who colored the news to promote a particular party most likely believed in their political causes and thought that using the press to promote the party was for the good of the country. But they also gained much: They "could walk with senators and presidents and find recognition and satisfaction in appointments to ministries or high office."[24] In return, party leaders funded their businesses through advertisements, subscriptions or through government printing jobs or post office jobs.[25]

After the American Revolution, the new country's political leaders promoted the idea of informing the public about issues of the day by encouraging newspapers, recognizing the dissemination of news as a common good. In 1792, Congress declared "newspapers as a favored instrument of national communication" and subsidized the cost of mailing newspapers.[26] The first newspaper to appear daily in America debuted in 1783, the *Pennsylvania Evening Post*. It lasted only seventeen months but was quickly succeeded by another daily, the *Pennsylvania Packet and Daily Advertiser*, which had already successfully transitioned from weekly to tri-weekly.[27]

Some early newspapers did print what today would be considered news-worthy, but the political ranting in newspaper pages exasperated even Thomas Jefferson, long a proponent of a free press. He complained in a letter to a friend that his political opponents "fill their newspapers with falsehoods, calumnies and audacities...We are going fairly through the experiment of whether freedom of discussion, unaided by coercion, is not sufficient for the propagation and protection of truth, and for the maintenance of an administration pure and upright in its actions and views...I shall protect them in the right of lying and calumniating."[28]

By 1800, 234 newspapers were publishing in the United States. By 1833, newspapers numbered 1,200. The growth was fueled by better, faster printing presses and, after 1817, paper made by machines instead of by hand.[29] In addition, as Americans pushed into western lands, they wanted to read newspapers to inform and entertain them, to tell them where they could buy and sell goods, to make them feel connected to their communities. Businessmen responded. Many of these papers were weekly and rural, with reports that largely promoted local businesses and economic development, which still tends to be true with small and weekly newspapers. Editors and reporters of rural newspapers, closer to their audiences than big-city papers, reported specifically on items that they knew these people cared about: the weather, crops, road conditions, parties, weddings, religious revivals, illness and death.[30]

The Specialized Press

Smaller newspapers also could be more concerned with the information needs of specific social groups than newspapers that served the teeming masses in large cities. For example, the Industrial Revolution created a class of city workers, meaning that a newspaper could devote itself to labor issues. The first successful labor paper, The *Mechanic's Free Press*, began publishing in 1828.[31] Because America was a country of immigrants, foreign-language newspapers covered events of the old country and the new. In 1860, there were 300 foreign-language newspapers; by 1880 there were 800.[32]

On March 16, 1827, *Freedom's Journal*, the country's first newspaper for blacks, began publishing in New York in response to white-owned newspaper editorials attacking black people as "indolent," "uncivil" and "an abominable nuisance." In its first edition, the editors explained to readers that what constituted news for people of color had been ignored by white-owned newspapers: "Too long have others spoken for us. Too long has the publick been deceived by misrepresentations, in this which concern us dearly, though in the estimation of some mere trifles."[33] This paper did not survive long, but about forty abolitionist newspapers sprouted between 1827 and the end of the Civil War.[34] The brave publishers who printed anti-slavery views might well be attacked or killed and their presses might be destroyed.

The most famous black newspaperman was former slave Frederick Douglass, a popular speaker of the day who would introduce himself as a thief ("I stole this head, these limbs, this body from my master, and ran off with them").[35] Douglass bought a press and started the *North Star* in Rochester, New York, in 1847, and its nameplate proclaimed: "Right is of no Sex—Truth is of no Color—God is the Father of us all, and we are all Brethren."[36] Douglass spent more than $12,000 of his own money before he had to shutter the paper because of mounting bills in 1860. His writing was passionate, and he took pride in editing his copy. "There has just left our office, an amiable, kind, and intelligent looking young woman, about eighteen years of age, on her way from slavery," he told readers in his first issue. "A rehearsal of her sad story thrilled us with emotions which we lack words to express. On her right arm between her wrist and elbow, the initials of the name of her infernal master, is cut in large capitals. Oh! The wretch!" While Douglass did challenge his readers to overthrow slavery and took strong positions about how blacks could fight back, black-owned newspapers also reported on the education and lifestyle of middle-class blacks during the Civil War, apparently hoping that the stories would lead to their acceptance into white society.[37]

However, the abolitionist press had started well before Douglass. In 1835, the American Anti-Slavery Society mailed 175,000 copies of its four monthly newspapers to Southerners in an effort to promote its message. When pro-slavery people in Charleston learned that some of these newspapers had arrived in a postal bag in a ship in the harbor, they burned them and touched off anti-abolition rallies throughout the South. The U.S. postmaster general eventually banned mailing of abolitionist papers to the South, but the organizers claimed it had garnered 15,000 new subscriptions for the society's papers.[38]

Since slavery was "the most convulsive issue in nineteenth century America,"[39] proprietors of abolitionist newspapers engendered fierce reaction from anti-abolitionists. Elijah Lovejoy correctly framed the conflict as a fundamental First Amendment issue. Lovejoy, who studied at Princeton Seminary, had moved to St. Louis in 1833 to preach and publish the religious paper, the *Observer*, in which he wrote fervently against slavery. Some St. Louis citizens fervently disagreed. They warned him "freedom of speech does not imply a moral right…to freely discuss the subject of slavery…a question too nearly allied to the vital interests of the slaveholding states to admit to public disputation."[40] After receiving threats to his wife and child, Lovejoy moved his press to Alton, in the free state of Illinois. There, refusing to attend a Fourth of July celebration, he chided those who did:

Alas! What bitter mockery is this. We assemble to thank God for our own freedom, and to eat and drink with joy and gladness of Heart, while our feet are on the necks of nearly three millions of our fellow men. Not all our shouts of self-congratulation can drown their groans. Even the very flag of freedom that waves over their heads is formed from materials cultivated by slaves, on a soil moistened with their blood drawn from them by the whip of a republican taskmaster.[41]

Lovejoy's *Observer* continued its abolitionist lecturing until a mob descended upon his office in August 1837 and destroyed his printing press. He ordered a replacement, which was promptly destroyed when he was out of town in September. In response, Lovejoy attempted to form an anti-slavery society and ordered yet another printing press. In November, community leaders in the Market House asked him formally to stop publication. He responded:

I do not admit that it is the business of this assembly to decide whether I shall or shall not publish a newspaper in this city. The gentlemen have, as the lawyers say, made a wrong issue. I have the *right* to do it. I know that I have the right freely to speak and publish my sentiments, subject only to the laws of the land for the abuse of that right. This right was given to me by my Maker; and is solemnly guaranteed to me by the constitution of the United States and of this state.[42]

The final confrontation would surround Lovejoy's printing press. He and some followers got their guns and guarded it in a warehouse by the river. A mob gathered outside. Threats were hurled. A window was broken, and shots were fired. One of the people outside was killed. Others set the warehouse on fire. When Lovejoy appeared near a doorway, he was shot dead. News of the death spread nationwide, and another abolitionist paper, *The Emancipator*, in Cincinnati, Ohio, printed 161 editorials denouncing the killing. A member of the Illinois House of Representatives, Abraham Lincoln, asserted that whenever "the vicious portion of population" who "burn churches, ravage and rob provision stores, throw printing presses into rivers, and shoot editors, and hang and burn obnoxious persons at pleasure, and with impunity; depend on it, this Government cannot last."[43]

The Penny Press

While the abolitionist press continued up to and through the Civil War, another type of newspapering was developing in America's cities. While the country's first newspapers had been aimed at upper class elites, news aimed at the common man grew in the 1830s with the penny press, named for its affordable daily price. While many penny papers printed exaggeration and half-truths, they also expanded what constituted news in ways that persist today. Rather than merely print the politicized messages of the powerful, the penny press took it upon itself to write for the working class. As one commentator noted, "For the first time in the history of

Northern America, newspapers became totally integrated into the culture of their respective communities."[44] Benjamin Day's *New York Sun* encouraged reporters to find stories from the police, items such as a "Melancholy Suicide," a tale of an ordinary man (like the reader) who ended his life with opium after his beloved rejected him. Unfortunately for journalism, Day's paper was not limited to printing only the truth; one series of articles detailed life on the moon.[45] Even when covering Earthly events, the penny press often took a rather breathless approach in its coverage, and the papers became wildly popular.

Day's rival, James Gordon Bennett, who started the *New York Morning Herald* as a penny paper in 1835, devoted many column inches to crime, business and foreign news but also to society, religion and sports.[46] Bennett's contemporaries could not agree whether the *Herald*, the most successful of the papers of its day, succeeded "because it was so good or because it was so bad."[47] While Bennett was esteemed for his cleverness in gathering news that people wanted to read, his biographer, James Parton, wrote of Bennett: "That region of the mind where conviction, the sense of truth and honor, public spirit, and patriotism have their sphere, is...mere vacancy."[48] Bennett started the *Herald* in 1835 as its only employee, reporting the news, printing it and delivering the paper. His coverage of financial news from Wall Street garnered an international following because of its reliability, and he correctly predicted the stock market crash of 1837.[49]

On the other hand, his reportage of a hatchet murder of a prostitute in 1836 delved into gory details about the corpse and the brothel, which he had convinced police to let him enter. Bennett was innovative in finding information, printing a question-and-answer story from perhaps the first formal journalistic interview with the madam of the brothel where the murder occurred. He named Richard Robinson as the "cold-blooded villain" responsible; Bennett had changed his mind about his guilt by the time Robinson was acquitted.[50] With stories like these, the *Herald's* circulation boomed, and so did its staff. During the Civil War, Bennett spent a half million dollars on a cadre of sixty-three war reporters who sent back timely reports from battlefields, competing aggressively with the *New York Sun* to get the news of the war first to its readers. At Bennett's death in 1872, Horace Greeley, editor of the rival *New York Tribune*, said of him, "He developed the capacities of journalism in a most wonderful manner, but he did it by degrading its character. He made the newspaper powerful, but he made it odious."[51] Nevertheless, the news in the penny press focused on useful information that ordinary people needed in a capitalist country and a democracy:

> At that point, news became an intimate part of citizenship and politics. At that point, news in newspapers became not the extension of gossip but an institutionalized, competitive marketplace commodity. It also became a public good, a collective and visible good, important in part precisely because it did not pass, like rumor, from person to person but, like divine instruction, from a printed text to hundreds of people at once.[52]

News Travels Fast

At that point as well, old news was no longer sufficient. Timeliness had become an important characteristic of news. The percentage of newspaper reports older than a month declined from 28 percent in 1820 to 8 percent in 1860, according to one study.[53] Editors first used carrier pigeons and pony express to speed the news from distant points to the home office and then took advantage of new technology—steamships, railroad and finally the telegraph—to gather and report the most recent events. In fact, the telegraph became crucial to newsgathering. The organization that would become the Associated Press (AP), which would propel almost instantaneous news to subscribing papers in the hinterlands, was founded in New York in 1846 and sent its bulletins and stories via wire.[54] In 1844, Samuel F.B. Morse's first telegraph line was completed, connecting Washington and New York. Soon a web of telegraph wires connected cities along the East Coast. Newspaper editors formed cooperatives to share the cost of using this expensive new invention, which could send news practically instantaneously across the country. The first news sent along the wires was on February 3, 1946, when the *Utica Gazette* carried news items from Albany, N.Y. By the time the line was completed to Buffalo on the Fourth of July of that year, newspapers along the wire were already sharing their news as well as the expense. By 1849, the telegraph was sending tentacles toward Chicago, Baltimore and Halifax, Nova Scotia.

Recognizing the telegraph's potential for fast, distant newsgathering, six of the largest of New York City's dailies formed a cooperative venture, the Associated Press, to gather and transmit "telegraphic news." Its first general manager, Alexander Jones, wrote and edited the news himself, but he soon hired reporters from Cincinnati to Toronto. AP correspondents gathered and transmitted telegraphic news up and down the eastern seaboard, where other Associated Presses had formed. In 1861, the telegraph line over the Potomac was severed, cutting access to Confederate news gathered by the Southern AP. After the war, telegraphic news continued expanding when a cable beneath the Atlantic Ocean connected America to Europe for immediate transmission of foreign news. Through the 1860s and 1870s, press associations covered news in Texas, California and points in between and sent it nationwide. The news had become fast and national.[55]

By the middle of the nineteenth century, larger newspapers were covering prizefights, horse races and other sporting events. At the time of the Civil War, baseball's popularity soared. It was reporters, in fact, who created box scores and other statistics to follow the game.[56] Although only big-city newspapers had regular sports coverage in the 1880s, by 1910 almost all papers prominently covered major athletic events. In 1920, the Associated Press hired a dozen reporters to cover nothing but sports.[57] In fact, during the 1920s, dailies devoted 12 to 20 percent of their news coverage to sports,[58] and the decade would become known as America's Golden Age of

Sports—although one researcher believes it more accurately should be described as the Golden Age of Sports Writing.[59] Sports reporting, after all, was less likely to offend readers and advertisers than politics or religion or scandal, and "it offered the spirit and excitement of conflict and struggle in a politically trivial area."[60]

Yellow Journalism

Big-city newspapers had become big businesses and mass media. While plenty of small-town newspapers were one- or two-person operations, in the largest cities, in the early 1800s newspapers hired hundreds of reporters and divided them into beats to compete to get the freshest news. Newspapers covered not only "hard news" stories of politics and crime, but they also incorporated "soft news," or human interest pieces. For instance, the stories published in the *Pittsburgh Leader* on a single Sunday in April 1898 included "how to eat with chopsticks, gold speculation in British Columbia, big game hunting, identical twins in Michigan, spring fashions for men, gossip about former President Grover Cleveland and his family, fashion (including "April wraps: Novelty coats and capes that captivate feminine fancy" and the startling news that "the all-conquering blouse has suffered its first defeat and threatens to disappear altogether"), women polar explorers, amateur baking, egg farming, women firefighters, traveling in Europe, prominent species of American trees, insect life and fiction."[61]

Yellow journalism stained reportage in many big-city newspapers after the Civil War. William Randolph Hearst, the newspaper mogul most associated with yellow journalism's bellowing headlines, emotion-laden copy and occasionally fabricated stories, entered the news business after being expelled from Harvard for putting professors' pictures on chamber pots.[62] The public loved Hearst's brand of sensational news. The number of readers of his *Morning Journal* newspaper were said to have jumped by 125,000 in New York in a single month (although newspapers routinely lied about their readership statistics in those days), lured by such headlines as "A Marvellous New Way of Giving Medicine: Wonderful Results from Merely Holding Tubes of Drugs Near Entranced Patients," "Why Young Girls Kill Themselves" and "Strange Things Women Do for Love."[63] Hearst's name is forever tied, as an embarrassment, to newspaper history for his *New York Journal's* coverage leading up to the Spanish-American War in 1898. Hearst spent lavishly on reporting to produce stories that promoted war with Spain. For weeks, the paper published overwrought and embellished stories about such events as a strip-search of a woman by Spanish officials on a boat in Havana harbor (complete with a sketch by artist Frederic Remington of the nude woman surrounded by men, which did not happen); about a beautiful eighteen-year-old Cuban revolutionary languishing in jail; about the death of a Cuban man who had become an American citizen and who returned to the island to die mysteriously in a Spanish jail.[64]

Then on February 15, 1898, the American battleship *Maine* blew up in Havana harbor. Hearst's *Journal* printed fake stories: about a cablegram sent by the ship's captain to the secretary of the Navy, saying that the explosion was not an accident; a story that a mine had blown up the ship; a map showing all Spanish mines in the harbor. Yet, even though Hearst's yellow journalism has been blamed for pushing the country into a war that cost 5,000 American lives, many historians believe he is given far more credit for the war than he deserves. As David R. Spencer noted, "In spite of the popular myth that William Randolph Hearst provided a war for *The Journal* to exploit, it remains clear to most observers that one newspaper or newspaper editor could hardly have mustered up support for a war if the underpinnings of that support did not exist in the first place."[65]

Joseph Pulitzer's *World* was in many ways the equal of Hearst's *Journal*, but it also used a crusading style that attempted to change some urban evils. Pulitzer came to New York having left his mark first on his newspaper in St. Louis, the *Post-Dispatch*. In one series of stories aimed at getting that city's government to actually collect taxes on personal property to perform essential city services, such as paving the mud streets, the newspaper had listed how much money well-to-do citizens had claimed on their tax returns. Many had reported no income and so paid no taxes, and Pulitzer's paper noted next to their names, "Money on hand, not a cent. Money deposited in bank or other safe place, not a dollar."[66] In New York, Pulitzer continued this type of journalism with the *World*, although his paper also produced plenty of tawdry journalism. One of Pulitzer's crusades to improve conditions in tenements after hundreds of children died during a heat wave featured a story with the headline: "How Babies Are Baked."[67] The *World* also sponsored journalistic stunts, such as reporter Nellie Bly's trip around the world to see if she could beat the challenge in Jules Verne's then-popular novel, *Around the World in Eighty Days*. She did.

Rather than simply selling newspapers, yellow journalism was also a hook to get people to read the paper and find the thoughtful editorials, which he considered the newspaper's soul.[68] Pulitzer wrote into his 1904 will that his fortune would endow prizes for excellence in journalism, education, letters and drama and for four traveling scholarships. He also set up a Pulitzer advisory board, giving it the authority to change the prizes as appropriate, which it did. Since the prizes were given, beginning in 1917, the board increased the number of prizes to twenty-one and, in 1999, allowed newspapers to submit their online presentations for consideration.[69]

As yellow journalism hollered and wept in certain newspapers at the end of the nineteenth century, other papers, such as *The New York Times*, began to encourage its reporters to be objective. The *Times'* operating plan of 1860 declared a newspaper's "proper business is to publish facts in such a form and temper as to lead men of all parties to rely upon its statements of facts." Within thirty years, about one-third of newspapers in the country also announced that they were independent, neutral or local.[70] News people had begun to realize that to give an honest account of the day's events required them to not only be independent of government and politics but also be responsible and honest.

While it is true that the corrupt politicians of Tammany Hall paid equally corrupt journalists in New York City more than a million dollars for them to print certain stories favorable to the political machine, it is also true that the *New York Times* turned down a $500,000 bribe from Boss Tweed to ignore documents that proved the politician's criminality.[71] The *Times'* series of articles starting in 1871 exposed the ring—and helped to bring it down.

A newspaper critic writing in the 1850s charged that newspapers were still highly partisan, withholding information that conflicted with the editor's political stance, publishing misleading stories or simply deceiving people purposely.[72] Harlan S. Stensaas found that about 40 percent of news stories were objective between 1865 and 1874, about two-thirds were objective between 1905 and 1914, and 80 percent were between 1925 and 1934.[73] By 1905, editorials were likely to be segregated from the news and subordinated to it.[74] In 1923 the American Society of Newspaper Editors adopted a code of ethics, following this type of criticism from its readers:

> You and your reporters take an ounce of fact and a pound of imagination and give us the mixture under a date line. That is what the novel writers do, but they call the stuff fiction, while you print obvious fiction and label it "fact." We want the FACTS, the bare, bald facts. We are tired to death of fictionized news![75]

Some view the goal of objectivity merely as a method that capitalist owners used to keep news inoffensive and so to garner as many advertisers as possible, but that is a deeply cynical interpretation. Fair and balanced news reporting, focusing on facts, also respects an audience, ceding to readers the authority to analyze issues for themselves. In a cycle of converged interests, news coverage from a politically independent press attracted readers, and that in turn attracted advertisers who wanted to reach the most people, and so more reporters were hired to find more news for more readers. Melville E. Stone, editor of the *Chicago Evening Daily News,* said in the late 1800s a newspaper's focus should be on news first, with opinion second and entertainment third. In this model of newspapering, which became standard in the twentieth century, the advertising side of the paper operated separately from the reporting side. This meant the newspaper could objectively cover striking railroad workers and subsequent riots in 1877 Chicago while supporting the position of the strikers against the wishes of its advertisers on its editorial pages. Importantly, its circulation increased, and advertisers did not flee.[76]

The Price of Competition

The number of newspapers in America peaked between 1910 and 1914 at 2,200 English-language newspapers and a huge number of weeklies—14,000.[77] But after World War I, a trend toward consolidation and competition from radio and then television trimmed that number. By 1929, the U.S. Census found 1,944 dailies.[78] The newspaper business suffered with other businesses during the Great Depression, and the number of papers shrank to 1,911 in 1933. Victims of the Great Depression were Pulitzer's *New York World,* which merged with another paper and became the *New York World-Telegram,* and the *Philadelphia Public Ledger*, which had helped to pioneer the era of the penny press.[79]

Franklin D. Roosevelt initiated sweeping changes in the country during his four terms in the White House, and he also initiated changes in how a president dealt with the press. Roosevelt gave reporters more access than any president before or since, meeting with them an average of eighty-three times a year during his fourteen years as president and held 340 press conferences in his first term (1933–1937). Ronald Reagan, the "Great Communicator," averaged six per year while president between 1981 and 1989.[80]

Roosevelt's accessibility may have made him popular with reporters, but he angered the publishers with other efforts. Signing a Daily Newspaper Code that newspaper editors drafted with government regulators, he criticized the publishers' wrapping their minimal changes in working conditions for newspaper workers in language about the First Amendment, saying, "The freedom guaranteed by the Constitution is freedom of expression and that will be scrupulously respected—but it is not free to work children, or to do business in a fire trap or violate the laws against obscenity, libel and lewdness."[81]

By 1933 the American Newspaper Publishers Association was worrying about how the new medium of radio would cut into the scarce advertising dollars that newspapers wanted. It recommended that papers that owned radio stations keep their news broadcasts brief and suggested that press associations not sell any news to radio networks. The Associated Press, United Press (UP) and the International News Service (INS) all followed that advice until 1935 when UP and INS relented, and then in 1940, the AP followed suit. After radio and television started broadcasting news bulletins, newspapers' "extra" editions were no longer necessary. Newspaper reporters were encouraged to give more background and context to their reports, which the broadcasters could not do as well.[82] Another effect was that advertising dollars that had solely gone to newspapers were being diverted, and between 1937 and 1944, 362 daily newspapers merged or closed.[83]

Investigative Journalism and Improved News Design

Throughout the twentieth century, sensationalist newspapers still found an audience, but others tried to inform and entertain their readers with more restrained and credible news reports; some attempted to serve as watchdogs against corruption on behalf of the ordinary citizen. As one of the past century's most famed journalists, H.L. Mencken, wrote in his memoirs, "I recall crusades against sweat-shops, against the shanghaiing of men for the Chesapeake oyster fleet and against dance-halls that paid their female interns commissions on the drinks sold."[84] The crusading spirit waxed and waned in newspapers of the twentieth century. Pulitzer Prizes, set up in the will of the editor whose sometimes sensationalistic newspaper also sponsored crusading journalism, were won by the Waterbury (CT) *Republican & American*'s stories that exposed municipal graft in 1940, the *Chicago Daily News* and *St. Louis Post-Dispatch*'s divulging the fact that thirty-seven Illinois newspapermen were on the Illinois State payroll in 1950, and for Scripps-Howard Newspaper Alliance's revelations about nepotism in the Congress of the United States in 1960.[85]

The investigative newspaper series that would shake the country, however, was the story that made a couple of reporters almost as famous as the movie stars who would play them in the movie about their exploits. *The Washington Post*'s Carl Bernstein and Bob Woodward, nicknamed "Woodstein," started with a story about a break-in of the Democratic Party headquarters in the Watergate Hotel in Washington. Through dogged reporting over many months, they traced the crime back to top aides of the president and ultimately to a cover-up directed from the White House. President Richard Nixon was forced to resign in 1974. Their Watergate reporting was, according to media critic Ben Bagdikian, "the single most spectacular act of serious journalism of the century."[86] Yet, critics debate whether the president would have been forced to resign without the *Post*'s reports. Even Woodward said that it was nonsense to say that only the press brought down Nixon, adding, "the press always plays a role, whether by being passive or by being aggressive, but it's a mistake to overemphasize" its importance. Nevertheless, Bernstein said he believes that "the press coverage played a very big role in making information available that the Watergate break-in was part of something vast and criminal and directed from or near the Oval Office against President Nixon's opponents." Bernstein conceded that his and Woodward's role in unseating the president "has been mythologized" because "in great events people look for villains and heroes."[87]

Watergate spurred renewed interest in newspaper reporting for a time, but the look of the paper itself did not change much, until September 15,

1982, when a new national, general-interest newspaper was launched, one that was called "the most significant innovation in the newspaper business since the invention of the rotary press in the 19th century."[88] With its splashy color pages, bold graphics, including a full-color national weather map, extensive sports reporting, short stories and pithy "factoids" of information, *USA Today* shook the newspaper industry. It was sold on the street in boxes designed to look like television sets, metallic symbols that it was designed for the TV generation. Many newspaper journalists ridiculed it, calling it "McPaper." Its own editor later joked that the paper "brought new depth to the meaning of the word 'shallow.'"[89]

But it proved popular with its audience, who were busy, educated working people who traveled, and in December 1999 it overtook the *Wall Street Journal* as the largest circulation newspaper in America.[90] It had cost its publisher, Gannett Company, Inc., about a billion dollars before it broke even.[91] To be fair, as the paper grew, it matured. It hired more reporters, and it allowed more stories to run in depth rather than in outline only. As *USA Today* succeeded, ridicule faded and newspapers countrywide copied the paper's innovations, redesigning their pages and using color to be attractive to readers; requiring crisper writing and more stories; emphasizing sports coverage, which draws readers to newspapers; and cutting foreign coverage, a move that has been criticized as myopic.

The Decline of Newspapers

The latter part of the twentieth century was full of bad news for newspapers. Paid readership of daily newspapers had peaked at 63.3 million readers in 1984 and then spiraled to 48.6 million by 2008, about the level of 1945.[92] As a deep recession took hold in 2008, advertisers, who had been deserting newspapers as readers stopped reading them, continued their exodus. While the overall newspaper industry turned a profit in 2008,[93] many weakened papers folded, cut the number and size of news pages or entire daily issues, and laid off reporters. The Internet also was a potent competitor, and journalists fumbled at least initially in harnessing it for news reporting.

Some of the dreadful news about newspapers was self-inflicted. In 2003, Jayson Blair plagiarized or fabricated parts of about three dozen stories at *The New York Times*. In 2004, Jack Kelley did much the same at *USA Today*. In 1981 *The Washington Post* returned a Pulitzer Prize that its reporter, Janet Cooke, had won for a profile of an eight-year-old heroin addict after it discovered the story was a concoction. These were the most egregious events, but there were more incidents of unethical behavior, often reported by the newspaper employers themselves. The effect of these scandals on the newspaper reader was not clear, however. Even though the percentage of people who favorably viewed the press had fallen to a new low by June

2005 and the number who said the press was professional and cared about what they did also fell, the number of people who said the press was inaccurate had not changed, according to an analysis by representatives of Project for Excellence in Journalism and the Committee of Concerned Journalists. The authors surmised that either the reputation of journalists was so poor that these ethical violations made little impression or that readers were pleased by how vigorously newspapers seemed to expose those who violated the tenets of ethical journalism.[94] Still, favorable ratings for the institution of journalism continued a slow slide. In the 2007 survey by the Pew Research Center for the People and the Press, 61 percent of Americans ranked national newspapers favorably, down from 81 percent in 1985. Those who ranked their local paper favorably were 78 percent, down from 88 percent in 1985.[95]

Walter Pincus, a reporter for fifty years and an aide to the late Sen. J. William Fulbright in the 1960s, criticized journalists for losing readers because of their "narcissism." His colleagues at *The Washington Post* won nineteen Pulitzer Prizes in a decade, he wrote, but some of those resources could have been better spent writing stories more likely to tell stories that matter to readers. Pincus criticized newspapers for being "artificially distant" from public figures and becoming "common carriers, transmitters of other people's ideas and thoughts, irrespective of import, relevance, and at times even accuracy." He called for journalism to return to its activist roots, to write stories that truly affect people's lives.[96]

Truth be told, fear for the future of journalism has been voiced for decades. The final chapter in a history of the press published in 1961 was titled, "The Vanishing Newspaperman?" In that chapter, Bernard Weisberger wrote: "The newspaper claimed to be the voice of the locality, but except for advertisements, scandal, and crime was almost completely filled with matter that bore no relation whatever to the paper's home city....The newspaper claimed to be the lively literature of the commonalty, but its relentless quantitative demands filled it with banalities and formulas." Nonetheless, he ended with hope that a "new American newspaperman" might emerge to carry on.[97]

By the end of the twentieth century, journalists spent a lot of time listening to such criticism and adding their own, trying to figure out how to salvage their profession. Yet the decline in the number of newspapers continued inexorably. According to the Newspaper Association of America, in 1940, there were 1,878 morning and evening newspapers in the country, a number that would never be seen again. The number of papers slid to about 1,750 between 1955 and 1980, but then a more precipitous drop began. By 2008, only 1,408 dailies operated nationwide, the smallest number in history.[98]

The Pew Project for Excellence in Journalism declared that the newspaper industry had experienced "a harrowing 2008 and entered 2009 in something perilously close to free fall." Publicly traded newspapers lost on average 42 percent of their value between 2005 and 2007. Then, in 2008, they lost another 83 percent of what was left.[99] A worldwide economic recession combined with high debts at some news companies, and newspapers folded. Nevertheless, even where the parent companies had large debt, many newspapers themselves made money. Even in 2008, newspapers earned about nine dollars out of every ten from the paper product, rather than from digital formats, while printing and delivering that paper averaged about 40 percent of newspapers' costs. Pew's annual report on the "State of the News Media" concluded, "For now, it doesn't add up to sacrifice potentially 90 percent of revenues to save 40 percent of costs."[100]

Journalists wrote many stories in 2008 about their colleagues being laid off, as dailies shed 5,900 newspaper jobs. It was the largest decline since the American Society of Newspaper Editors started counting in 1978, and was on top of a loss of 2,400 full-time professional jobs the previous year.[101] The *Los Angeles Times* cut forty of its 900 newsroom jobs in February 2008. Then it let go another 135 in July 2008, and then seventy-five in October 2008, and another seventy in February 2009. Gannett Inc., which published eighty-four dailies and 850 non-daily newspapers, including *USA Today*, announced in 2008 cuts of 10 percent of its 3,000 workers, although not all would be reporters and editors. Then it announced that employees would have to take two weeks unpaid leave in the first half of 2009. In July 2009, it announced another round of cuts of 1,400 jobs nationwide from its community publishing unit.[102]

As bad as this sounds, what may be even worse is the relationship that the press appears to have lost with its readers. Fewer than half of Americans polled in March 2009 said that the closing of their local newspaper would hurt their community's civic life a lot. Only one-third said that if their local paper closed, they would miss it. The title of the report on these survey findings appears to have said it all: "Many Would Shrug if Their Local Newspaper Closed."[103]

However, closing newspapers means that fewer stories are written about how politicians spend tax money, or about what development project is coming to town, or how well schools educate children. It is possible that the movement toward "citizen journalism," where citizens report for their communities themselves, could take the place of professional journalists. But it is not likely. While it is not hard to imagine parents writing news about their children's sports teams or gardeners reporting which vegetables are best to grow in a particular climate, it is considerably more difficult to imagine a citizen having the time to cover an important, daylong hearing on a proposed tax increase at the statehouse or possessing the professional obligation to report on it fully, fairly and accurately. As the Project for Excellence in Journalism put it, "Fewer people and less space equates to significant erosion of the serious, accountability reporting that newspapers do more than any other medium."[104]

And yet, working as a newspaper journalist remains a profoundly interesting occupation. Newspaper reporters and editors have access to the mighty whose decisions affect thousands and to individuals whose stories can help people connect with each other to form a community. Despite the stresses on the industry, some newspapers probably will survive, even if smaller in form, for the foreseeable future. Citizens can only hope that serious, professional reporting continues as well.

Notes

1. Michael Emery, Edwin Emery and Nancy L. Roberts. *The Press and America: An Interpretive History of the Mass Media* (Boston, Mass.: Allyn & Bacon, 2000, 9th ed.), 24.
2. Charles E. Clark, "The Newspapers of Provincial America," in John B. Hench, ed., *Three Hundred Years of the American Newspaper* (Worcester, Mass.: American Antiquarian Society, 1991), 377.
3. Jill Lepore, "Back Issues: The day the newspaper died," *The New Yorker,* posted on January 26, 2009, available at http://www.newyorker.com/arts/critics/atlarge/2009/01/26/090126crat_atlarge_lepore.(accessed June 13, 2009).
4. *Publick Occurrences Both Forreign and Domestick*, September 25, 1690, http://nationalhumanitiescenter.org/pds/amerbegin/power/text5/PublickOccurrences.pdf (accessed June 13, 2009).
5. Clark, *supra* note 2, at 375.
6. *Publick Occurrences, supra* note 4.
7. Jeffery A. Smith, "James Franklin," in Perry J. Ashley, ed., *American Newspaper Journalists, 1690–1872. Dictionary of Literary Biography* (Detroit, Mich.: Gale Research Co., 1985), 214.
8. Michael Kirkhorn, "Benjamin Franklin," in Perry J. Ashley, ed., *American Newspaper Journalists, 1690–1872. Dictionary of Literary Biography* (Detroit, Mich.: Gale Research Co., 1985), 196.
9. Dennis S. Kahane, "Colonial Origins of Our Free Press," *American Bar Association Journal* (February 1976), Volume 62, Issue 2, 202–206.
10. Smith, *supra* note 7, at 217.
11. Kahane, *supra* note 9.
12. Smith, *supra* note 7, at 217.
13. Kahane, *supra* note 9.
14. Clark, *supra* note 2, at 382.
15. Emery, *supra* note 1, at 27.
16. Lepore, *supra* note 3.
17. Emery, *supra* note 1, at 95.
18. Lepore, *supra* note 3.
19. Bernard A. Weisberger, *The American Newspaperman* (Chicago: The University of Chicago Press, 1961), 27–28.
20. Ibid., 29–30.
21. Frederick B. Farrar, "Benjamin Russell," in Perry J. Ashley, ed., *American Newspaper Journalists, 1690–1872. Dictionary of Literary Biography* (Detroit, Mich.: Gale Research Co., 1985), 409.
22. Ibid., 410.
23. Ibid., 413.

24. Ted Curtis Smythe, *The Gilded Age Press*, 1865–1900 (Westport, Conn.: Praeger Publishers, 2003), 18.

25. Ibid., 17.

26. David Paul Nord, "Newspapers and American Nationhood," in John B. Hench, ed., *Three Hundred Years of the American Newspaper* (Worcester, Mass.: American Antiquarian Society, 1991), 397.

27. Emery, *supra* note 1, at 79.

28. Ibid., 78.

29. Carol Sue Humphrey, "The Press of the Young Republic: 1783–1833," in James D. Startt and Wm. David Sloan, ed. *The History of American Journalism.* (Westport, Conn.: Greenwood Press, 1996), 133–134.

30. Thomas D. Clark, *The Rural Press and the New South* (Baton Rouge, La.: Louisiana State University Press, 1948), 12.

31. Emery, *supra* note 1, at 91.

32. Ibid., 228.

33. Patrick S. Washburn, *The African American Newspaper: Voices of Freedom* (Evanston, Ill.: Northwestern University Press, 2006), 18.

34. Richard Campbell, Christopher R. Martin and Bettina Fabos, *Media & Culture* (Boston, Mass.: Bedford/St. Martin's, 2005), 282.

35. Washburn, *supra* note 33, at 28.

36. Ibid., 30.

37. Ibid., 36.

38. Bertram Wyatt-Brown, "The Abolitionists' Postal Campaign of 1835," *The Journal of Negro History* (October 1965, Volume 50: 4), 227–238.

39. Allen H. Merriam, "Elijah Lovejoy and Free Speech." Paper presented at the Annual Meeting of the Speech Communication Association (73rd, Boston, Mass., November 5–8, 1987).

40. Ibid., 2.

41. Ibid., 3.

42. Ibid., 6.

43. Ibid., 9.

44. David R. Spencer, *The Yellow Journalism: The Press and America's Emergence as a World Power.* (Evanston, Ill.: Northwestern University Press, 2007), 25.

45. Ibid., 117.

46. Emery, *supra* note 1, at 102.

47. Warren Francke, "James Gordon Bennett," in Perry J. Ashley, ed., *American Newspaper Journalists, 1690–1872. Dictionary of Literary Biography* (Detroit, Mich.: Gale Research Co., 1985), 31.

48. Ibid.

49. Ibid., 39.

50. Ibid., 35–36.

51. Ibid., 42.

52. Michael Schudson, "Preparing the Minds of the People, in John B. Hench, ed., *Three Hundred Years of the American Newspaper* (Worcester, Mass.: American Antiquarian Society, 1991), 435.

53. Emery, *supra* note 1, at 109–110.

54. "The News Cooperative Takes Shape," Associated Press, available at http://www.ap.org/pages/about/history/history_first.html (accessed June 24, 2009).

55. William David Sloan and Lisa Mullikin Parcel, eds., *American Journalism: History, Principles and Practices* (Jefferson, N.C.: McFarland & Company, 2002), 154–156, available at http://books.google.com/books?id=JOItkXKZ-3EC&pg=PA146&lpg=PA146&dq=American+Journalism+telegraph&source=bl&ots=OQK_5TL

14G&sig=ZXh66WEM917FGTALZ576hwKlwIc&hl=en&ei=KBhKSs3LDJL GMNrW0a4B&sa=X&oi=book_result&ct=result&resnum=1.

56. Robert McChesney, "Media Made Sport: A History of Sports in the United States," in Lawrence A. Wenner, ed. *Media, Sports and Society* (Thousand Oaks, Calif.: Sage, 1989), 94, available at http://books.google.com/books?id= d6HhgJDGXtQC (accessed June 16, 2009).

57. Ibid., 56.

58. Ibid., 58.

59. Ibid., 55.

60. Ibid., 57.

61. Gerald J. Baldasty, "The Nineteenth-Century Origins of Modern American Journalism," in John B. Hench, ed., *Three Hundred Years of the American Newspaper* (Worcester, Mass.: American Antiquarian Society, 1991), 414.

62. Emery, *supra* note 1, at 193.

63. Ibid., 196.

64. Spencer, *supra* note 44, at 134–138.

65. Ibid., 142–150.

66. Smythe, *supra* note 24, at 86.

67. Emery, *supra* note 1, at 175.

68. Spencer, *supra* note 44, at 103.

69. Seymour Topping, "History of the Pulitzer Prizes," available from www.pulitzer.org/historyofprizes (accessed June 30, 2009).

70. "Background," *CQ Researcher* (March 27 2009, Volume 2:1), 282–286.

71. Smythe, *supra* note 24, at 11–12.

72. Harlan S. Stensaas, "Development of the Objectivity Ethic of U.S. Daily Newspapers," *Journal of Mass Media Ethics* (1986, Volume 2:1), 50–60.

73. Ibid.

74. Ibid.

75. Ronald R. Rodgers, "'Journalism is a Loose-Jointed Thing': A Content Analysis of Editor & Publisher's Discussion of Journalistic Conduct Prior to the Canons of Journalism, 1901–1922," *Journal of Mass Media Ethics* (2007, Volume 22:1), 66–82.

76. Smythe, *supra* note 24, at 78–80.

77. Emery, *supra* note 1, at 288.

78. *Historical Statistics of the United States: Colonial Times to 1970* (Washington, D.C.: U.S. Dept. of Commerce, Bureau of the Census, 1975), 809.

79. Weisberger, *supra* note 19, at 194.

80. Emery, *supra* note 1, at 303.

81. Alfred McClung Lee, *The Daily Newspaper in America: The Evolution of a Social Instrument* (New York: Octagon Books, 1973), 243.

82. Weisberger, *supra* note 19, at 190–192.

83. Ibid., 195.

84. Baldasty, *supra* note 61, at 417.

85. "The Pulitzer Prizes," http://www.pulitzer.org/ (accessed June 23, 2009).

86. Mark Feldstein, "Watergate Revisited," August/September 2004, available at http://www.ajr.org/Article.asp?id=3735 (accessed June 23, 2009).

87. Ibid.

88. John Morton, "Short Term Losses, Long Term Profits," *American Journalism Review* (2007, Volume 19: 7), 60.

89. James McCartney, "USA Today Grows Up," *American Journalism Review* (2007, Volume 19: 7), 18.

90. "*USA Today* Circulation Moves Ahead of *Wall Street Journal*," *Quill*, December 1999, 3.

91. Lauren Janis, "A $1 Billion Gamble, A New Newspaper," *Columbia Journalism Review* (November/December 2001, Volume 40:1), 93.

92. "Total Paid Circulation," Newspaper Association of America, available at http://www.naa.org/TrendsandNumbers/Total-Paid-Circulation.aspx (accessed June 14, 2009).

93. "Project for Excellence in Journalism," The State of the News Media 2009, available at http://www.stateofthemedia.org/2009/narrative_newspapers_intro .php?cat=0&media=4 (accessed June 16, 2009).

94. Tom Rosenstiel and Bill Kovach, "The Public'sCcomplicated Views of Press Point to Solutions," The Pew Research Center for the People and the Press, posted on June 26, 2005, available at http://people-press.org/report/?pageid=971 (accessed July 1, 2009).

95. "Internet News Audience Highly Critical of News Organizations: Views of Press Values and Performance: 1985–2007, Summary of Findings," *The Pew Research Center for the People and the Press*, posted on August 9, 2007, available at http://people-press.org/report/348/internet-news-audience-highly-critical-of-news-organizations (accessed July 1, 2009).

96. Walter Pincus, "Newspaper Narcissism," *Columbia Journalism Review* (May/June 2009), 54–57.

97. Weisberger, *supra* note 19, at 202.

98. Newspaper Association of America, *supra* note 92 (accessed July 2, 2009).

99. Rick Edmonds and the Pew Project for Excellence in Journalism, "The State of the News Media 2009: An Annual Report on American Journalism," available at http://www.stateofthemedia.org/2009/narrative_newspapers_intro.php?cat=0&media=4 (accessed July 2, 2009).

100. Ibid.

101. American Society of Newspaper Editors. "U.S. Newsroom Employment Declines," posted on April 16, 2009, available at http://asne.org/article_view/smid/370/articleid/12/reftab/101.aspx (accessed July 2, 2009).

102. Greg Bensinger, "Gannett to Cut about 1,400 Newspaper Jobs by July 9 (Update 1)," available at http://www.bloomberg.com/apps/news?pid=20601103&sid=akQlyUshJpjs (accessed July 2, 2009).

103. News Interest Index, Pew Research Center for the People and the Press. "Many Would Shrug if Their Local Newspaper Closed," available at http://people-press.org/report/497/many-would-shrug-if-local-newspaper-closed (accessed July 2, 2009).

104. Project for Excellence in Journalism, *supra* note 93. Michael Emery, Edwin Emery and Nancy L. Roberts. *The Press and America: An Interpretive History of the Mass Media* (Boston, Mass.: Allyn & Bacon, 2000, 9th ed.), 24.

3

Why Freedom of the Press Is Essential

When the military took over the government of the Pacific nation of Fiji and a court declared the action unconstitutional, the government began removing stories from news websites and controlling the content of news stories. The *Fiji Times* kept publishing in 2009, but readers found swaths of white space where a military "sub-editor" had removed the story.[1]

It's called censorship.

Ever wonder what it would be like to pick up a newspaper and find it full of one-sided news, all praising the government? Ever wonder why when you pick up a newspaper that it has an opinion page where people debate the mayor's tax proposal or the way the police conducted an investigation or the government's bailout of an auto giant? Or when you read a story on the newspaper's website that comments of other readers often accompany the story?

The answer lies in the First Amendment: "Congress shall make no law…abridging the freedom of speech or of the press…." The First Amendment's promises that all Americans can speak their political convictions without fear of fines or imprisonment and that the media can report the news without government interference are part of the American heritage.

These freedoms, probably more than any other Constitutional right, symbolize America's commitment to liberty under law by posing a seemingly insurmountable obstacle to government censorship of ideas.[2]

Freedom Around the World

But freedom of the press is enjoyed today by fewer than 20 percent of the world's people, according to Freedom House, an independent organization that has monitored press freedom since 1980. According to Freedom House, "a free press plays a key role in sustaining and monitoring a healthy democracy, as well as in contributing to greater accountability, good government, and economic development."[3]

Freedom House explains what this means: "in the rest of the world, governments as well as non-state actors, control the viewpoints that reach citizens and brutally repress independent voices who aim to promote accountability, good governance, and economic development."[4]

The 2008 annual survey categorized seventy nations as offering freedom of the press, sixty-one nations as partly free, while sixty-four were rated not free. Based on the study's criteria, 17 percent of the world's citizens live in countries that enjoy a free press. The percentage is low, even though more than a third of the nations offer press freedom, because of nations like China, which is rated "not free," and India, which is rated "partly free." They are two of the world's most populous nations.[5]

Freedom and Democracy

Freedom of expression is a foundational right in a democracy; other rights lose their significance if citizens are not free to express opinions and if journalists are not free to publish the news of the day. One commentator has called it the "virtual linchpin of our constitutional culture."[6]

These rights are guaranteed as an essential part of American democracy. Democracy cannot function without a free press because democracy requires citizens who are informed so they can participate in the decision-making process. A free press cannot function without a democracy because few governors are willing to share the truth with their citizens.

Columbia University sociologist Herbert Gans has spelled out the importance of the role journalists play in a democracy:

> The country's democracy may belong directly or indirectly to its citizens, but the democratic process can only be truly meaningful if these citizens are informed. Journalism's job is to inform them. As *New York Times* columnist Anthony Lewis ended his last column before retirement, "The most important office in a democracy, Justice Louis Brandeis said, is the office of citizen."

Gans also pointed to an earlier column Lewis wrote in which he defined the journalist's role: "The theory of democracy is that the citizens are the ultimate sovereign. But in today's world, individuals cannot personally observe events and reach decisions in a forum, as in ancient Athens. They necessarily depend on the press to be informed."[7]

James Madison, who played key roles in the creation of the Constitution and the Bill of Rights, wrote after he left the White House of the importance of informed citizens. "Knowledge will forever govern ignorance and a people who mean to be their own governors must arm themselves with the power which knowledge gives."[8]

The Supreme Court of the United States also has acknowledged the primacy of the role of the press in a democracy and the reason for the protection bestowed on it by the First Amendment:

> Enlightened choice by an informed citizenry is the basic ideal upon which an open society is premised, and a free press is thus indispensable to a free society. Not only does the press enhance personal self-fulfillment by providing the people with the widest possible range of fact and opinion, but it also is an incontestable precondition of self-government.[9]

Theories of the Press

More than sixty years ago, three journalism scholars wrote a series of essays seeking to differentiate the role of the media under different forms of government.[10] The essays focus on four theories, but in reality the writers identify two different roles of the media under two different types of government.

The authoritarian theory, which reflects the practice of most governments through history, holds that only the government has the freedom to decide what information can and should be disclosed to its citizens. The modern corollary, labeled the Soviet communist theory by the essays, asserts that the government controls information not by licensing those who would publish ideas but by being the sole authoritative publisher and forbidding any other voices.

The second theory is the libertarian theory, which has developed more recently. The government espouses freedom of expression for its citizens in order that they can be informed and participate in their own governance. As a consequence, the government is restricted from interfering with the activities of the agencies and individuals that report news to the public. A modern corollary is the social responsibility theory, which argues that the press is morally responsible for serving the public and carrying out mass communications activities for the benefit of society.

The authors argue the different forms the media take in different countries are less a matter of technology, education and journalistic skill and almost exclusively a function of political and social control.

The Authoritarian Press Theory

The first theory of the press, the authoritarian theory, portrays the press as a "servant of the state responsible for much of its content to the power figures in charge of the government," whether those figures operate under a religious, military or otherwise totalitarian mandate.[11] Those in power communicate information—both truth and lies—that they want dispersed to instruct the governed what policies they should obey and support. The act of publishing generally requires some license or other government sanction; to violate that license has often resulted in imprisonment and death to those who dared publish something other than the authorized information. But censorship has seldom been completely effective. With the invention of the printing press, it became easier to publish material and distribute it discreetly. Today, the advent of technologies that make communication even more pervasive—satellite transmission and the Internet, for example—diminishes the ability of authoritarian rulers to control media messages.

But that doesn't mean they won't try. Countries such as China, Cuba, Burma, Eritrea and Uzbekistan have found one sure way to intimidate those involved in practicing journalism that criticizes the government. They are the top five countries for jailing journalists, according to a report by the Committee to Protect Journalists. The organization reported that in 2008, 125 journalists, including fifty-three reporters, editors and photographers who had worked for newspapers, were in jail around the world. The committee also reported that in 2008 the number of online journalists exceeded the number of newspaper journalists for the first time.[12]

Advanced technology allows messages to ignore political boundaries and be accessible to anyone who has the appropriate receiver. The authoritarian press has been predominant since the development of the printing press in the seventeenth century, but today most countries guarantee, or claim they guarantee, some press rights.

The authoritarian press theory rests on four postulates. First, people can reach their full potential only through their membership in a society, which thus gives greater importance to the community than to the individual.[13] "(T)he state became the summation of all desirable attributes." Second, the state superseded the individual in value since individuals can accomplish their purposes only through the state. Third, the state was essential to the full development of people, for "without the state the individual was helpless in developing the attributes of a civilized state." Finally, knowledge could be discovered by "wise men" and should be channeled for the good of everyone through the state. The state could operate successfully for the good of all but only through a unity of intellectual activity.

The "role" of the press in an authoritarian society has changed. Some of today's totalitarian states promote their own positions by publishing and broadcasting their own version of the news and their positions through state-run newspapers and broadcast outlets. The result is known as propaganda.

Propaganda was certainly the product of the press in the twentieth century corollary of the authoritarian press—the Soviet communist version. The idea that the press can function as a watchdog or coequal branch of government is not allowed in a system in which the role of the press is to broadcast the official view of the government. The concept that the press facilitates a debate about ideas is not consistent with the role of the press because the government's view is the view that is right.

Karl Marx, whose philosophic writings became the basis of socialism and communism, viewed the press as an indispensable weapon in the hands of the capitalists as an agent of social control. So long as the capitalistic class controlled the press, Marx said, the working class would never have access to the channels of communication. Marx, who was a journalist at the beginning of his career, believed the press helped capitalists maintain the status quo by concealing from the workers the true nature of the world they lived in; by not providing workers an accurate picture of the exploitation, it lulled them into contentment.[14]

Marx saw the press as a medium to change society, and his newspaper work demonstrates it. He thought the press should reveal to the working class how to throw off its chains. His call for revolution would have included putting the press in the hands of the working class to carry out meaningful reform. Of course, under the Leninist/Stalinist incarnation of Marx's socialism, the press was viewed as an instrument of the state.

The Libertarian Press Theory

The other press theory and its corollary rely on non-authoritarian forms of government, essentially democracy.

The libertarian theory holds that the press functions as a political institution to inform and to entertain citizens. Essential to its role is the independence of the press from government. Freedom of the press is essential because government officials usually have some stake in the outcome of a public debate and because giving government exclusive access to the channels of communication—as happens in authoritarian and communist governments—necessarily forces other voices and ideas to seek underground media.

In a landmark ruling, the Supreme Court of the United States said the nation was committed "to the principle that debate on public issues should be uninhibited, robust, and wide-open."[15] That principle requires the government not to control, or censor, the channels of debate, the media.

Like the authoritarian theory, the libertarian theory is rooted in its postulates about people and society and a theory of government. Libertarians hold that people are capable of mental reasoning, that they are rational; the goal of society is the happiness and well-being of the individual. Libertarians believe that people, as rational beings, are capable of creating society around them that will advance their interests and that they are capable of making decisions that will maintain society in the same manner. "The fulfillment of the individual therefore became the ultimate goal—the goal of man, of society, and of the state."[16]

In a libertarian government, the press functions to inform and entertain citizens so that they can fulfill their role within a democratic system. "Basically the underlying purpose of the media was to help discover truth, to assist in the process of solving political and social problems by presenting all manner of evidence and opinion as the basis for decision."[17]

The media were seen as a vehicle for public discussion of issues, and public discussion was seen as a vital part of the duty of a citizen. Supreme Court Justice Louis Brandeis declared that "public discussion is a political duty...this should be a fundamental principle of the American government."[18]

To protect voices and ideas expressed in the pursuit of truth, the founders of the American government created guarantees in many early state constitutions and in the federal Bill of Rights for freedom of expression— the freedom of speech, the freedom of the press, the freedom to assemble peaceably, the freedom to petition the government and the freedom of religion. Scholars have argued the prominent position given freedom of expression in American jurisprudence is essential to democratic government. "The special position that the First Amendment is granted in our system is a recognition of the paramount importance of the free exchange of ideas to self-government. Freedom of speech and press provisions of the First Amendment are designed to prevent interference with the exchange of information if citizens are to make intelligent decisions when choosing public officials and shaping policy."[19]

This principle—that citizens of a democracy should be able to exchange information and ideas without government interference—lies at the heart of the First Amendment. Legal scholar Alexander Meiklejohn argued that the First Amendment protects more than the act of expression; it protects the entire process before and after expression that is essential for self-government, including the critical role of the press. He argued that self-government could not be effective unless the "selves" of self-government were informed. Voting, he argued, was the final act in a process citizens follow to fulfill their responsibility for making the decisions that a democracy requires of them. Self-government can function properly only when the voters "acquire the intelligence, integrity, sensitivity, and generous devotion to the general welfare that, in theory, casting a ballot is assumed to express."[20]

> We, the people who govern, must try to understand the issues which, incident by incident, face the nation. We must pass judgment upon the decisions which our agents make upon those issues. And, further, we must share in devising methods by which those decisions can be made wise and

effective, or, if need be, supplanted by others which promise greater wisdom and effectiveness.

But the manner in which the press has fulfilled this role of supplying information to citizen-governors has been heavily criticized. Social responsibility theory, the corollary of the libertarian theory of the press, developed in the twentieth century as an answer to the criticisms leveled against the media. The major premise of the theory is that freedom carries with it certain obligations.[21]

Problems of 'A Free and Responsible Press'

A special task force, The Commission on Freedom of the Press, conducted one of the most influential evaluations of the role of the press. The commission published its report, *A Free and Responsible Press*, in 1947, summarizing "the problem" confronting the country in its first pages. The commission argued that freedom of the press faced danger for three reasons:

- First, the importance of the press to the people has greatly increased with the development of the press as an instrument of mass communication. At the same time the development of the press as an instrument of mass communication has greatly decreased the proportion of the people who can express their opinions and ideas through the press.

- Second, the few who are able to use the machinery of the press as an instrument of mass communication have not provided a service adequate to the needs of society.

- Third, those who direct the machinery of the press have engaged from time to time in practices which the society condemns and which, if continued, it will inevitably undertake to regulate or control.[22]

After concluding that the press was not meeting the needs of American society, the commission laid out what it called a free society's "requirements" of a free press:

1. a truthful, comprehensive and intelligent account of the day's events in a context that gives them meaning
2. a forum for the exchange of comment and criticism
3. projection of a representative picture of the constituent groups in the society
4. presentation and clarification of the goals and values of the society
5. full access to the day's intelligence

Those requirements, the commission argued, are necessary for informed citizens, who are essential to liberty. The basic theory of media and democracy holds that a free press and a democratic government cannot exist without each other. A democratic government depends on the participation of informed citizens; that information is obtained most of the time through the news media although other channels exist. In order for that information to be free of government control, it must come through a press that is independent.

Of course, the United States is not a pure democracy. In ancient Athens, the free citizens were able to gather in order to debate the issues of the day. But in a nation of 300 million, all the citizens of the United States—or even most of them—cannot gather in St. Louis to collectively question the candidates for president. Today's democracies function with citizens electing representatives who will make laws and oversee the government on their behalf. The United States, therefore, is a representative democracy; voters choose those who will make the decisions and serve as the chief executives of the country, the states and the cities.

A Press Free to Inform Citizens

For citizens to participate in the deliberations of their government, they must be informed of the issues, the actions of their governors and the outcomes of government's decisions.[23]

First, voters must understand the issues. But issues in the twenty-first century—issues such as health care, monetary policy, America's growing trade deficit and creating jobs in the global economy—are increasingly complex. Second, voters must come to their own convictions about the best approaches to those issues. Deciding which approach is better requires reading about the issue, the competing potential solutions, and the debate about those approaches. Third, voters must understand who the candidates are and what they stand for. Voters should know how candidates seeking re-election have handled the office and whether the votes they cast were consistent with the values they proclaimed on the campaign trail.

Because it is not realistic for most voters with their own resources to examine carefully the candidates and many of the issues, they are dependent on accounts that explain the candidates' stands and the issues. In that most important way, the news media facilitate the central function of a democracy: citizen involvement.

As the amount of information available multiplies and voices compete more loudly on cable news networks and ideas duel on blogs, citizens will find it increasingly important to locate sources that aggregate information and distill it in a manner that is both digestible and balanced.

Political scientists have argued that newspapers fail to effectively communicate important information to readers on the basis of repeated surveys that show citizens have little information about government. But another study concluded, "Although political knowledge levels are, in many instances, depressingly low, they are high enough among some segments of the population, and on some topics, to foster optimism about democratic possibilities."[24] Further, the study concluded that the overall political knowledge level has changed little in the past fifty years.[25]

The news media likewise serve as a conduit for public officials; newspapers have for decades provided a forum for elected representatives to speak to citizens. Some newspapers print regular updates written by officials. Public officials periodically write op-ed pieces that are published selectively. Reporters often interview officials, elected and appointed, and candidates about important issues. But with the birth of talk radio, the ever-watchful eyes of C-SPAN on congressional meetings, and the advent of the Internet and the rapid increase in its usage, public officials can communicate directly—without a reporter filtering the message—with voters.

Newspapers continue to provide important information that enables citizens to voice their opinions and vote their convictions. How would citizens know a school board was planning to close schools if the news media didn't report it? When a president desired to pressure members of Congress to pass tax reform legislation, the tactic would have little effect if the media failed to cover and report his speeches and travels to rally support for that proposal. How would citizens know the dangers of traveling to countries of the world where a deadly disease was being spread if the media didn't report it? It is difficult to protect yourself against some danger if no one has informed you about that danger.

Newspapers report all kinds of news people need and want to know. For example, on June 10, 2009:

> *The Aniston (Ala.) Star* reported the state's crops were in peril as farmers had trouble planting because of all the rain.
>
> *The Redding (Calif.) Searchlight* informed residents of four hamlets that they would soon be driving to Redding for fingerprinting, buying dog licenses and applying for a concealed weapons permit because, as a result of budget cuts, a sheriff's station was being closed.
>
> *The Ft. Collins Coloradoan* said that three fatal accidents involving drivers over the age of seventy highlighted the risks presented by older drivers.
>
> *The Hour* in Norwalk, Conn., reported on the governor's plan to increase public transportation fares by 40 percent.

A Press Not Always Free

While a democracy requires a free press to inform citizens and the First Amendment has guaranteed freedom of the press since 1791, the press has not always been free in the United States. History demonstrates that the great guarantee has not proven ironclad and that Congress has found ways to nullify it. One period of our history illustrates the fragility of freedom of the press.

The idea of a free press developed slowly. The First Congress, at the dogged insistence of U.S. Rep. James Madison of Virginia, proposed that great list of liberties known as the Bill of Rights, and the states quickly ratified it by the end of 1791.[26] Almost immediately, Congress moved to violate it. Fighting an undeclared war on France, the Quasi-War, the Federalists in Congress with the support of President John Adams, enacted the Alien and Sedition Acts of 1798. Adams later wrote that he considered the acts war measures and that they were needed. [27]

One provision of the acts originally declared war on France, but it was deleted before passage. Congress had authorized an army of 35,000 men, and Adams laid plans for construction of two ships, the *United States* and the *Constitution*. Congress levied a tax to pay for the army and the ships.[28]

The provisions of the Alien Law included increasing the residence requirement for immigrants from five to fourteen years because Federalists feared immigrants would vote against their party's candidates.[29] A second act authorized the president to deport or imprison resident aliens considered a danger to the peace or safety of the country.[30] Adams did sign deportation orders for three men, all Frenchmen who the administration later learned already had fled the country.[31] A third act authorized the president to deport resident aliens if the United States declared war on their home countries, an act that is still part of U.S. law.[32]

The Sedition Law, passed after the other three, made it a criminal offense to incite opposition to the laws or "to write, print, utter or publish…any false, scandalous or malicious writing…against the government of the United States, or either house of the Congress of the United States, or the President of the United States with intent to defame them or to bring them…into disrepute." Convictions could result in fines of up to $2,000 and imprisonment for up to two years.[33]

Even in the twenty-first century, it is hard to understand the bitterness of the political rivalries at the end of the eighteenth century. Both parties included men who had signed the Declaration of Independence and the Constitution. They had stood together to throw off the yoke of British imperialism and had worked together through the long hot summer of 1787 to craft a Constitution that created the union, and while the Constitution has been altered infrequently, the union it created has lasted and its citizens are among the freest on earth. Of course, in 1798, as the members of Congress debated the Alien and Sedition Laws, in the middle of what Adams considered a half-war, they could not see that what they had created together a decade before was being threatened by their efforts for national security.

During the administrations of George Washington, the ruling class divided into two parties, although they did not organize as such or resemble the parties of the current era. A major factor in the split was Alexander

Hamilton and the policies he advocated as Washington's secretary of the treasury. In the cabinet, he clashed with Thomas Jefferson and Madison over the financial goals he advocated for the country and a foreign policy that featured a strong relationship with Great Britain. He advocated a liberal interpretation of the Constitution that would energize the national government. Jefferson and Madison and their allies stressed development of agriculture, a foreign policy focused on France, and an interpretation of the Constitution that would limit national power.[34]

The lines were clearly drawn by the end of Washington's second term. The Federalists were led by Hamilton and John Adams until Hamilton's extra-marital affair was uncovered and he resigned from his post. The Republicans were led by Jefferson and Madison. In the election of 1796, Adams was elected president and Jefferson, because he finished with the second-highest number of electoral votes, became vice president.[35]

Despite the bonds of liberty that united these early statesmen and politicians, the internal disputes had reached a point that would serve as a model for politicians of every era. "The political tricks of the day—name-calling, allegations of guilt by association, and the like—were so similar to those employed within present memory that twentieth-century demagogues of either the right or left would have felt very much at home, no doubt, if translated to the late eighteenth century."[36]

What was not similar is the way newspapers cover politics. While a common but untrue assertion is that Republicans watch only Fox News and Democrats watch only CNN, the newspapers of that day were highly partisan. The eighteenth-century newspapers, especially during the Revolutionary War and the post-Washington presidency, were just as biased as the politicians themselves. The twentieth-century ideal of objectivity, that newspapers should strive to tell all sides of a story and leave the editorializing to the editorial page, had not been conceived.

The political motive behind the odious sedition law was the 1800 presidential election. Federalists loathed Jefferson and his beliefs, and they rightly feared that the vice president would seek the presidency again.[37] The targets of the law, however, were Republican newspapers because of their ability to influence readers and build support for Jefferson and Republican candidates. Jefferson, in a letter to Madison, expressed the belief that the newspapers were the best vehicle for toppling Adams and the Federalists in the election of 1800.[38]

This effort to silence criticism of Adams and his administration by suspending the First Amendment's guarantee of freedom of the press failed to enrage the Federalist newspapers. "It is patriotism to write in favor of our government," proclaimed the *Albany Centinel,* and "sedition to write against it." The *Gazette* of New York demanded that editors of Republican newspapers "be ferreted out of their lurking places and condemned" to punishment. The *Salem Gazette* argued that the safety of the country depended on the Sedition Act. One editor even compiled a list of Republican abuses for the benefit of government prosecutors.[39] A majority of the Federalist newspapers saw no conflict between the First Amendment and the Sedition Act.[40]

Secretary of State Thomas Pickering, who is said to have scoured Republican newspapers daily to find targets, did not view the Sedition Act as a threat to freedom of the press but as a measure necessary to exterminate "the pests of society and disturbers of order and tranquility."[41] As the election of 1800 approached, Pickering prepared to spring into action. In the summer of 1799, he laid plans to prosecute the editors of every leading Republican newspaper who had not already been prosecuted under the Sedition Act. With the approval of President Adams, he took personal charge of the prosecution of William Duane, editor of *The Aurora* of Philadelphia, the leading Republican newspaper. He wrote letters in August 1799 to district attorneys in New York where the *Argus* was published, in Baltimore where the *American* was published, and in Richmond where the *Examiner* was published, encouraging them to scrutinize those Republican papers and to prosecute them for any seditious libels they discovered.[42]

The editor of a fifth newspaper had been pursued before Pickering went to work. Thomas Adams, editor of the Boston *Independent Chronicle*, second in importance only to *The Aurora* among Republican newspapers, was indicted for his repeated blasts against the Sedition Act, the first important Republican editor hauled into court. Before he could be tried, however, he died. Abijah Adams, the bookkeeper for his brother's newspaper, also was indicted and found guilty of seditious libel. He was convicted, sentenced to thirty days in jail and forced to pay court costs.[43]

By focusing on the five major newspapers in the months before the election year, Pickering was able to keep the Republicans and their criticism of the president in the news. If, as in the case of the editor of the *Argus* in New York, the trial was held in May 1800, the newspaper and its editor would be consumed with the trial and little able to launch many attacks on Adams. These newspapers represented geographical centers, so news of the indictments and trial would spread throughout the various regions of the country. In that era, smaller newspapers often subsisted by republishing stories the editors found in larger newspapers from the population centers of the young country.[44]

Historians disagree on the exact numbers, but twenty-five people were arrested, fifteen of them were indicted, and ten of them were convicted, including a congressman. Seven of those who were convicted were journalists.[45] Pickering's scorecard: Two Republican newspapers—the New York *Time Piece* and the Mount Pleasant *Register*—folded and several others—such as the *Bee* of New London, Conn.—had to suspend publication while their editors served time in jail.[46] Violations of the law ran the gamut from circulating a petition for repeal of the repressive act to a drunken wish that a cannonball would strike the president in his behind.[47]

One of the most notorious trials involved Congressman Matthew Lyon of Vermont, who in a letter to the editor of the *Journal* of Windsor, Vermont, said the Adams administration had demonstrated "an unbounded thirst for ridiculous pomp, foolish adulation and selfish avarice." For that he was sentenced to four months in jail and fined $1,000.[48] The Republican was re-elected from jail and became almost a folk hero in his district. But the Sedition Act failed to have the desired effect. Before the Federalists pushed the law through Congress in June and July of 1798, 28 percent of the nation's press was Republican. By the time of the 1800 election, that number had climbed to 40 percent.[49] Most convincingly, the Federalists lost congressional control and, in one of the closest elections in the history of the United States, Jefferson was elected president by a vote decided in the House of Representatives.

One of the Virginian's earliest acts as president was the pardon of two men charged under the Sedition Act. Later in the year, he would halt proceedings against William Duane, the editor of *The Aurora* of Philadelphia.[50] James Thomas Callender had just completed his nine-month sentence, but Jefferson made sure his $200 fine was returned to him. Callender, writing for the South's leading Democratic-Republican newspaper, the Richmond *Examiner*, in 1800 compiled material for *The Prospect before Us*, a pamphlet advocating the election of Jefferson. Callender described the administration of John Adams as "one continued tempest of malignant passions. As President he has never opened his lips, or lifted his pen without threatening and scolding; the grand object of his administration has been to exasperate the rage of contending parties, to calumniate and destroy every man who differs from his opinions."[51]

David Brown had received the most severe punishment under the law, a sentence of eighteen months and a fine of $480. Brown was described as a vagabond radical who went around proclaiming the evils of the Federalist administration. In Dedham, Mass., he helped erect a pole similar to those erected during the Revolutionary period. The practice was a favorite one of the Sons of Liberty, led by Samuel Adams, before the Revolutionary War to protest what they considered a tyrannical act of the British monarchy. The Republicans revived the practice during the Adams administration. To the pole Brown attached a placard declaring "No Stamp Act. No Sedition Act. No Alien Bills. No Land Tax, downfall to the Tyrants of America; peace and retirement to the President; Long live the Vice-President." Even though Brown pleaded guilty, Justice Samuel Chase, who presided at the trial, insisted on a full trial and demanded that Brown identify those who helped him erect the pole. When he would not do it, Chase handed down the toughest sentence of the Alien Act prosecutions. When Jefferson took the oath of office on March 4, 1801, Brown was still in jail because he could not pay his fine.[52]

In 1840, Congress voted to refund the heirs of Rep. Matthew Lyon his

$1,000 fine and $60.96 court costs plus interest. Ten years later, Congress refunded to the heirs of Dr. Thomas Cooper, a Pennsylvania pamphleteer, his $400 fine and interest.[53]

The constitutionality of the Sedition Law of 1798 was never tested in the Supreme Court. Its prospects would not have been dim because three of the six members of the Supreme Court presided over sedition trials and never found the law violated the First Amendment.[54] But the principle of judicial review did not even exist in 1798 and would have to wait until a Federalist congressman, Virginia's John Marshall, appointed as chief justice of the United States by Adams in 1801, handed down the Court's decision in *Marbury v. Madison*, establishing the role of the judiciary as final arbiter of the law in 1803.[55]

History affords us few clues how the early Marshall court would have ruled on the question of the Sedition Act directly violating the rights of citizens guaranteed under the First Amendment's freedom of speech and freedom of the press clauses. Marshall was not a member of the U.S. House of Representatives in 1798 when the Sedition Act was passed. But when he ran for a seat in Congress in autumn of 1798 to represent his Virginia constituents, he made it clear that while a Federalist, he opposed the Alien and Sedition Acts and would have voted against them if he had been a member of Congress when they were considered. He did vote with the Republicans in 1800 on a failed motion to repeal the sedition law.[56] His opposition, however, was based on his belief that the law was "calculated to create unnecessary discontents and jealousies."[57]

Jefferson, of course, was certain the act was unconstitutional. It had expired on the day before he was inaugurated as the nation's third president, and his allies in Congress beat back an attempt by the Federalists to renew it.[58] In an 1804 letter to Abigail Adams, wife of the former president, Jefferson explained his belief about the unconstitutionality of the Section Act. "I discharged every person under punishment or prosecution under the Sedition Law because I considered, and now consider, that law to be a nullity as absolute and as palpable as if Congress has ordered us to fall down and worship a golden image; and that it was my duty to arrest its execution at every stage, as it would have been to have rescued from the fiery furnace those who should have been cast into it for refusing to worship their image."[59]

The expiration of the Sedition Act did not, of course, bring an end to debate on the meaning of the First Amendment, but in no other era of this nation's history has the government prosecuted editors for criminal sedition. During the first half of the twentieth century, the history of the First Amendment was a story primarily of dissidents whose ideas were anathema to the majority and the efforts of state and federal governments to punish those dissidents and limit their right to freedom of expression. The defendants in the early free speech cases from the World War I era were primarily anti-war demonstrators and socialists usually tried either for advocating the overthrow of the government or for advocating interference with the war effort.

In one of those cases, the issue of sedition arose again in a dissent written by Associate Justice Oliver Wendell Holmes: "I wholly disagree with the argument of the Government that the First Amendment left the common law as to seditious libel in force. History seems to me against the notion. I had conceived that the United States through many years had shown its repentance for the Sedition Act of 1798, by repaying fines that it imposed."[60]

The final word on the Sedition Act came in 1964 in a powerful opinion written by Supreme Court Justice William Brennan Jr. *New York Times v. Sullivan* was a libel action by a city official in Montgomery, Ala., who claimed an advertisement seeking support for the civil rights movement had damaged his reputation. In his opinion for a unanimous Court overruling the official's victory in the lower courts, Brennan declared the lawsuit was a way to re-establish sedition as a civil action since it was not available as a criminal action. Citing Jefferson's pardons and letter to Mrs. Adams, the repayment of fines, the statement of Justice Holmes and other justices, he declared, "These views reflect a broad consensus that the Act, because of the restraint it imposed upon criticism of government and public officials, was inconsistent with the First Amendment."[61]

If Brennan's opinion puts to rest the issue of the constitutionality of the Sedition Act, it doesn't preclude the possibility that a national crisis could revive sedition. Despite the age and history of the Constitution and the Bill of Rights, freedom is a delicate matter. The breadth of First Amendment protection that journalists and speakers enjoy is not carved in stone, and public opinion on what freedom of the press should mean ebbs and flows. Politicians today do not enjoy the biting criticism they receive through the media. Editorial writers and columnists are capable of over-the-top criticism. But criticizing the government is not a crime today.

The strangest news about the First Amendment is not that most of the world does not enjoy the right to freely express themselves, nor that during times of war it has taken a back seat to national security concerns. What is most surprising is that Americans fail to appreciate it fully.

Since 1997, the First Amendment Center at Vanderbilt University has been conducting an annual public opinion poll that seeks to measure American attitudes toward the First Amendment. The 2009 results, issued on Constitution Day, September 17, continue to show a level of support inconsistent with the importance of freedom of the press.

The survey, conducted by telephone, found that 16 percent of the 1,003 people who responded were able to name freedom of the press as one of the rights guaranteed by the First Amendment. Astoundingly, 84 percent could not. When they were asked whether the First Amendment guaranteed the right amount of freedom to the press to enable it to do what it wants, 48 percent agreed. But 39 percent said the press had too much freedom and 7 percent said it didn't have enough.

The survey did find some good news. Forty-eight percent of those surveyed strongly agreed with a statement that the media's role as watchdog of the government is important, and 25 percent more mildly agreed.[62]

Notes

1. *The Sydney Morning Herald*, "Media Draw Blank as Fiji Told to Watch This Space," posted on April 13, 2009, available at http://www.smh.com.au/national/media-draw-blank-as-fiji-told-to-watch-this-space-20090412-a41x.html.

2. Cass Sunstein, *Democracy and the Problem of Free Speech* (New York: Simon & Schuster, 1995), xi.

3. Freedom House, "Freedom of the Press," available at http://freedomhouse.org/template.cfm?page=16 (accessed November 19, 2009).

4. Ibid.

5. Karin D. Karlekar, Freedom House, "Press Freedom in 2008: Restrictive Laws and Physical Attacks Fuel Further Declines," downloadable at http://freedomhouse.org/template.cfm? page=16.

6. Vincent Blasi, "Free Speech and Good Character," *UCLA Law Review* (1999, Volume 46), 1567, 1568. See also Sunstein, *supra* note 2 at 121. "Every democrat places free expression at the catalogue of legally protected rights."

7. Herbert J. Gans, *Democracy and the News* (New York: Oxford University Press, 2003), 1.

8. James Madison, "Letter to W. T. Barry, August 4, 1822," in Saul K. Padover, ed., *The Complete Madison* (New York: Harper & Brothers, 1953), 337.

9. *Branzburg v. Hayes*, 408 U.S. 665, 726–727 (1972) (*Stewart, J., dissenting*).

10. Fred S. Siebert, Theodore Peterson and Wilbur Schramm, *Four Theories of the Press* (Urbana, Ill.: University of Illinois Press, 1956, 1963), 1.

11. Ibid.

12. The Committee to Protect Journalists, "CPJ's 2008 Prison Census: Online and in Jail," posted on December 4, 2008, available at http://www.cpj.org/imprisoned/cpjs-2008-census-online-journalists-now-jailed-mor.php (accessed June 10, 2009).

13. Siebert et al., *supra* note 10, at 10–12.

14. Herbert J. Altschull, *From Milton to McLuhan: The Ideas Behind American Journalism* (New York: Longman, 1990), 198–204.

15. *New York Times v. Sullivan*, 376 U.S. 254, 270 (1964).

16. Siebert et al., *supra* note 10, at 40.

17. Ibid., 51.

18. *Whitney v. California*, 274 U.S. 357, 375 (1927) (*Brandeis, J., concurring*).

19. Richard Labunski, *The First Amendment Under Siege* (Westport, Conn.: Greenwood Press, 1981), 3.

20. Alexander Meiklejohn, "The First Amendment Is an Absolute, *Supreme Court Review* (1961), in Kent Middleton and Roy Mersky, eds., *Freedom of Expression: A Collection of Best Writings* (Buffalo, N.Y.: William S. Hein & Co., 1981), 75.

21. Siebert et al., *supra* note 10, at 74.

22. Robert D. Leigh, ed., *A Free and Responsible Press: Report of the Commission on Freedom of the Press* (Chicago: University of Chicago Press, 1947), 1.

23. Stephen Breyer, *Active Liberty: Interpreting Our Democratic Constitution* (New York: Random House, 2005), 1–2.

24. Michael X. Delli Carpini and Scott Keeter, *What Americans Know about Politics and Why It Matters* (New Haven, Conn.: Yale University Press, 1996), 269.
25. Ibid.
26. Richard Labunski, *James Madison and the Struggle for the Bill of Rights* (New York: Oxford University Press, 2006), 178–241.
27. David McCullough, *John Adams* (New York: Simon & Schuster, 2001), 504–507.
28. Michael Emery, Edwin Emery and Nancy L. Roberts, *The Press and America: An Interpretive History of the Mass Media* (Boston: Allyn & Bacon, 2000, 9th ed.), 71.
29. Ch. 54, 1 Stat. 566 (1798) (repealed on April 14, 1802).
30. Ch. 58, 1 Stat. 570 (1798) (expired).
31. John Ferling, *Adams vs. Jefferson: The Tumultuous Election of 1800* (New York: Oxford University Press, 2004), 122.
32. Ch. 66, 1 Stat. 577 (1798).
33. Ch. 74, 1 Stat. 596 (1798) (expired on March 3, 1801).
34. William J. Watkins, *Reclaiming the American Revolution: The Kentucky and Virginia Resolutions and Their Legacy* (New York: Palgrave Macmillan, 2004), 1–25.
35. Under the Constitution, the candidate who received the most votes in the Electoral College became president, and the runner-up became vice president. This meant the top contenders, and bitter opponents, in 1796 took the top two offices. The Twelfth Amendment, ratified in 1804, changed that system.
36. Dumas Malone, *Jefferson and the Ordeal of Liberty* (Boston, Mass.: Little, Brown & Co., 1962), 391.
37. Geoffrey R. Stone, *Perilous Times: Free Speech in Wartime* (New York: W.W. Norton & Co., 2004), 48.
38. Ferling, *supra* note 31, at 143.
39. Stone, *supra* note 37, at 46.
40. William David Sloan, ed., *The Media in America: A History* (Northport, Ala.: Vision Press, 2008), 116.
41. Ibid.
42. James M. Smith, *Freedom's Fetters: The Alien and Sedition Laws and American Civil Liberties* (Ithaca, N.Y.: Cornell University Press, 1956), 186.
43. Ibid., 247–255.
44. Ibid., 185–187.
45. Eric Burns, *Infamous Scribblers* (New York: PublicAffairs, 2006), 362.
46. Anthony Lewis, *Make No Law: The Sullivan Case and the First Amendment* (New York: Vintage Books, 1991), 63.
47. Lance Banning, *Sacred Fire of Liberty* (Ithaca, N.Y.: Cornell University Press, 1995), 385–386.
48. Lewis, *supra* note 46, at 63.
49. Ferling, *supra* note 31, at 144.
50. Dumas Malone, *Jefferson the President* (Boston, Mass: Little, Brown & Co., 1970), 35.
51. Smith, *supra* note 42, at 339; Stone, *supra* note 37, at 61–63.
52. Smith, *supra* note 42, at 286.
53. Lewis, *supra* note 46, at 66.
54. Ibid., at 65.
55. *Marbury v. Madison*, 5 U.S. 137 (1803).
56. Gregg Costa, "John Marshall, the Sedition Act and Free Speech in the Early Republic," *Texas Law Review* (1999, Volume 77), 1011.
57. Malone, *supra* note 36, at 417.
58. Malone, *supra* note 50, at 153.

59. Ibid., 155.
60. *Abrams v. United States*, 250 U.S. 616, 630 (*Holmes, J., dissenting.*).
61. *New York Times Co. v. Sullivan*, 376 U.S. 254, 276 (1964).
62. First Amendment Center (2009), "Traditional News Media Still 1st Source on Big Stories," available at http:// www.firstamendmentcenter.org/news .aspx?id=22071 (accessed November 19, 2009).

4

The Roles of a Free Press

The Newspaper is an Institution developed by Modern Civilization to present the News of the day, to foster Commerce and Industry, to inform and lead Public Opinion, and to furnish that check upon Government which no constitution has ever been able to provide.

That was the credo of *The Chicago Tribune* in 1924 written by its publisher, Colonel Robert Rutherford McCormick. He is best remembered for the crucial role he played in ensuring the Supreme Court of the United States considered *Near v. Minnesota*,[1] the case that more than seventy-five years later is the foundation of the First Amendment's prior restraint doctrine.[2] While McCormick was not a communications scholar, many of his ideas resonate with today's theories on the role of the newspaper. Newspapers present the news of the day, whether it originates in Beijing or Washington; newspapers report on business and carry advertising for products and services; they report on important issues and debates, editorialize on such debates and carry columns written by syndicated journalists and other opinion leaders; newspapers still serve as watchdogs on the powerful.

In a real sense, newspapers are also a means of entertainment. Apart from the news of the day, they offer movie and music reviews, celebrity news, puzzles, how-to features on topics as diverse as investing and gardening, personal advice columns, baseball scores and a myriad of sports statistics and dozens of other topics that are not essential to the life of the average reader.

Some of the newspaper's daily content is essential for the maintenance of a democratic government. In addition to the jobs newspapers provide for reporters, editors, photographers, cartoonists, advertising and circulation personnel, and the money it earns for those who own them, newspapers play a significant part in the democratic government of the United States.

Four of those roles underscore the importance of newspapers.

- Newspapers examine what public officials are doing, a process that discourages the powerful from abusing their public trust. This enables citizens to hold their governors accountable for their behavior and their conduct of the duties of their offices. This is known as the **watchdog role** of the media.

- Newspapers inform citizens of what is happening now-in their communities, in their cities, in their states, in their country, in the world. Citizens need to understand the issues and the problems confronting society. They need to know what their elected representatives are doing about those problems. This is known as the **informative role** of the media.

- Newspapers publish stories about issues and points of view so that they can be debated. This provides an opportunity for citizens to look at the various perspectives on an issue. This is known as the marketplace of ideas or the **deliberative role** of the media.

- Newspapers hold a searchlight on pressing public issues that editors and reporters believe should be addressed by government. This means the government cannot control the public policy agenda. This is known as the **agenda-setting** role of the media.

To facilitate the informative role of newspapers and the media and to facilitate the watchdog role, government must be open to public observation. To ensure openness, states have adopted open records and open meetings laws, so-called "sunshine laws." The Kentucky Open Meetings Law (KRS 61.800) begins with a preamble that declares, "The General Assembly finds and declares that the basic policy of (the open meetings law) is that the formation of public policy is public business and shall not be conducted in secret...."

To make sure that public business is not conducted as private business, reporters act as surrogates for the public, attending meetings, examining public documents, interviewing sources to understand what government is doing. Without open government and sources, journalists could not fulfill their responsibilities to democracy. One of those responsibilities, serving as a watchdog on government and society's institutions, is the most basic function of the press.

The Watchdog Role

More crime, immorality and rascality is prevented by the fear of exposure in the newspapers than by all the laws moral and statute ever devised.[3]

At least that was the belief of Joseph Pulitzer, publisher of the *St. Louis Post-Dispatch* and the *New York World*. There is no way of proving his contention, and public corruption seems to be fairly common despite the omnipresence of the media. Nevertheless, reporters often produce stories that expose activities that the governed or other authority figures would like to hide from scrutiny. If the governors are to be accountable to those who elected them, citizens must be informed about their performance. A basic rule of human behavior is that when people believe they are accountable they do a better job. Or, put another way, power corrupts.

Jennifer Hewlett, reporter for the *Lexington Herald-Leader*, reported in November 2008 that the executive director of Lexington's Blue Grass Airport, the 117th busiest in the country, spent more than $200,000 on travel on behalf of the airport between January 2006 and March 2008 in addition to his $220,000 annual salary and benefit package. Her reporting led to the director's resignation and a shake-up of the airport's organization.[4] Prompted by the newspaper's reporting, the state's auditor's office did its own investigation and announced that airport administrators had spent nearly $500,000 in "questionable or unsupported" expenses between January 2006 and December 2008.[5]

David Barstow, reporter for the *New York Times*, reported in April 2008 that the Pentagon had attempted to influence public opinion about the war in Iraq by providing the media with access to "military experts," most of them retired military officers, to generate positive news coverage of the war. And most of the media who interviewed those officers failed to disclose to the audience that many of these experts had ongoing ties to military contractors and their preparation by the Pentagon. For his reporting, Barstow won a Pulitzer Prize.[6]

The Washington Post reporters Anne Hull and Dana Priest won a Pulitzer Prize in 2008 for their reporting on the deteriorating conditions for treatment of veterans at Walter Reed Hospital, which resulted in quick action by the Defense Department to improve conditions.[7] It was Priest's second Pulitzer for shedding light on the secretive actions of the federal government. Her first was for "her persistent, painstaking reports on secret 'black site' prisons and other controversial features of the government's counterterrorism campaign."

All the above are examples of watchdog journalism. One definition of watchdog journalism holds it is "independent scrutiny by the press of the activities of government, business, and other public institutions, with an aim toward documenting, questioning, and investigating those activities in order to provide publics and officials with timely information on issues of public concern."[8] Another definition describes it as "revealing abuses in the exercise of state authority."[9]

Some scholars argue that the watchdog role is the primary democratic responsibility of the press, overriding the other roles in importance.[10] Regardless of how it is defined or what it is called—advocacy journalism, adversarial journalism, investigative reporting or muckraking—the watchdog role of the press has been and remains a part of journalism. One list of the accomplishments of watchdog journalism includes pressing the government to end slavery, promoting women's rights, integrating baseball and supporting the civil rights movement, bringing to an end American involvement in Vietnam, exposing the accounting abuses of Enron and revealing the flaws in the selection process of Olympic host cities. No list would be complete, of course, without an entry for Watergate and exposing the cover-up created by the White House.[11]

But that impressive list of contributions to American life doesn't overshadow its list of failures, most notably its failure to warn of the impending collapse of the housing market in 2008, the gigantic losses on the stock market and the rise of unemployment, the worst economic recession since 1929. Analysts point to industry conditions that contributed to the failure. "The disintegration of the financial media's own financial underpinnings could not have come at a worse time. Low morale, lost expertise, and constant cutbacks, especially in investigative reporting—these are not conditions that produce an appetite for confrontation and muckraking." At the same time, veteran Wall Street regulators were leaving, depriving the remaining reporters of tips that could have put them on the trail of the looming crash.[12] Former *New York Times* Investigative Editor Steve Engleberg told National Public Radio that another reason the media watchdogs largely failed to bark was that they did not understand the complexity of the financial markets.[13]

And what happens when the press sounds the alarm but no one listens? In an amazing five-part series in June 2002, the *New Orleans Times-Picayune* laid out the disaster that was awaiting the arrival of Hurricane Katrina on August 29, 2005, taking more than 1,800 lives, inundating most of New Orleans and creating a political maelstrom of epic proportions.[14] The warning tragically went unheeded.

For all the glamour of high-profile reporting and Pulitzer Prize nominations, most of the watchdog function is performed by reporters at local newspapers, as part of routine but eminently important monitoring of local government.

Reporters will examine the city's new budget to see how the money is going to be spent. That makes the city officials accountable to taxpayers. Reporters will also check the list of winners in the budget against the list of campaign contributors to city officials. That ensures taxpayers learn who is being rewarded and who is wielding influence in city government.

How public money is spent should never be secret. It is taxpayer money, and it has been paid to the city or county or state government. Those holding office were elected by voters or appointed by those who were elected by the voters. Their jobs involve the public welfare. Each element of that equation strengthens the demands for public accountability of how the money is spent. What is more difficult to ferret out is whether political power is being exercised improperly.

Public support for the news media's role as a watchdog increased from 2003 to 2005. Six in ten Americans responding to a 2005 survey for the Pew Research Center for the People and the Press said that when news organizations criticize political leaders it keeps politicians from doing things that should not be done. That represented an increase from 2003 when 54 percent endorsed the role of the press as a political watchdog. In the 2005 survey, respondents had a favorable image of their local newspaper by an 80–20 percent margin.[15] In a 2008 survey, the Pew Center found that the number of local journalists who believe the press is playing its watchdog role well had more than doubled since 2004, from 9 percent of local print journalists to 23 percent. In 2004, 5 percent of national journalists said the press was fulfilling its watchdog role well, and that rose to 9 percent in the 2008 survey.[16]

The Supreme Court also has recognized the importance of the watchdog role of the media. Justice Hugo Black wrote one of the fullest discussions in a decision upholding the right of a newspaper to run on Election Day an editorial that expressed the paper's policy on an issue on the ballot. He began by acknowledging that while legal scholars differ on the interpretation of the First Amendment, almost everyone agrees that one major purpose was to ensure that Americans could freely discuss government affairs.

> The Constitution specifically selected the press…to play an important role in the discussion of public affairs. Thus the press serves and was designed to serve as a powerful antidote to any abuses of power by governmental officials and as a constitutionally chosen means for keeping officials elected by the people responsible to all the people whom they were selected to serve. Suppression of the right of the press to praise or criticize governmental agents and to clamor and contend for or against change…muzzles one of the very agencies the Framers of our Constitution thoughtfully and deliberately selected to improve our society and keep it free.[17]

This role of the media as an independent check on those who govern explains the power and rationale of the First Amendment. In November 1974, just months after the resignation of President Richard M. Nixon, Supreme Court Justice Potter Stewart delivered a speech in which he argued that the framers had created a constitutional guarantee of a free press to set up another institutional check on the three branches of government.

Freedom of speech and freedom of the press exist to keep in check the power of the government in relation to its citizens. Justice Stewart quoted the free press clause of the Massachusetts Constitution, which was drafted by John Adams, who became the nation's second president: "The liberty of the press is essential to the security of the state."[18]

Therefore, any ability of the government to regulate the press would eat away at the independent role of the press and its ability to serve as a watchdog. The Supreme Court of the United States declared unconstitutional a Florida law that created a "right of reply," which required a newspaper to publish a reply from a political candidate whose character or record is criticized by the newspaper.[19] The Florida law was supported by those who argued that it was the government's responsibility to ensure that the widest possible variety of views reached the public, even though the First Amendment's wording appears rather clearly to close off government intervention: "Congress shall make no law…abridging freedom of the press.…"[20]

The argument over a right to access is still alive.[21] But Justice Byron White, never a strong voice on behalf of the media, scoffed at the very idea that a "right of reply" could survive "the virtually insurmountable barrier between government and the print media."[22] He went on to argue that the United States "has learned, and continues to learn, from what we view as the unhappy experiences of other nations where government has been allowed to meddle in the internal editorial affairs of newspapers…and (we) remain intensely skeptical about those measures that would allow government to insinuate itself into the editorial rooms of this Nation's press.…"[23]

The Informative Role

These and other cases raise the question of] whether peace is best preserved by giving energy to the government, or information to the people. This last is the most certain, and the most legitimate engine of government. Educate and inform the whole mass of the people.…They are the only sure reliance for the preservation of our liberty.

The importance of the informative role of the press was spelled out by Thomas Jefferson in a letter to James Madison in 1787. He reiterated his conviction in another letter, two years later: "Whenever the people are well-informed, they can be trusted with their own government." However, it was also Jefferson who wrote "the man who never looks into a newspaper is better informed than he who reads them, inasmuch as he who knows nothing is nearer the truth than he whose mind is filled with falsehoods and errors."[24]

Of course, Jefferson was writing 200 years ago, long before the mass media found their way across the airwaves and onto the information superhighway. But even today, most of what people know about what is happening in the world, apart from their own circle of personal experiences, they know because newspapers or television told them, or they heard it from someone who heard it on the radio or read it in a newspaper or on the Internet.

According to the libertarian theory, the news media function as a political institution to inform citizens. This is essential for democracy in a nation of almost 300 million people living within 3.8 million square miles. It might have been possible for all the ruling class in ancient Athens to gather to discuss an issue of great importance, but it is impossible today except in the smallest of towns. "Ideally, the media should inform people about the issues confronting their society and the world and about the policy alternatives for trying to resolve them."[25]

As an example, look at the front page of *The New York Times* on July 1, 2009, which carried stories headlined "Minnesota Court Rules Democrat Won Senate Seat," the decision in the November 2008 race between Republican incumbent Norm Coleman and the victorious challenger Al Franken, a Democrat; "Iraq Celebrates U.S. Withdrawal From Its Cities," as American troops turned over responsibility for patrolling in urban areas; and "Ban Is Advised On 2 Top Pills For Pain Relief," as an advisory panel recommended that the Food and Drug Administration ban two common prescription pain medicines.

Daily newspapers cover a gamut of topics. Readers can learn about government, education, crime, business, sports, the arts and entertainment and dozens of other topics. Newspapers provide information on a broad range of topics. But specialty newspapers are focused. *The Wall Street Journal* is one of the nation's sources for business news. *The Chronicle of Higher Education* focuses on news of interest to university administrators and educators. *The Sporting News* is a must-read for fans of baseball, football and many other sports. In addition, several newspapers—the *New York Times, The Washington Post, USA Today* and *The Christian Science Monitor*—are recognized as national newspapers, intended for wide circulation around the country.

Local newspapers, from dailies to weeklies, report national and international news, usually by publishing stories from wire services. Depending on their publication schedule and their circulation area, they use most of their reporters and news hole to focus on local news, and their readers are able to develop a sense of their community's strengths and weaknesses. That knowledge enables citizens to discuss—with their leaders, their neighbors and the candidates—how to address those problems. But if they are uninformed, citizens can't effectively participate in their own government, can't help solve problems and can't be mobilized to defend their own way of life.

The information can serve not only to enable citizens to participate in self-government but also to reassure them, especially during times of crisis. In the hours after the assassination of President John F. Kennedy in November 1963, the assassination attempt on President Ronald W. Reagan in March 1981 and the terrorist attacks on the United States in September 2001, citizens watched and read to learn the latest. What they saw were steps being taken to ensure the government was continuing to function and the crisis was being addressed. Citizens learned events were not spiraling into chaos.

Signaling the Importance of Events

One product of this informative role is that readers gain an understanding of what is important. As media scholar Walter Lippmann outlined it, a primary role of the press in reporting the news is to signal the important developments as soon as possible. It is this role that puts the stress on getting information and publishing it first.[26] "There is a reason it is called news," is one way to stress that the passage of time diminishes the importance of any story in a competitive media market. And newspapers are largely focused on reporting breaking news as it happens. The move to the Internet has dramatically enhanced the ability of newspapers to compete with the breaking news features of their radio and television. What once could be accomplished only through an "extra" published outside the newspaper's normal schedule can now be accomplished with relative ease on a newspaper's website.

This clearly affects what people talk about. A study of the media coverage of the 2000 presidential election found a close association between the amount of coverage of the campaigns and the extent to which people discussed and thought about the campaign. As the media paid more attention to the candidates, those who were surveyed reported having seen, read or heard election news stories. That study led the author to this conclusion: "If the coverage in 2000 had been as heavy as it was in 1992, people would have talked and thought more about the campaign. As a result, they also would have been better informed about the candidates and issues." The author suggested there was evidence that more coverage would have produced higher voter turnout.[27]

The Gate-Keeping Function

"All the news that's fit to print," the motto of *The New York Times*, is simply an impossibility; the events in more than one hundred nations on seven continents could not be chronicled entirely. No newspaper has the space to handle all those accounts or the reporters and editors to process them. Far more news is available than news space, and that demands that reporters and particularly editors make choices every day about what is going to be published.

The gate-keeping function of the media is a corollary to the informative role; that is, from the many happenings of a day, reporters and editors choose events, issues and people and present them as the most important information for the news consumer on that particular day. Some of the choices they make are dictated by the power of events and the audience members who read the newspaper. When Michael Jackson died, when President Barack Obama visited Russia, when Iranians took to the street to protest an election they thought was fixed, when Roger Federer won his sixth Wimbledon tennis title and his record fifteenth grand slam championship, news editors knew they had to provide those stories for their readers.

Regional differences matter, too. Any story about the thoroughbred industry will receive the attention of news editors in Kentucky. In New York, any story about Israel will be a priority. News editors in Illinois, Iowa, Nebraska and Kansas will jump on a story about corn prices and ethanol.

Of course, reporters fail to cover many stories. The reasons are many, but they can be simplified to two: First, a newspaper has limited space and can publish only so much material unless it decides to become the *Reader's Digest* of daily news. Second, newspapers have a limited amount of reporting and editing time. Good news stories require time for reporters to interview and search public records as well as time to organize and write the stories.

Some stories are never reported because journalists never learn of them or never have enough sources to publish the story with authority and credibility. Some stories may go unreported because the newspaper isn't interested in the story or the subject, or the editor feels readers are not interested. Some stories may even go unreported because of pressure from influential power brokers.

Today, the gate-keeping power of newspapers has been diminished because of alternate sources of media communication. Anyone with a Web page or a blog can tell a story today. Callers to radio call-in programs likewise can call attention to an otherwise unreported story. With copy machines, any pamphleteer can hand out a message.

Serving the News Makers

The informative role of the press serves more than the people who read newspapers. It serves the newsmakers and policy-makers as well. While many newspapers have pulled back their reporting resources overseas, readers often learn within hours of a plane on its way from Brazil to France that disappears from radar; of new demonstrations in China; of a tsunami in Asia that kills thousands; of a new war between rival tribes in Africa; of the death or election of a world leader.

In providing this notice of war, disaster, disease and elections, the media provide notice to policy-makers, often conveying more information initially than can be obtained in any other way. Reporters on the scene have direct access to eyewitnesses and police sources while a military officer or a policy-maker in the State Department may not. Officials may use the information they gather from media reports to make decisions in a crisis that does not allow time for independent information-gathering or reflection. More than half of foreign policy officials who believe the media have a large impact at the earliest stage of policy development said policy-makers rely on the news media very much for information.[28]

The media also serve as a conduit for diplomats and national leaders, who are able to send, through the media, signals and messages to one another. Famously, President Ronald Reagan stood in front of the Brandenburg Gate, part of the Berlin Wall that separated East Germany from West Germany, and demanded, "Mr. Gorbachev, tear down this wall." The general secretary of the Communist Party of the Soviet Republic was not in Berlin that day in June 1987, but he got the message through the news media.

The Deliberative Role

Before there was an Internet, there were newspaper columnists. Before the back-and-forth format of cable television news programs, there were letters to the editor. Before there were blogs and bloggers, there were editorials and editorial writers. This idea of exchanging opinions is another major reason that the United States enjoys freedom of the press.

University of Kentucky Professor Richard Labunski argued that the protection given freedom of expression by American courts is essential to democratic government. According to Labunski, "The special position that the First Amendment is granted in our system is a recognition of the paramount importance of the free exchange of ideas to self-government. Freedom of speech and press provisions of the First Amendment are designed to prevent interference with the exchange of information if citizens are to make intelligent decisions when choosing public officials and shaping policy."[29]

That concept of the free exchange of ideas is enshrined in First Amendment Supreme Court decisions as the marketplace of ideas, a metaphor for debate within a democracy. The assumption is that many will participate in the debate, and, in the end, the best ideas will prevail. The weaker ideas, the ideas that develop little or no public support, will not prevail. The theory provides a major argument against government censorship; if the best ideas win out, the government should not preclude the discussion of any idea because bad and dangerous ideas will quickly be discarded.

The news media provide a forum in which the important issues can be debated. "(I)t is a fundamental tenet of democracy that the validity of ideas about what is proper and just in a society should be established through the exchange of informed opinions."[30] Essential to this role is the independence of the media from government control because government officials usually have some stake in the outcome of a public debate and because giving government exclusive access to the channels of communication—as happens in authoritarian governments—necessarily forces other voices and ideas to seek underground media.

The marketplace of ideas, while not an American creation, has been elevated to the capstone of democracy and individual liberty by a long string of judicial decisions. Supreme Court Justice Oliver Wendell Holmes introduced the concept of the marketplace of ideas into American jurisprudence in a World War I free speech case:

> But when men have realized that time has upset many fighting faiths, they may come to believe even more than they believe the very foundations of their own conduct that the best test of truth is the power of the thought to get itself accepted in the competition of the market, and that truth is the only ground upon which their wishes safely can be carried out. That at any rate is the theory of our Constitution. It is an experiment, as all life is an experiment.[31]

In this decision, the majority of the Court upheld the conviction of five Russian immigrants for violating the Espionage Act of 1917 by printing and then circulating two different pamphlets criticizing the Wilson administration policies. Most of it was done by throwing copies out the windows of tall buildings in New York City. While the marketplace metaphor was introduced in Justice Holmes's dissent, his view ultimately triumphed, and it has over the years become a dominant concept in interpreting the breadth of First Amendment freedom of expression.

No metaphor is more often used in First Amendment jurisprudence than the "marketplace of ideas," to the point that one scholar has complained that the theory "consistently dominates the Supreme Court's discussions of freedom of speech."[32] But scholars argue that the metaphor is inept; it fails to protect expression because it is inherently flawed, and justices who continue to rely upon it are naive, unthinking, or both. Critics argue the metaphor is based on false assumptions: (1) that everyone has access to the debate in the market, (2) that truth is objective and discoverable and not subjective and chosen or created, (3) that truth is always among the ideas being debated in the marketplace and always survives, and (4) that people are rational and able to perceive the truth.[33]

But one scholar who studied the Supreme Court's use of the metaphor in free speech and free press cases came to a different conclusion. First, by studying the Court's decisions from 1919 to 1995, he found the Court had begun using it more frequently, particularly since the 1970s. Secondly, he found no effort by the justices to explain the marketplace metaphor but concluded the Court has accepted that the "metaphor is effective because the rationale upon which it is built—that the best way to discover truth is through a robust competition of a multitude of voices—is sound." And third, he concluded, the way the Court has used the metaphor has changed dramatically until today the Court recognizes not one marketplace but several "mini-marketplaces," each having its own audience, dynamics and parameters.[34]

Critics argue that mega-media companies dominate the marketplace, making it hard for lesser voices to be heard. That point and others like it may be moot, however, because the Internet has given birth to endless opportunities for those voices to be heard. Whether these developments improve or diminish the ability of Americans to learn about issues, understand the differing viewpoints and distill all of that into their own viewpoints remains to be seen.

The Agenda-Setting Role

The press may not be successful much of the time in telling people what to think, but it is stunningly successful in telling people what to think about.[35]

The news media also have the power to publish and broadcast stories about issues that result in widespread public attention to those issues, issues that otherwise would be ignored by leaders in a community. Stated another way, the media have the power not to tell citizens what to think but to tell citizens what to think about.

Journalist Walter Lippmann wrote in the 1920s that ordinary people had limited opportunities to see important events first-hand and they were thus dependent on the media to provide them with accounts of these events. Lippmann wrote about "The World Outside and the Pictures in Our Heads."[36] His thesis was that the news media—which then consisted of newspapers, magazines and radio broadcasters—are the principal connection between what transpires in the world and the pictures of those events drawn in our heads.

Two researchers at the University of North Carolina developed the agenda-setting theory. During the 1968 presidential election, they selected one hundred undecided voters in Chapel Hill, North Carolina. Each was personally interviewed during a three-week period before the election. They were asked, "What are you most concerned about these days? That is, regardless of what politicians say, what are the two or three main things that you think the government should concentrate on doing something about?" Five main themes—foreign policy, law and order, fiscal policy, public welfare and civil rights—emerged as the major concerns. Those were also the major themes in the election coverage in the nine media outlets—five newspapers, two network TV news broadcasts and two weekly news magazines—that served Chapel Hill. What they found when they compared the two lists was that the concerns of the voters almost exactly matched the subjects of the media reports.[37] The study, of course, had its weaknesses, but it was ground-breaking. Agenda-setting theory was a major turning point in communication research because it focused the attention of researchers on the process by which the media play a significant part in generating a common culture.

Agenda-setting allows the news media to call attention to issues that need public attention that otherwise might go unaddressed. Nursing home abuses and deteriorating education systems are just two of the issues that have been highlighted over the years by the local and national media. The first step is that the newspaper recognizes a problem exists in the community or in the state, perhaps as a result of a reporter's discovery, a disaster or a visit from a concerned citizen. The second step involves the newspaper focusing attention on that problem by repeatedly reporting on the story or perhaps by a special front-page series of stories, complete with a logo and special layout, that focuses on the problem, followed usually by editorial columns and editorials. The third step involves public recognition of the problem as people discuss what they have read in the newspaper's emphasis on an issue. As people discuss the issue and perhaps write letters to the editor about it, a consensus begins to grow that this problem needs to be addressed. When citizens start talking about a problem, public officials start talking about it, too, and suddenly the issue becomes part of the public policy agenda. There are, of course, variations, and it is easier for one newspaper to focus on a problem in its community than on a state or national basis. Some agenda-setting is driven by special interest groups and some by policy advocates.

But the agenda-setting theory is not just about how one issue becomes part of the public agenda but also about why one issue makes the public agenda while another issue remains ignored for a longer period.[38] For example, why was abuse of senior citizens virtually ignored as a public issue for years after child abuse was a hot issue? For that matter, why did it take the media so long to recognize the extent of child abuse? It is because other issues were competing for the media attention that would propel the issue into the public agenda.

Journalism Through the Eyes of Journalists

The roles the press, and more broadly the news media, play in a society have been widely studied by communication scholars for most of the past century. One common designation is the journalist as neutral observer; the reporter serves as an informer and interpreter and a channel as government communicates with citizens. Another role of the journalist is as a participant, what is more commonly referred to as the press as the fourth estate, as critic and watchdog of the government, as representative of the public and as an advocate for policies.[39]

When reporters are surveyed about their own role conceptions, two roles rise to the top in importance. When journalists were asked to assess different functions in 2002, getting information to the public quickly and investigating government claims both were rated extremely important by a large majority. The same two received the most support in the 1992 survey with one significant difference: Investigating government claims was first in 2002 (71 percent) but second in 1992 (67 percent). Getting information to the public fell from first in 1992 (69 percent) to second in 2002 (59 percent), probably as a reflection of the near-instantaneous news market today based on satellite and Internet technology.[40]

Notes

1. *Near v. Minnesota*, 283 U.S. 697 (1931).
2. Fred W. Friendly, *Minnesota Rag: Corruption, Yellow Journalism, and the Case That Saved Freedom of the Press* (New York: Random House, 1981), 76.
3. Judith Serrin and William Serrin, eds., *Muckraking: The Journalism That Changed America* (New York: New Press, 2002), xx.
4. Jennifer Hewlett, "A Sky-high Expense Account: It's Worth It, Board Chair Says," *Lexington Herald-Leader*, November 23, 2008.
5. Jennifer Hewlett, "Ex-airport Manager to Be Paid Severance," *Lexington Herald-Leader*, June 26, 2009.
6. David Barstow, "Behind TV Analysts, Pentagon's Hidden Hand," *New York Times*, April 20, 2008.
7. Dana Priest and Anne Hull, "Soldiers Face Neglect, Frustration at Army's Top Medical Facility," *The Washington Post*, February 18, 2007.
8. W. Lance Bennett and William Serrin, "The Watchdog Role," in Geneva Overholser and Kathleen Hall Jamieson, eds., *The Press* (New York: Oxford University Press, 2005), 169.
9. James Curran, "Mass Media and Democracy Revisited," in James Curran and Michael Gurevitch, eds., *Mass Media and Society* (New York: Oxford University Press, 1996, 2nd ed.), 83.
10. Ibid.
11. Bennett and Serrin, *supra* note 8, at 176.
12. Dean Starkman, "How Could 9,000 Business Reporters Blow It?," *Mother Jones*, January/February 2009 Issue, available at http://motherjones.com/politics/2009/01/how-could-9000-business-reporters-blow-it (accessed December 29, 2009).
13. David Folkenflik, "Where Were the Media as Wall Street Imploded?" *National Public Radio*, Morning Edition, posted on March 9, 2009, available at http://

www.npr.org/templates/story/story.php?storyId=104310605 (accessed November 22, 2009).

14. "Washing Away," *Times-Picayune,* posted on June 23–27, 2002, available at http://www.nola.com/hurricane/content.ssf?/washingaway/index.html (accessed November 22, 2009).

15. "Public More Critical of Press, But Goodwill Persists: Online Newspaper Readership Countering Print Losses," *Pew Research Center for the Public and the Press,* posted on June 26, 2005, available at http://people-press.org/report/248/public-more-critical-of-press-but-goodwill-persists (accessed November 22, 2009).

16. "Financial Woes Now Overshadow All Other Concerns for Journalists," *Pew Research Center for the Public and the Press,* March 17, 2008, available at http://people-press.org/report/?pageid=1269. (accessed November 22, 2009).

17. *Mills v. Alabama,* 384 U.S. 214, 218 (1966).

18. Potter Stewart, "Or of the Press," 26 *Hastings Law Journal,* 631 (1975), in Kent Middleton and Roy M. Mersky, eds., *Freedom of Expression: A Collection of Best Writings* (Buffalo, N.Y.: William S. Hein Co., reprinted in 1981), 425, 430.

19. *Miami Herald Publishing Co. v. Tornillo,* 418 U.S. 241 (1974).

20. Ibid., 247–248.

21. Gregory P. Magarian, "Reclaiming the First Amendment: Constitutional Theories of Media Reform: Market Triumphalism, Electoral Pathologies, and the Abiding Wisdom of First Amendment Access Rights," 35 *Hofstra Law Review* (Spring 2007, Volume 35), 1373.

22. *Miami Herald Publishing Co.,* 259.

23. Ibid.

24. Esther Thorson, "Mobilizing Citizen Participation," in Geneva Overholser and Kathleen Hall Jamieson, eds., *The Press* (New York: Oxford University Press, 2005), 204.

25. David L. Paletz, *The Media in American Politics* (New York: Longman, 2002, 2nd ed.), 1.

26. Walter Lippmann, *Public Opinion* (New York: Simon & Schuster, 1927, 1997 ed., 3–20.

27. Thomas E. Patterson, *The Vanishing Voter* (New York: Knopf, 2002), 90–91.

28. Patrick O'Heffernan, "Mass Media Roles in Foreign Policy," in Doris A. Graber, ed., *Media Power in Politics* (Washington, DC: CQ Press, 2000), 292–303.

29. Richard Labunski, *The First Amendment Under Siege: The Politics of Broadcast Regulation* (Westport, Conn.: Greenwood Press, 1981), 3.

30. Michael X. Delli Carpini and Scott Keeter, *What Americans Know about Politics and Why It Matters* (New Haven, Conn.: Yale University Press, 1996), 5.

31. *Abrams v. United States,* 250 U.S. 616, 630 (1919) *(Holmes, J. dissenting).*

32. C. Edwin Baker, *Human Liberty and Freedom of Speech* (New York: Oxford, 1989), 7.

33. W. Wat Hopkins, "The Supreme Court Defines the Marketplace of Ideas," *Journalism and Mass Communication Quarterly* (1996, Volume 73:1), 40, 43–44.

34. Ibid., 40–41.

35. Bernard Cohen, *The Press and Foreign Policy* (Princeton, N.J.: Princeton University Press, 1963), 13.

36. Lippmann, *supra* note 26.

37. Maxwell McCombs and Donald Shaw, "The Agenda-setting Function of Mass Media," *Public Opinion Quarterly* (1972, Volume 36), 176.

38. James W. Dearing, Everett M. Rogers and Steven H. Chaffee, *Agenda-Setting* (Thousand Oaks, Calif.: Sage, 1996), 2.

39. Denis McQuail, *Mass Communication Theory* (Thousand Oaks, Calif: Sage, 1994, 3rd ed.), 194–195.

40. David H. Weaver, Randal A. Beam, Bonnie J. Brownlee, Paul S. Voakes and G. Cleveland Wilhoit, *The American Journalist in the 21st Century* (Mahwah, N.J.: Lawrence Erlbaum Associates, 2007), 140–142.

5

The Role of the Rural Press

Thinking back, a neighbor of Los Angeles attorney Paul Morantz remembered something odd: She had seen two men approach his house and place something in his mailbox. She did not have time to warn him. On that day in October 1978, Morantz returned home from work and reached into his mailbox. Instead of mail, he pulled out a four-and-a-half-foot diamondback rattlesnake, whose rattle had been cut off to prevent it sounding a warning before it sank its fangs into his left hand. "I felt a sharp pain, and then it felt as though my hand was in a vise," he would later tell a reporter. Screaming, he ran to a neighbor's house, and from there he fell into shock and was rushed to a hospital, where he had to stay six days.

Authorities traced the snake attack to Synanon, which had begun as a residential drug rehabilitation organization in the rural area forty miles northwest of San Francisco but which also described itself as "an educational center, an agricultural operation and a religion."[1] Morantz had considered it a cult. He had just won a $300,000 judgment against Synanon after suing it on behalf of a woman who claimed it had imprisoned, brainwashed and tortured her.[2]

Soon, three members of Synanon would be charged in connection with the attempted murder. The incident (which CBS's Walter Cronkite would label "bizarre, even by cult standards")[3] made national news, but a tiny newspaper that covered a rural community along the Pacific Coast was way ahead of the national press on this story. Dave Mitchell, one of three employees at the *Point Reyes Light*, already had written more than one hundred stories and editorials[4] about Synanon, which operated a huge facility in the paper's circulation area. The stories had chronicled purchases of a $60,000 arsenal of weapons by some of its 900 members; its immense wealth generated from its business-es; its alleged beatings of people; its refusal to allow state child-abuse inspec-tors on its compound;[5] its three boats, six airplanes and "computer center appropriate for a large corporation";[6] and its propensity to sue news organ-izations that reported on its activities. The *Point Reyes Light's* reporting was so solid that, in 1979, the rural newspaper became one of a tiny minority of weekly papers to win a Pulitzer Prize.[7]

Although rural newspapers rarely win Pulitzers, they perform a vital service to their communities. Big city papers are not likely to cover Little League championships, the heaviest zucchini of the summer, the building of a village school's playground or even petty crimes. The rural press focus-es attention on items and events that large newspapers would probably not consider newsworthy but that local residents do care about, events and people that give a place a *sense* of place. Rural newspapers help to define news as being personal and local rather than political and distant. While they are likely to be boosters of their towns or counties, they also can be independ-ent and honest chroniclers of the life of the people. They not only help to identify problems in the area, but they also help to solve them.[8]

When Dave Mitchell and his wife, Cathy, bought the *Point Reyes Light* a few years before they won the Pulitzer, they "had developed a vision of what a weekly newspaper could accomplish. If we kept the *Light's* focus nar-row enough—covering only news involving the ten thousand people of West Marin—we could, we believed, be small and yet professional. We would provide readers not only with an objective record of local events, but also with editorials and features interpreting the significance of West Marin happenings."[9]

About 4,000 rural newspapers were publishing in the country as of 2007. These non-metropolitan newspapers excluded papers that covered a rural area but were located in a metropolitan area because of commuting pat-terns. The dailies ranged from the *Bisbee Daily Review*, with a daily circula-tion of 738, to the *Northeast Mississippi Daily Journal*, with a circulation of 35,500. About 270 of the weekly rural papers were even smaller than the *Bisbee Daily Review*. Only about 740 of the rural papers were dailies, but that figure constitutes more than half of the total number of daily newspapers in the United States. Rural newspapers employ an estimated 15,000 jour-nalists.[10]

People who read rural newspapers tend to know the people who pro-duce them because these journalists show up regularly at their civic club meetings, sporting events and county fairs. "There's a closer tie between the paper and the community," said Al Cross, director of the Institute for Rural Journalism and Community Issues, based at the University of Kentucky. "People say *our* paper, not *the* paper."[11]

Smart politicians recognize the value that readers place upon their rural paper. When Barack Obama started his presidential campaign in Iowa, he sent an emissary to the *Daily Times Herald* of Carroll, Iowa (circulation: 6,000). The spokesman spent two-and-a-half hours being interviewed, which conveyed to the newspaper a lot of information as well as goodwill. "When they showed us a lot of respect, I looked at it that they were showing Carroll a lot of respect," Doug Burns said.[12] *New York Times* political correspondent Jeff Zeleny recognized the importance of the small paper in community life: On the *Times'* political blog, he noted, "There is, perhaps, no better way to give an hourlong presidential visit far greater staying power than appearing on the pages of the weekly newspaper, particularly in an edition that is likely to be sitting on coffee tables at Thanksgiving time."[13]

Life in rural areas is distinct from urban life, and so reporting on it is different: Scholars note that rural areas became "depopulated" between 1940 and 1970, as the U.S. farm population declined 73 percent after people left, seeking higher education and jobs in metropolitan areas.[14] A study of how rural newspapers in Georgia covered development noted that the people who were left behind were more likely to be poor. Rates of illiteracy and infant mortality were higher, and access to health services was lower.[15] The study used a "development news paradigm" for mass communications articulated by Narinder Aggarwala. This model says journalists should have the goal of improving living conditions for the people they cover but must remain independent from business or government so that they can cast a critical eye on development plans. For improvements in the quality of life to take place, the entire community must be involved in decisions that affect their lives, not just the powerful, and that means reporting must cover all development plans from the initial planning stages and must seek opponents as well as proponents of plans.[16]

George McLean probably would have agreed with that model. McLean was owner of the *Northeast Mississippi Daily Journal*, the nation's largest paid-circulation rural newspaper, which covers seventeen counties and whose 35,500 circulation is larger than the population of its publication city, Tupelo. McLean created the Community Development Foundation to promote development in the rural region. He would rent movies and show them in rural towns on Saturday nights but would first give brief speeches about the quality of life in the area and encourage residents to cooperate, rather than compete, to promote development. McLean explained his philosophy in a column:

> The good newspaper is its community's encourager, which by making known what groups and individuals are doing, brings mutual support for each other's projects and invites still greater personal initiative. It is a com-

munity's semi-official provider of pats on the back through news stories, pictures or editorials. The good newspaper can contribute perhaps more than any other institution to development of an active, mutually serving citizenship.[17]

Partly because of efforts by a foundation he created, Toyota planned to build a plant in his newspaper's circulation area. Cross, of the Institute for Rural Journalism and Community Issues, commended the publisher's "great public service," but he noted that the *Northeast Mississippi Daily Journal*, which McLean had left to the foundation, had a serious conflict of interest in reporting the story. If it published what it knew about the plant's plans of locating to its area too soon, it could have fouled the project, and the community could have lost the plant entirely. So it withheld the news from its readers until the relocation was certain. Such conflicts occur regularly in rural journalism, Cross noted. So do such solutions. Whereas rural journalists sometimes must write critical reports or reports that anger powerful interests, in rural journalism there is no brick wall between being a booster and being a reporter. Instead, he said, the wall goes "up to about shoulder height."

For example, at a country paper west of Lincoln, Nebraska, the publisher, Dennis Berens, got wind of a new printing plant that was considering moving to the area. Cross said the publisher tried to get the two local banks to recruit the plant, but they told him that he was the best person to lure the new business. So, he went back to the newspaper office and told his staff that he would be working on a "special project" upstairs for a while, and if they found out about it, they should report it. They didn't, and the printer moved to town.[18]

Modern journalistic ethics discourage reporters from getting too close to any story because it can lead to biased reporting; being simultaneously a critical observer and a community booster is difficult to manage. Reporters everywhere must find the balance between cultivating knowledgeable sources who will tell them what is happening in the community and writing negative stories about those very same people or their friends when things go wrong. Finding this balance is especially difficult in rural areas where the newspaper editor may attend the same church as his sources or have children in the same schools or spouses working at the same factory. Yet, living in the community bestows on rural journalists a natural incentive to make that community succeed and a practical requirement to avoid alienating the reader, who could easily show up at the editor's desk to discuss the flaws in news stories.

The Rural Life

Working as a journalist at a country newspaper is hard. The pay is low, the hours long; the readers know where to find you to complain. Most rural papers can afford only a small staff, and these workers must develop skills across a variety of tasks to produce a paper on time every week. "We're all things at once in weekly publishing—printers, yet competent ad salesmen, sensitive photographers, knowledgeable reporters, successful businessmen," Bruce M. Kennedy wrote. "Yet we must also be on occasion society editor, mechanic, subscription taker, chief of the complaint desk, as well as the guy who sweeps out the front office." The profession calls it being "country trained." As Kennedy noted, "It means you know newspapering."[19]

Rural newspapers are the least homogenized news product around, so generalizations about them are difficult to make. Many rural papers are owned independently because they do not make enough money to be attractive to be bought by newspaper chains. They often reflect the editor's personality and ideas. The relationship of the editor with his readers also influences what the paper covers and how it covers it. Their audience relies on them for local information; a statewide survey in Louisiana in the late 1970s found that rural residents read the small weekly papers for information significantly more than they relied upon a daily paper.[20]

Although readers had been abandoning newspapers in large cities throughout much of the twentieth century, the situation was quite different for smaller papers, according to the National Newspaper Association, a trade group for small community newspapers. The association commissioned a survey in 2008 in communities of fewer than 50,000 people served by newspapers of under 25,000 circulation. It found the vast majority of residents—86 percent—said they regularly read a local newspaper.[21] Previous surveys had found similarly high readership for these smaller newspapers. In addition, more than five times as many people said the newspaper was their primary source for news and information in their local communities as those who cited the next-highest ranked source, television. Brian Steffens, executive director of the newspaper association, pointed out in a statement:

> Just about all of the research and news reports on the "struggling" newspaper industry have been based on what's happening at the top one hundred major metropolitan newspapers, maybe the top 250. That doesn't tell the story of the remaining 1,200 daily newspapers or 8,000 community weekly papers in America….Community newspapers remain the dominant source of local news, products and services—typically by a wide margin—over any other media.[22]

History of the Country Press

The tension between "boosterism" and journalism started early in newspapering. In the early 1800s, small weeklies across the country "represented state parties and state economic interests. More than ever before, newspapers became boosters of private business and the politics of economic development."[23] After the Civil War, weekly newspapers popped up all

over the country, and most of them in the newly settled West were pro-
moters of their communities. If the merchants succeeded, so would the
newspaper.[24] Pioneering editors glossed over swarming grasshoppers and
fights with Native Americans to support settlements. It was so expected that
newspapers would boost new western towns and that local businesses would
return the favor that the editor of *The Laramie Daily Sentinel* published this
disapprobation of businesses that did not support the newspaper: "Right
here in our town, small as it is, there are men trying to do business whose
existence is scarcely known because they do not keep themselves before the
public through the press, and such men ought to be ignored."[25]

In the 1700s, American newspapers had not carried much local news
because editors figured that people would not buy a newspaper for information they could get for free through word of mouth.[26] In the 1830s, the
penny press started reporting local news to city dwellers who could no
longer get such information in face-to-face encounters. David J. Russo
believes that one reason rural papers started emphasizing local news was to
compete with those big city papers that would ship weekly "country editions" to their markets. In 1880 more than 82 percent of daily newspapers
also printed weekly editions, and each averaged two and a half times more
circulation per issue than country weeklies published locally.[27] This was
extreme competition for a small rural newspaper, whose resources were
nowhere near those of a city paper. An Indiana newspaper, for example,
could charge up to $100 a year for a column of advertising, but the *New York
Tribune* could get $22,932 for the same advertising space.[28] As a result, some
newspapers in the 1840s appealed to their readers to support their local rural
paper instead of the city paper, which they argued simply could not provide
the same service as a big city paper "some two, three, or five hundred miles
distant."[29]

When the Civil War came, newspapers printed many letters home
from local soldiers. Sometimes, the soldiers, like Melvin Dwinell, had been
rural newspaper editors. Dwinell had edited a tri-weekly in rural Georgia,
the *Rome Courier*, when he joined the Confederate Army. "Dear Courier,"
he would begin each of the more than 200 perceptive and thoughtful mis-
sives to his newspaper. After writing one story about the Battle of First
Manassas, he followed up with more reflections about Union soldiers: "At
the first sight of the enemy, all the bug bear delusions that may have existed in the fancy of anyone, as to their appearance, were suddenly dispelled,
and they looked at the distance of three hundred or four hundred yards, precisely like so many of our men."[30]

The *Courier*, like many small papers then, had trouble collecting money
from subscribers during the war, and advertising revenues fell steeply. The
paper cut its pages from four to two, but it continued publishing throughout the war, sometimes including two of Dwinell's war letters in a single
issue. He skirted some sensitive stories, but he did report on deserters,

inadequate clothing and equipment, and crime and heavy drinking among soldiers. His "compelling and thorough" reportage and his "clear and straight-forward writing style puts him in the same league with the South's most skilled professional correspondents," according to Ford Risley, who also noted:

> Like the good newsman he was, Dwinell also knew what readers wanted more than anything: the condition of family, friends and neighbors serving in the army. He rarely sent correspondence that did not mention the health of soldiers from northwest Georgia, especially the "Floyd Boys," as he called residents of the county. Soldiers from the area who were killed in the fighting or who died later from wounds or sickness usually received special mention in his letters back to the *Courier*.[31]

During the Battle of Gettysburg, Dwinell was shot in the arm. He returned home to recuperate, and townspeople convinced him to run for state representative. He handily won the election and soon began sending stories back to the paper from the state capital, but the war was not over for him. In an act that must have galled him, Union soldiers stopped in Rome during Gen. William T. Sherman's march to the sea and used his printing press to publish their own newspaper, the *Union Flag*. Then they destroyed the press. Dwinell rebuilt the newspaper office, purchased a new press and continued as editor of the *Courier* for another twenty years.[32]

In the period after the Civil War and continuing to this day, virtually any out-of-the-ordinary event could be noted on the pages of a rural newspaper. As the editor of the *Eufaula (Alabama) Times and News* reminded his correspondents, "...when anybody dies, gets married, runs away, steals anything, builds a house, makes a big sale, breaks his leg or gets the senses kicked out of him by a mule, or does anything that is in anyway remarkable, and you have reason to believe you know as much about the occurrence as anybody else, don't wait for someone else to report it, or trust us to find out by instinct, but come and tell us about it, or send the fact on a postal card."[33]

Country readers and editors (and probably most readers anywhere) loved stories about the strange. "One of the easiest ways for a constituent to get his name into the news, aside from getting married or shooting someone, was to discover and deliver to a newspaper office a freak of nature," noted Thomas D. Clark, who studied the rural press in the New South. Hence, rural papers ran stories about eggs that looked like baseballs, complete with strange "stitching," eggs with human faces, eggs with a "W" on them (which some said signified war). Readers would also haul to their rural newspaper offices "the carcasses of deformed animals, strange bugs, long, sinuous snakes, roots of trees which gave the appearance of everything from a cross to the Hunchback of Notre Dame, old-fashioned tools, guns, and pieces of weird local whittling."[34] When Gene Roberts, then editor of *The New York Times* but who also had been executive editor of *The*

Philadelphia Inquirer, won the Columbia University Journalism Award in 1996, his speech recommended that beginning journalists seek employment on small newspapers for the education to be found in the craft of recounting rural life. Roberts, who wrote the farm column for the Goldsboro *News-Argus* in Wayne County, North Carolina, reminisced with fondness of his stories "about the first farmer of the season to transplant tobacco plants from the seedbed to the field; about the season's first cotton blossom. I wrote about picnic tables sagging at family reunions under the weight of banana sandwiches, banana pudding, chicken pastry, sage sausage, fried chicken, and collard greens. I wrote of hailstorms and drought. I once wrote about a sweet potato that looked like General Charles de Gaulle."[35]

Country newspapers also often were political agents through the late 1800s, especially in the South. *The New York Times* surveyed one hundred Southern editors of rural papers in 1882 and found that they were mostly proponents of the Democratic Party, with an almost constant flow of partisan stories about Washington and state and local elections.[36] In West Virginia even at this writing some rural papers still register as Republican or Democratic to get legal ads, in a system that guarantees such ads to papers of both parties.[37]

Nevertheless, other rural editors saw their role to be purveyors of a variety of information to educate the citizenry and to be a forum for divergent ideas. Many printed letters to the editor from all viewpoints. After the South Dakota *Reporter and Farmer* bought a competing paper in the 1940s, it invited the other paper's editor to write a standing column on its own editorial page, noting:

> We have done so because we feel that the Democrat viewpoint should be represented on our editorial page. Whether you agree or disagree with his opinions is for you to decide, just as we accord you the same privilege concerning the views in our editorial column. If occasionally there are varying thoughts expressed in adjoining columns, just remember that this is America.[38]

To cover their large geographic areas, rural editors have had to rely on correspondents, who often were paid only with a free subscription. When big city dailies flourished in the middle 1800s, their advertising revenue grew and their publishers could hire many reporters. But in the country, editors often had to beg for subscriptions as well as ads, and newspapers were lucky to afford an editorial assistant to cover local news.[39]

Clark wrote that Southern country editors in the middle of the nineteenth century had "vigilant maidens" who, under pen names, such as "Dad's Pet" or "Little Mary," would forward bits of news for publication.[40] The practice of publishing news sent from these rural correspondents continues today, but it is fading. In 2005, Waid Prather, editor of the *Carthaginian* in Carthage, Mississippi, wrote that he used Christmastime hams to pay a stable of correspondents, whom he called "country cousins," to send him brief items about illnesses, marriages and other life events of his readers. "It beats the stew out of who Madonna is sleeping with today," Prather was quoted as saying. "Nobody around here cares. But the guy with the stent in his heart, folks know him, and they're worried about his health."[41]

Rural Journalism Today

Some rural editors lament the difficulty in finding reporters willing to move to or stay in the country, where salaries are typically lower. One editor in Montana mourned that the country paper acts as a training ground for those with talent, who then move away. They often follow the pattern of one recent university journalism graduate who wrote well and made good contacts on the Crow Reservation, but left for a job on a bigger paper and a 40 percent raise.[42] Yet, the rural journalist can have a better chance of getting into management or ownership in rural markets as well as have more of a connection with readers and an influence on their lives. In 2003, the general manager of new media for the largest daily newspaper in Florida, *The St. Petersburg Times*, quit the city paper to return to his roots in rural journalism at *The High Springs Herald*, a weekly with a circulation of only 5,000. "I've missed the impact that a small-town newspaper can have on its community," Ron Dupont was quoted as saying. "When I was [previously] editor of *The High Springs Herald*, we did some world-class journalism on our way to doubling the circulation and being named the best small weekly paper in Florida, four years straight."[43] The *Herald's* website noted the contradictions in rural life today: "… a newspaper article on farming can sit side-by-side on the newspaper's front page with a story on a new technological advancement made at the local research center, where an advertisement for a fancy, high-priced development can sit on the same page as an ad for a tractor dealer."[44]

The Feisty Rural Press

Rural journalism is broad and varied. Stories about the annual pumpkin harvest may appear in the same issue with editorials that blister the powers-that-be. Mississippi has several such rural papers that follow this tradition. Ray Mosby, editor of the *Deer Creek Pilot*, won the Mississippi Press Association's special award for best editorial in 1999 for his saucy chastening of the local Board of Supervisors. The board wanted to use tax money to buy a bankrupt cotton gin, even though one board member was part owner of it. Mosby rebuked them for the conflict of interest, labeling the plan a "purely pernicious act of public policy which from more than one angle looks to be as crooked as a one-eyed, spastic snow snake." If the supervisors, he wrote, "conspire, meet illegally or otherwise grease the wheels of bureaucracy" to buy the gin "in spite of the ethical fungus so obviously growing on it...somebody is going to the penitentiary, or somebody is going to pay back lots of money, or both....So what's it gonna be? Are you feeling lucky?"[45]

Another Mississippi editor from an earlier era, Hazel Brannon Smith, was contemptuously labeled by a state politician in the early 1960s as a "female crusading scalawag domiciled in our midst" for her editorials. Smith owned four Mississippi weeklies in rural Mississippi during the struggle for civil rights.[46] For more than a decade, she wrote fierce editorials decrying injustice and racism in her front-page column, "Through Hazel Eyes." For her words, she was subjected to boycotts, threats and violence. In 1964, Smith became the first woman to win the Pulitzer Prize.

To the paper and the region, the prize made no difference. One of her weekly papers, the *Northside Reporter* in Jackson, Mississippi, was bombed. A few years later, someone set fire to her printing plant, but she printed a miniature version of *The Advertiser* on a smaller press, with an editorial declaring, "When I am no longer free to print the truth unafraid, then you are no longer free to speak the truth without fear."[47]

Yet, in the early 1950s, Smith had argued in favor of segregation, a view espoused by newspapers throughout the South: "We know that it is to the best interest of both races that segregation be maintained in theory and in fact—and that where it isn't maintained, trouble results."[48] But in 1954, the sheriff shot an unarmed black man who was running away from him, and Smith's opinions began changing. She wrote an editorial calling for the sheriff's resignation, declaring that most Holmes County residents would not countenance such violence based on race. The sheriff sued her for libel, but Smith won, arguing truth as her defense.[49]

When white advertisers boycotted her paper, Smith started printing a civil rights newspaper and took printing jobs for the black community. She also hired blacks to work in her printing plant and continued writing for civil rights. About two years after Smith won the Pulitzer Prize in 1964, the boycott had so hurt her financially that journalists and the black community started fund-raising campaigns to help support her. Smith wrote editorials urging white parents to take their children out of private schools and put them back in public schools. In 1968, she wrote almost despondently about the assassination of Martin Luther King, saying that "there has been little change in the white man's mind and virtually no change in the white man's power structure."[50] She died in 1994 in a nursing home, nearly destitute.

Another rural Mississippi newspaper took courageous steps to attempt to heal some of the wounds suffered during the civil rights era. In Philadelphia, Miss., civil rights workers James Earl Chaney, Andrew Goodman and Michael Schwerner disappeared in June 1964. The disappearance set off national media coverage until forty-four days later, when the Federal Bureau of Investigation found their bodies buried near the Neshoba County fairgrounds. The local papers' coverage at the time was not exemplary. An analysis of how the rural newspapers covered the disappearance at the time said that *The Meridian Star*, a daily, and *The Neshoba Democrat*, a weekly, "contributed to the community's belief that the trio's disappearance was a hoax." The *Meridian Star* frequently reported rumors that the disappearance was a publicity stunt; the *Democrat* unquestioningly printed what the sheriff said and never implied that the civil rights workers could have met with foul play, even when their car was found incinerated.[51]

For years, Mississippi never prosecuted anyone for the crime, and many residents of Neshoba County wanted to forget that dreadful time. But on the twenty-fifth anniversary of the killings in 1989, Stanley Dearman, one of several reporters who had covered the initial story of the disappearance of the three men for the *Star* but who in 1989 owned and edited the *Democrat*, thought otherwise. He spearheaded an effort to hold a memorial service, and he called Goodman's mother to find out what type of person her son had been. Dearman was so impressed with Carolyn Goodman's words describing her son's athleticism, his flair for dramatic arts and his compassion that he ran the interview verbatim. The story caught the attention of James E. Prince III, a journalist in Alabama who was three months old when the men had been killed, who moved to work that summer at the *Democrat* and who bought the paper in 2000.[52]

A few years later, Prince worked with the head of the local NAACP to rally the community for another memorial for the fortieth anniversary of the killings. The paper issued a call for justice in the killings, campaigning for a continued investigation and prosecution of people responsible for the murders. "Stan and Jim carried the torch to get the case reopened, which was not a popular stand. Nobody in Philadelphia gave a damn what *The New York Times* had to say, but when the local newspaper started pushing for a grand jury, that had impact," said Sid Salter, a columnist for the *Clarion-Ledger* in Jackson, Miss.[53]

Eventually, the grand jury indicted a former Klansman in connection with the deaths, and Prince ran daily coverage of his trial and his conviction, using the newspaper's website. "We had a former mayor who said on the stand that the Klan was a good thing. People needed to know that," he said. "They needed to read about it in our paper." The emphasis that the editors put on the story of the murders cost the newspaper some advertisers and readers, Dearman acknowledged, but he said he believed that pushing for a resolution to the story instead of ignoring it benefited the community. When he retired as editor, virtually the entire town turned out to see him off, and Carolyn Goodman came to speak.[54] For this series of reports, the *Neshoba Democrat* won the 2008 Tom and Pat Gish Award for public service and for "courage, tenacity and integrity" from the Institute for Rural Journalism and Community Issues at the University of Kentucky.[55]

The Institute for Rural Journalism and Community Issues

The institute was founded by a retired weekly publisher and Kentucky public-television commentator, Al Smith, and journalist Rudy Abramson, who died in 2008. Abramson worked for *The Tennessean* and the Washington bureau of the *Los Angeles Times*, but he never forgot his rural roots. While he was writing about Appalachia in 2001, Abramson noticed that many rural papers "lacked the vigor" necessary to adequately cover issues that afflict country people as much as urban dwellers, "poverty, disease, drug abuse, poor schools, local corruption." So Abramson and Smith conceived of the institute to help rural journalists, and it began operating in 2004 from headquarters in the School of Journalism and Telecommunications at the University of Kentucky.[56] At a memorial service for Abramson at the Newseum, a museum about journalism in Washington, D.C., Smith quoted Abramson's philosophy of rural journalism: "We are not about crafting pretty paragraphs. We want to change lives for the better." And political commentator Mark Shields remembered, "Rudy never, never forgot where he came from, or the people from whom he came. Rudy understood that the one demographic group that could be caricatured, could be ridiculed and could be condescended to with total impunity, are the white working-class Americans that did not go to college, and who often live in the rural United States."[57]

Rural journalists resist and resent the caricatures of country folk. Tom and Pat Gish, publishers of *The Mountain Eagle* for whom the award is named, respected their readers. The Gishes said they did not buy *The Mountain Eagle* in 1956 to become crusading reporters, but in addition to writing the typical weekly fare of who had chocolate cake for their birthday or who made the honor roll at the high school, they wrote stories about coal mining companies and corrupt officials, and they suffered for it. Before they had taken over *The Eagle*, the school board, which was the largest public employer in the county, had grown used to doing business in secret, calling people in to speak and dismissing them so the board could make decisions out of public view. The school board tried to ban the press from its meetings, but Pat Gish stood in a corner of the meeting room and reported what they said. The Gishes also reported on the nearly seventy one- and two-room schools in the county, most of which they said were not fit for human habitation. The *Mountain Eagle* reported on coal companies' strip mining practices and on the poverty of the people. They changed the *Eagle's* slogan on the nameplate from "A Friendly Non-Partisan Weekly Newspaper Published Every Thursday" to "It Screams." Eventually, the school board spearheaded a boycott of the newspaper at a time when its advertising and finances were declining. Once, the newspaper office was firebombed. The next day, Tom Gish sat on his porch and typed stories for the paper, which appeared on time with an altered nameplate: "It Still Screams."[58]

The rest of the country seemed to have discovered Appalachian issues during the 1960s, and the first stop for many out-of-town reporters was *The Eagle*. While they were gracious in educating visitors about the local people, Tom and Pat Gish were also sensitive to their readers. They never published a photograph that demeaned local people, according to the rural institute's Al Cross. Cross conceded that a country editor must hold up a mirror to its readers, which shows blemishes as well as beauty, yet "they held up the mirror in text—but not in photos. I think avoiding that little piece of business that could be deemed sensational served them really well. People in Letcher County knew the paper was their paper; it looked out for their interests."[59]

The Point Reyes Light

Many rural editors do look out for their community's interests. While editor Dave Mitchell owned the *Light*, which had won a Pulitzer for its coverage of the Synanon cult, he ran virtually every letter to the editor, some of which ran for pages, recognizing that the newspaper was a public forum for community views.[60] Mitchell sold *The Light* in 2005, and the new editor made some changes. He ran only selected letters from readers. He also hired smart young journalism students as unpaid interns, but they were not familiar with the region or its people. The readers noticed, and many did not appreciate this different style of journalism. At a town meeting in 2006 at which residents met to discuss what they wanted from their newspaper, one citizen said, "When people used to complain to me about Dave Mitchell, I'd say, '*The Point Reyes Light* is what holds this community together. It is the center. It is the glue.'...I don't find that to be the case anymore. It breaks my heart." Another said of the interns, "They know how to write. But they don't know how to write for the community."[61]

Jonathan Rowe, a West Marin County resident who wrote an essay about the changes at the *Light*, argued that journalism should be about serving the community, not about "hotshot" editors and reporters making names for themselves. The rural journalism institute reported on the changes at the *Light* in one of its newsletters, noting that a good rural newspaper does not have to report only what citizens want to hear, but it does have to know its readers and its place in the community: "The best community newspapers recognize their connection to their readers and work to strengthen it."[62]

Still, the story of rural journalism in West Marin County may have a happy ending, at least for journalists. In the summer of 2007, another rural weekly was born to serve the people of West Marin County: *The West Marin Citizen*. In August 2008, the National Newspaper Association awarded *The Citizen* six national awards for excellence.[63]

Notes

1. Dave Mitchell, Cathy Mitchell and Richard Ofshe, *The Light on Synanon* (New York: Seaview Books, 1980), 38.
2. Ibid., 179.
3. Ibid., 201.
4. John Hatcher, "Were Those the Days? Revisiting the Pulitzer-winning Efforts of Community Newspapers in the 1970s," *American Journalism* (Winter 2007, Volume 24:1), 89–118.
5. Mitchell, *supra* note 1, at 173–174.
6. Ibid., 22–24.
7. Hatcher, *supra* note 4, at 98.
8. Bob Giles, "Community Journalism's Pathway to the Future," *Nieman Reports* (Spring 2006), 3.
9. Ibid., 5.
10. Al Cross, Vaughan Fielder, Christine Noel Tigas and Beth E. Barnes, "A Survey of Training Backgrounds and Needs at Rural Newspapers in the United States." Paper presented at the National Summit on Journalism in Rural America (Shaker Village of Pleasant Hill, Ky., April 20, 2007).
11. Al Cross, director, Institute for Rural Journalism and Community Issues, interview by author, June 30, 2009.
12. The Institute for Rural Journalism and Community Issues, "Obama Worked Rural Papers in Iowa, and It Paid off," *Rural Report* (Spring 2008), 2.
13. Jeff Zeleny, "On the Road: Obama Caters to Small-Town Media," *The New York Times*, http://thecaucus.blogs.nytimes.com/2007/11/20/on-the-road-obama-caters-to-small-town-media/?scp=1&sq=Zeleny%20weekly%20newspaper&st=Search (accessed June 30, 2009).
14. William F. Griswold and Jill D. Swenson, "Development News in Rural Georgia Newspapers: A Comparison with Media in Developing Nations," *Journalism Quarterly* (Fall 1992, Volume 69: 3), 580–590.
15. Ibid.
16. Ibid.
17. "Miss. Publisher Spurs Economic Boost for Rural Area Via Paper, Foundation," *Good Works 2006*, http://www.ruraljournalism.org/ (accessed June 30, 2009).
18. Cross, *supra* note 11.
19. Bruce M. Kennedy, *Community Journalism: A Way of Life* (Ames, Iowa: The Iowa State University Press, 1974), 3–4.
20. George M. Winford, "Newspaper versus 'Newspaper': A Statewide Study of the Weekly," *Journalism Quarterly* (Spring 1978, Volume 55:1), 135–139.
21. "86% of Adults 18-plus Read America's Community Newspapers Weekly," Donald W. Reynolds Journalism Institute, updated on April 15, 2009, available at http://rji.missouri.edu/research/stories/2008-study/index.php (accessed July 5, 2009).
22. Ibid.
23. David Paul Nord. "Newspapers and American Nationhood," in John B. Hench, ed., *Three Hundred Years of the American Newspaper* (Worcester, Mass.: American Antiquarian Society, 1991), 404.
24. Ted Curtis Smythe, *The Gilded Age Press*, 1865–1900 (Westport, Conn.: Praeger Publishers, 2003), 31.
25. Kimberly Mangun, "The (Oregon) *Advocate*: Boosting the Race and Portland, Too," *American Journalism* (Winter 2007, Volume 23:1), 7–34.
26. David J. Russo, "The Origins of Local News in the U.S. Country Press,

1840s–1870s," *Journalism Monographs* (February 1980, No. 65), 1–43.

27. Smythe, *supra* note 24, at 32.
28. Smythe, *supra* note 24, at 33.
29. Russo, *supra* note 26, at 6.
30. Ford Risley, "Dear Courier: The Civil War Correspondence of Editor Melvin Dwinell," *Journalism History* (Fall 2005, Volume 31: 3), 162–170.
31. Ibid.
32. Ibid.
33. Thomas D. Clark, *The Rural Press and the New South* (Baton Rouge, La.: Louisiana State University Press, 1948), 14.
34. Ibid., 41.
35. Joan Konner, "From Rural Ramblin' to a Bunker in Hue," *Columbia Journalism Review* (September/October 1996), 4.
36. Clark, *supra* note 33, at 20–25.
37. Al Cross, director, Institute for Rural Journalism and Community Issues, correspondence with author, July 15, 2009.
38. "The Country Newspaper: Symbol of Democracy," *Saturday Evening Post* (May 25, 1946), 160.
39. Russo, *supra* note 26.
40. Clark, *supra* note 33, at 10.
41. Julia Cass, "Wonderful Weeklies," *American Journalism Review* (December 2005/January 2006), 20–29.
42. Dick Crockford, "Finding Writers Poses Tough Challenge for Rural Weeklies," *Grassroots Editor* (Spring 2008), 12–13.
43. Carl Sullivan, "Web Ace Gets Back to His Rural Roots," *Editor & Publisher* (July 14, 2003), 24.
44. "Our Coverage Area," *High Springs Herald*, available at http://www.highspringsherald.com/advertise/coverage/ (accessed July 1, 2009).
45. Cass, *supra* note 41.
46. Bernard Stein, "This Female Crusading Scalawag: Hazel Brannon Smith, Justice and Mississippi," in *Profiles in Journalistic Courage—Media Studies* (2001): 55–65.
47. Ibid.
48. Ibid.
49. Ibid.
50. Ibid.
51. Laura Richardson Walton, "In Their Own Backyard: Local Press Coverage of the Chaney, Goodman, and Schwerner Murders," *American Journalism* (Summer 2006, Volume 23:3), 29–51.
52. Cass, *supra* note 41.
53. Ibid.
54. Ibid.
55. "Annual Report 2008," Institute for Rural Journalism and Community Issues, availableat http://www.uky.edu/CommInfoStudies/IRJCI/AnnualReport2008 .pdf (accessed June 30, 2008).
56. Al Cross, "From the Director," *Rural Report* (Spring 2008), available at http://www.uky.edu/CommInfoStudies/IRJCI/RuralReportSpring2008.pdf (accessed June 30, 2009).
57. Ibid., 4.
58. "Publishers of Mountain Eagle Get Award Named for Them," Institute for Community Journalism and Rural Issues, available at http://www.Rural Journalism.org (accessed June 30, 2009).
59. Al Cross, *supra* note 11.

60. Jonathan Rowe, "The Language of Strangers: How a Hotshot Editor with Big Ideas Failed to Comprehend the Soul of Community Journalism," *Columbia Journalism Review* (January/February 2008), 36–40.

61. Ibid.

62. The Institute for Rural Journalism and Community Issues, "An Exemplar of Rural and Community Journalism Changes, Offering Essential Lessons in the Craft," *Rural Report* (Spring 2008), 12–13.

63. "Looking ahead: Counting the Steps along the Path," *The West Marin Citizen*, available at http://www.westmarincitizen.com/page7.htm (accessed July 1, 2009).

6

Newspaper Readership

Readers are the reason newspapers exist. Readers buy a newspaper for news, of course, to learn about events in their cities, their nation and the world, to read opinions about the meaning of social issues, to seek stories of human interest. But readers are not only a newspaper's customers; they are also its stock in trade. Newspapers have made most of their money not by selling news to the readers, but by selling readers to advertisers. Advertisers trying to reach a mass audience know that readers buy the paper to find information about where to go for entertainment, about which stores are promoting sales or about which local business has the item that they need. In short, readers buy the paper for advertisements, too. In fact, newspapers traditionally have made about 80 percent of their revenue from selling advertising. The rest comes from subscriptions.[1] The two are intertwined: The more readers a newspaper has, the more money it can command for advertisements and the healthier it is as a business.

Readers also are crucial to newspapers for a more noble reason. Many journalists regard their jobs not only as a career but also as a calling. They believe that reporting on daily events and issues, and on how they affect readers, is a duty and a trust. For a democracy to work, people need to know how their government and other institutions are meeting, or failing to meet, their needs.

For those reasons, newspaper managers and journalists have worriedly watched as fewer and fewer readers have bought newspapers. The total paid circulation of daily newspapers in America has decreased every year between 1984 and 2008, with the exception of one small upward blip, according to the Newspaper Association of America. In 1984, the paid circulation was 63.3 million; four years later, it had dropped to 48.6 million, a 23 percent decline.[2] If you consider the penetration of daily newspapers, the percentage of households that subscribe, the peak for newspaper readership was in the early 1920s.[3] What's worse is that such circulation figures count only people who paid for newspapers. The number of Americans who told pollsters that they simply looked at a paper the day before plunged from 58 percent in 1994 to 34 percent in 2008.[4]

Advertisers also deserted daily newspapers. A communications industry report for 2009 found that advertising spending was declining, down 2.9 percent in 2008, to $210 billion. For 2009, the private equity firm Veronis Suhler Stevenson predicted advertising would decline another 7.6 percent and 1 percent in 2010. The worst hit in 2009, the report predicted, would be newspapers, down 18.7 percent to $35.5 billion. In 2004, the total was $65.3 billion.[5]

Forced to cut costs, daily newspapers have laid off workers, reduced the number of days they publish or closed entirely. In 2008, about 5,900 full-time journalists lost their jobs as newspapers closed or cut back. That followed the loss of 2,400 jobs the year before.[6] Of course, journalists fear for their jobs, but they also express a sense of sadness about being unable to fulfill their duty as chroniclers of the American experience for their readership, especially during the severe financial crisis that started in 2007. Just before Reid Forgrave of Gannett's *Des Moines Register* started his mandatory, unpaid, weeklong furlough at the paper, Forgrave said a source told him about a seventy-year-old woman who was evicted when her house went into foreclosure. "Those are the stories that I'm most scared of losing," Forgrave said. "You can always say foreclosures are up 4.2 percent, but when you show it happening to an old woman who's on her front lawn with her granddaughters going through her stuff...."

The dreadful worldwide recession hurt newspapers as much as their readers, which, in a sad way, might prove to be a good thing, Forgrave said. "It will probably have been good for us to have had the spotlight shone on us. For once, we'll feel more in tune with the people we're covering...down to the level of what newspaper writers used to be and back to the people that we should be writing about more—the voiceless."[7]

The Disappearing Reader

This downward trajectory of readership has worried newspaper publishers, owners and journalists for decades. Yet almost 50 million Americans paid for a newspaper in 2008, and many more read the paper than bought it. To counter all the bad publicity the industry was getting about the loss of readers, more than 400 newspapers ran advertisements the day after the Super Bowl in 2009 proclaiming that readership of newspapers, estimated at 100 million, was still higher than the audience of the premier football game. Newspapers were using the tools of public relations and advertising to attempt to minimize an undeniable decline in readership.[8]

Who Reads Newspapers?

Reading a daily newspaper is increasingly an older person's habit. For years, older people have read newspapers at higher rates than the young, but even older readers started kicking the habit by the end of the twentieth century. In 2008, the Pew Research Center for the People and the Press conducted a nationwide survey, asking people, "Did you get a chance to read a paper yesterday, or not?" Among people born before 1946, more than half, 53 percent, said they had read a newspaper "yesterday." Ten years earlier, that number had been 65 percent.[9] The research center said, however, that some people who stopped reading the daily newspaper were instead getting their news online.

Researchers know that children who have grown up in households where the newspaper was read and who attended schools where newspapers were used as teaching aids tend to become newspaper readers as adults.[10] Hence, many newspapers sponsor Newspapers in Education programs, sending copies to teachers in the schools with advice about incorporating them into the curriculum. But that effort is fighting another trend: the drop in the number of households that subscribe to newspapers, and a general decline in reading, watching or listening to news among all Americans. The percentage of people under twenty-five years old who told researchers that they typically consumed no news *at all* from any medium increased from 25 percent in 1998 to 34 percent a decade later.[11] In fact, the proportion of people who got no news increased across *all* age groups over those years, except for the fifty to sixty-four age bracket, where it held steady at 14 percent.[12]

Clearly, the culture of reading the daily newspaper at home has faded. A survey of Americans conducted by the Readership Institute of Northwestern University between 2003 and 2004 found that more than half of people over the age of thirty-five remembered that newspapers had been read or discussed almost every day in their home when they were children. But younger people did not: Only slightly more than a third of eighteen- to twenty-four-year-olds grew up in homes where the newspaper was read daily.[13] Many journalists and newspaper managers have believed that as people mature, they will realize the importance of the news in public life and start reading newspapers. But the Readership Institute called this a "major myth." In fact, what has happened is that people who read less replaced older people who were frequent readers.[14]

What Readers Want

The Readership Institute also studied what motivated readers to pick up a newspaper and what discouraged them from reading. It found in 2004 that most readers who believed that a newspaper "looks out for my civic and personal interests," "gives me something to talk about" or "makes me smarter" were motivated to read more. These motivated readers told the researchers such things as "I count on this newspaper to investigate wrong-doing" or "Reading this newspaper makes me feel like a better citizen" or "I bring up things I've read in this newspaper in conversations with many other people." On the other hand, some readers believed the newspaper had just too much information or it "discriminates and stereotypes." These people told the researchers such things as "I worry that other people reading this paper will get the wrong impression of minority groups" or "They only target minorities for their money. They don't really care about them." The study concluded that if newspapers could better explain to readers how the newspaper looked out for their civic interests and helped them become smarter by reading, they might be able to increase their readership.[15]

The Pew Research Center Biennial News Consumption Survey in 2008 discovered interesting insights into what people wanted in their news and how they consumed news: Two-thirds of Americans, regardless of their political beliefs or their demographics, said they wanted news that was free of a political point of view.[16] Checking in on the news appears to be a habit: People who consumed news at particular times of the day were more likely to pick up a paper, either a daily or a weekly.[17]

People perceive the news differently. More than four of every ten people said they thought news organizations were all the same, but college graduates (69 percent) were much more likely to trust particular news sources than high school graduates (44 percent).[18] The survey also revealed a political gap that affected readers' perceptions of a news organization's credibility: A greater percentage of Democrats said they believed all or most of what was published in *The New York Times* and in their daily newspaper than Republicans did. In contrast, a greater percentage of Republicans believed what was in the *Wall Street Journal* than Democrats did.[19] Overall, the highest rating any newspaper received in this believability measure ("you can believe all or most of what the organization says") was the 29 percent given to their local newspapers, a terribly low rating for a profession dedicated to reporting the truth.

The survey pointed out a gender gap in news preferences: Men were more likely to prefer news about science and technology, sports, business and

finance, international affairs and Washington politics. More women read news about celebrities, entertainment, health and religion.[20]

The Early Newspaper Readers

The primary audience of America's earliest newspapers was educated white men in leadership positions, but the papers also circulated in coffee houses, businesses and homes, where people also presumably read and discussed them.[21] The range of items advertised for sale in colonial Philadelphia or New York makes it evident that not only the well-to-do or powerful read those papers.[22] As newspapers were passed around and read, they helped to narrow "the cultural gap between the learned and the merely literate and the information gap between the privileged and the merely competent."[23] In the newspapers' efforts to disseminate views and information, they became instruments of democracy and could have generated a sense of citizenship and community.

In the early 1800s, advertisers took on a bigger role in using newspapers to reach readers. Half of the dailies between 1810 and 1820, in fact, had the word "advertiser" in their names, and 60 to 80 percent of their contents were ads.[24] Some of these commercial newspapers grew to two feet wide and a yard long and were called "blanket sheets," according to historian Bernard A. Weisberger. They printed news, but their readers were generally merchants and businessmen. Their columns carried a plethora of ads in minute type: "ship owners besought cargoes, jobbers offered to buy and sell commodities in wholesale lots; farmers described acres for sale; retailers announced the supremacy of their hats, shoes, coal, garden seeds, coffins, cork legs, and cough medicines… the 'Commercials' and 'Advertisers' were primarily expensive bulletin boards for a small trading clientele."[25]

Specialty newspapers reached smaller segments of the mass audience. Newspapers endowed by political parties served partisans and politicians, and their news made no effort to be impartial. Many religious groups published newspapers carrying items about their denomination's current events, scripture and Sunday school lessons, including the followers of William Miller, who led a group that believed the world would end in the 1840s. Farmers found out about new machinery and agricultural techniques and science in the pages of such newspapers as the *American Farmer* in Baltimore in 1818 or the *Plough-Boy* in New York in 1821. Abolitionists could read anti-slavery tracts in the *Genius of Universal Emancipation* or the *Liberator.*[26]

When newspapers grew into big businesses reaching a mass audience in the bustling cities of the nineteenth century, they also expanded their coverage to include other things that readers, particularly middle- and upper-class women, cared about. After all, these were the readers who, then as now, did most of the shopping for families, and newspapers were making lots of

money through advertising. "The word 'quality' was often used in describing the reading audience of various publications and was meant to signify the ability to spend money," wrote communication scholar Gerald J. Baldasty.[27]

By the middle decades of the nineteenth century, readers flocked to newspapers, especially in the cities. The country's urban population grew 767 percent between 1850 and 1900, but over that same period, the circulation of daily newspapers exploded by 1,879 percent.[28] On average, papers sold 2.61 copies per urban dwelling.

Historian Ted Curtis Smythe found multiple reasons for the leap in readership in the nation's cities. One was content. Before the Civil War, about half of the news space in a group of large dailies had been devoted to politics, Smythe noted, and political journalism "was not popular journalism." After the Civil War, newspaper publishers realized that to reach a mass audience, they needed to cover more than just politics and so added feature stories and news about crime to attract more readers. Another boon to newspaper readership was improved education and thus a higher literacy rate. Cities that annexed other areas also helped expand the local readership for a newspaper. Even improved public transportation, including trains and streetcars, helped make newspaper readers of city dwellers; they bought newspapers for the commute to and from their jobs downtown. Many newspapers created the position of circulation manager, and these men systematically promoted newspapers sales. Falling prices for wood pulp for paper and improved printing technology meant that newspapers could be printed more cheaply. Competition fomented price wars in the last couple of decades of the nineteenth century; readers in city after city could not pass up buying two or more of the urban papers for a penny or two apiece. The Packard Motor Company studied New York car owners' and stock exchange members' newspaper reading habits from 1892 to 1893, discovering they bought an amazing number of newspapers: on average, two papers in the morning, two in the afternoon and two on Sunday.[29]

The Audit Bureau of Circulations

Because the circulation of a newspaper was tied to how much it could charge for advertising, newspaper publishers frequently lied. They inflated their circulation rates to generate more income. Until the late 1890s a publisher had the only figures about how many readers paid for the newspaper, but because of lax accounting practices, even the publishers' statistics might have been faulty.[30] The Audit Bureau of Circulations, or the ABC, was formed in 1914 with a membership that included representatives from newspapers, advertisers, advertising agents, magazines, trade papers and farm publications. A major goal of this bureau was to standardize how to

count paid circulation figures so that advertisers could figure the value of their investment when they purchased an ad. Some newspaper publishers were skeptical and others grumbled about increased paperwork, but many recognized the importance of providing honest figures about their readership and a standard way of counting them.[31]

Since then, advertisers have relied on the ABC for reliable circulation statistics, as a group that standardizes the definition of paid circulation. The group periodically changes its definition of what can be included. The ABC changed its rules April 1, 2009, allowing newspapers to count even papers sold for a penny a copy to count toward paid circulation.[32]

The Changing Readership

In the middle of the twentieth century, when many men worked in factories and came home at 4 P.M. to a wife who worked only in the home, afternoon newspapers were popular. But lifestyles changed, women became wage earners and circulation of afternoon papers plummeted. In 1982, the total circulation of morning papers exceeded that of afternoon papers for the first time; by 2002, the circulation of morning papers was five times that of evening papers.[33] Afternoon newspapers, faced with traffic gridlock, changing job markets, distribution problems, increasing competition from television news and changing lifestyles, dramatically declined.[34] According to *Editor & Publisher*, the number of afternoon newspapers decreased from 1,498 in 1940 to 546 in 2008 while the number of morning newspapers grew in that same period from 380 to 872.

To understand their readers, newspapers began conducting focus groups, telephone surveys and in-person interviews with readers in the middle of the twentieth century, although it proved controversial. Some news professionals believed that learning the characteristics of readers and what they wanted to read would lead to pandering to them rather than reporting the news that journalists believed they needed to be good citizens. However, without such studies, newspaper managers had a hard time knowing their customers' needs. Perhaps because of that conflict, seventy-eight editors surveyed in 1991 about how they used readership research said they were most likely to make changes based on reader research for the comics and news about sports, entertainment and business. They said they were least likely to affect content decisions for hard news on national government, international affairs and science.[35]

Studies of modern newspaper readers have shown they are "generally older, better educated and wealthier than non-readers."[36] The number of newspaper readers increased after World War II and then leveled off from the 1960s through the middle 1980s. Yet the population of the country kept increasing, so the number of paid subscriptions should also have climbed.[37]

Academic researchers have theorized why people seemed to be losing interest in reading the news. Some researchers found that newspapers were tied to city life, and as people moved to the suburbs, their communities splintered. Newspapers did not effectively follow them. Other researchers believed that exposure to newspapers and other media in fact helped them integrate into a community in the suburbs.[38] But a 1997 study that examined this idea closely found that interpersonal communication, rather than their use of local newspapers, radio or television, seemed to be the primary way that people became a part of their communities.[39] Still, newspapers may play a role in helping people integrate into their communities as they drift into a new place and settle down.[40]

News for Groups

The American Newspaper Publishers Association's News Research Center surveyed the content and the readership of American newspapers in June 1971. It concluded that newspapers ran three times to eight times as many news items for "men's news," devoted to business, sports and finance as for "women's news," which covered fashion, society, food, home and garden.[41] Perhaps as a reflection of a more leisurely lifestyle or less competition from other media, 92 percent of the readers in 1971 said they looked through the entire newspaper, sometimes at several sittings, with the median number of times they picked up each issue being 2.3.[42]

Readers' preferences for news changed over time. In 1961, people said they looked forward more to reading news (68 percent) than feature stories (28 percent). By 1987, however, only 46 percent said they preferred news over features, and 40 percent preferred features over news.[43] Newspapers' response to such findings was mixed. Eighteen percent of newspapers reported that they were emphasizing features more, although 10 percent reported they put more emphasis on hard news.[44]

Readership studies tried to measure whether editors were giving their readers stories that they actually would want to read. In 1977, people were asked how much space they would devote to each of 34 topics if they were editors of a "paper tailor-made to your own interests."[45] General news topics were omitted to reflect news stories that editors could more easily control. The survey found that few people would omit any of the topics, ranging from astrology and horoscopes to health and nutrition. More than seven out of ten men would give at least "some space" to "a lot of space" to best food bargains; health, nutrition, medical advice; human interest stories on people in the news; consumer news; the environment and sports. Seven out of ten women said they would devote space to those items as well—except for sports. Women preferred editorials. A similar percentage of men and women expressed interest in reading about men's fashions (something

advertisers had known).

But in the actual pages of newspapers, the editors' and readers' views of what deserved more column inches seldom jibed. Research suggested that readers wanted more space than had actually been published about best food buys, health, nutrition and medical advice, consumer news, environment, home maintenance and repair, letters to the editor, religion, home furnishing and decorating, travel, recipes and women's fashions. By contrast, newspapers published more than readers wanted about human interest stories, school news, sports or show business people, comics, hunting and fishing, crossword puzzles, astrology and sports. A similar disconnect had emerged in a previous study done in 1971. "The discrepancy...demonstrates the difficulty of improving on editorial judgments through the application of formulas," concluded readership researcher Leo Bogart.[46]

Nothing that editors tried in changing newspaper content convinced readers to keep buying the paper in the same numbers as they once had. In 1967, about three-fourths of American adults surveyed said they read a newspaper every day. By 1988, that proportion had dropped to about half.[47]

A task force at the Gannett Co. Inc. surveyed 115 readers of its papers across the country in 2007. It concluded: "The future of print within the next five years hinges firmly on our ability to satisfy newspaper readers over the age of 40—primarily baby boomers—because they're the ones most inclined to be regular newspaper readers." Of these readers, 98 percent said they most likely would still buy the paper five years later. They appreciated certain core values in a newspaper: "empowerment, engagement, 'a strong sense of ethics,' 'skepticism toward elected officials and government,' 'individualism, forever young, and instant gratification.'"[48] These readers most wanted to read hard news and local news, and the task force recommended that if newspapers had to cut content, to leave these items alone.

Young Readers

However, to stay viable, any business must also attract younger customers. In the newspaper business, young people with disposable income are attractive to advertisers, so newspapers have tried for decades to attract them and turn them into regular readers. One such effort started in 2002, when daily papers also started publishing tabloids aimed at the younger market, featuring entertainment news, bold graphics and sassy writing. In 2002, Gannett launched its youth-targeted tab, *Noise*, in Lansing, Michigan. Five years later, it followed with nine more tabloids in other cities. In October 2002, the *Chicago Tribune* started the *RedEye*, a tabloid full of short news stories about entertainment, sports and the "social buzz" for eighteen- to thirty-four-year-olds.[49] By 2009, the *RedEye* claimed to be "the leading vehicle in Chicago for advertisers wanting to reach young, urban professionals who are short on time and long on disposable income."[50]

Other daily newspapers countrywide launched similar weekly papers, often free, to attract younger people. Some young readers, such as Rachel Smolkin, a twenty-nine-year-old journalist herself, decried the trend among established newspapers to produce "self-consciously 'hip'" but intellectually weak editions aimed at young people, arguing that their editors apparently do not "grasp that youth and intelligence are not mutually exclusive." She contended that stories aimed at youth and older folks could and should exist in the same newspaper because people of any age could appreciate them.[51]

Despite such criticism, traditional newspapers continued to publish special editions aimed at particular groups of readers. In addition to *RedEye*, The Tribune Co., for example, also introduced *The Mash*, a weekly written by and about teens; *Hoy*, a Spanish-language paper published Monday through Friday; and *Fin de Semana*, a Spanish-language Sunday paper. The average circulation of *The Chicago Tribune*, the *RedEye* and these alternative newspapers totaled a massive 779,747 daily and 1,268,784 on weekends, according to the Audit Bureau of Circulations.[52] It wasn't enough. The Tribune Co., which was under an immense $13 billion debt created when billionaire Sam Zell purchased the company in 2007, filed for bankruptcy protection from its creditors in December 2008.[53]

In Cincinnati, in 2003, Gannett introduced a free tabloid, *CiN Weekly*, for younger readers. Five years later, it laid off the staff. In a move that may portend the future of joint publications, it replaced *CiN Weekly* with *Metromix*, produced with Tribune Media and featuring both national and local content.[54]

The *Chicago Tribune* and many other newspapers also tried to attract readers with less depressing and more human interest stories. Readers noticed. When a Chicago business publication published an online story about the "vertiginous losses" the *Tribune* had suffered in the first half of 2009, it generated this comment from a subscriber who said she had canceled her subscription after twenty years:

> It deserves to go under. Sam Zell has insulted Chicagoans by 'dumbing down' the paper, putting giant photos of kids with dogs on the front page, and relegating national news to bullets buried beneath masses of advertising. I miss having a real paper to read every morning—especially at a time of so much critical change in our world. I haven't abandoned print journalism—it has abandoned me![55]

Weekly Readers

For readers who did not find what they wanted in the daily newspapers, they could always turn to a weekly. Weekly newspapers had existed since the start of the country. Unlike dailies' readership, readership of weekly papers appeared to have held more steady. These papers are often called "community papers" because of their focus on local or even neighborhood news, such as high school sports, town government and school board actions. About a third of people surveyed said they read these weeklies in 2008, about the same number that read them since 2004.[56]

Another type of non-daily paper is the alternative weekly. The Association of Alternative weeklies started in 1978, and by 2008 it had 131 members and a Web portal, AltWeeklies.com. Readers of alternative weeklies tended to be younger than those who read traditional newspapers, but the newspapers themselves were diverse. The association's website noted that "what ties them together are a strong focus on local news, culture and the arts; an informal and sometimes profane style; an emphasis on point-of-view reporting and narrative journalism; a tolerance for individual freedoms and social differences; and an eagerness to report on issues and communities that many mainstream media outlets ignore."[57] However, by the start of the twenty-first century, many of these alternative "youth-targeted" papers had been around so long that they also began to worry that their readership was aging, and they, like traditional dailies, struggled with competition from online news.[58] Still, at least in 2007, the alternative weekly world outside of big-city markets was still drawing readers and "doing well."[59]

The Online Newspaper Reader

Most newspapers in America are tied to a place; for them, geography is destiny. People like to read local news, and local advertisers like to reach those customers. Even though the Internet is what Frances Cairncross has called "the death of distance,"[60] readers still want to feel connected to a community, even online. A study published in 2007 found some newspapers drew more than half their online readers from outside the traditional geographic market. To tap into advertising revenue, the researchers said, newspapers need to find out who these "outside" readers of their newspapers online were and why they came.[61]

For a while after the advent of the Internet, newspapers continued to simply send their news out to a passive audience. Then, at the bottom of news stories, newspapers added boxes where readers could comment about the stories and about each others' comments. Bloggers began to summarize news from multiple sites, adding commentary and sharing it with whole new audiences; other bloggers did their own reporting.

Newspapers eventually realized that much of their future was online. In an optimistic news release, the Newspaper Association of America reported that more than 73.3 million unique visitors went to newspaper websites in the first quarter of 2009, an increase of more than 10 percent over the same period in 2008. Many of these people were attractive to advertisers. Of the readers who said they had visited a newspaper website in the previous week, 28.2 percent had incomes of $100,000 or more, 34 percent had a post-graduate degree, 32.4 percent had bought a residence in the past year and 29.9 percent of people worked in management, business or finance.[62]

However, Martin Langeveld, who had thirty years' experience in newspapers before he began blogging for the Nieman Journalism Lab at Harvard University, pointed out that a closer look at those numbers was not reassuring to the newspaper industry. CNN, Yahoo and MSNBC each had drawn more than half the number of unique visitors of the entire newspaper industry to their own sites in one month, he noted. The total number of monthly views of newspaper pages accounted for less than one percent of the total U.S. page views, he contended. And if about one-third of high-wage, well-educated, professional homeowners had visited a newspaper website in the past week, he wrote, that meant that about two-thirds had *not*. Langeveld drew three "inescapable" conclusions:

- While newspapers have a substantial online audience, it is nothing like the audience attention owned by newspapers in pre-web days;
- Newspaper websites are far from dominant in the online news sphere;
- The newspaper site audience is insignificant compared with total web engagement.[63]

In fact, even though some readers have migrated to newspapers' online sites, those sites made less money because the advertising dollars did not follow to the same degree. One reason is that when people look for news online, they might also check such news aggregators as Google or Yahoo in addition to their local paper, thus splintering the traditional newspaper audience for advertisers. In addition, when people read the news in the newspaper, they read the ads willingly. Online, ads are annoyances. So the amount that newspapers can charge for an online ad is lower, and they make far less money from them.[64]

Many readers also expect newspapers to give away their content online, no matter whether the newspaper makes more or less money from online ads. One former reporter wrote to *Editor & Publisher*, a newspaper trade magazine, explaining why someone like him, who had been reading about the declining newspaper industry since he started as a cub reporter in 1968 and who suffered from "a lifelong addiction to the printed word," had deserted the newspaper for the free online product:

> I haven't bought a printed newspaper for years, almost a decade. Yet every day I relish reading my favorite newspaper in the world, *The Guardian*, along with the NYT [*The New York Times*] and the *Globe & Mail*.
>
> Of course, I regularly visit Crooks and Liars, the Daily Beast, Drudge and anything else that catches my eye. So it's hard to get misty-eyed at the deaths of the *Rocky Mountain News* or *Seattle P-I*, or the cutbacks at McClatchy.
>
> The point of all this is that I fully realize that I, and millions like me,

are to blame for the rapid demise of ink-on-paper journalism, but I don't care. All I care about is content, and I've got content coming outta my ears.[65]

In 2009, the debate about whether charging for newspaper content would drive readers away or would generate enough money to continue their existence raged. It seemed clear that unless most newspapers agreed to do it and could legally make such an agreement or unless a newspaper had unique content, readers would probably go elsewhere online for the same information for free.

Three Groups of News Consumers

After surveying Americans in 2008, the Pew Research Center for the People and the Press concluded that people's news consumption habits divided them into four groups: the Integrators, the Net-Newsers, the Traditionalists and the Disengaged (See Table 1).

The Disengaged are just what they seem, uninterested in local, national, international or business and finance news. They constitute about 14 percent of Americans, and they were the lowest paid and least educated of the groups. The other three groups, who are at least somewhat interested in the news, are these: [66]

The Traditionalists. Of the news consumers, this is the largest and oldest group. These people preferred getting news from television, and few got news online. They constituted 46 percent of news consumers and their median age was fifty-two. A large percentage of them, 43 percent, were unemployed, and six out of ten had no more than a high school education. Traditionalists were more likely to be Democratic but also more likely to say they were conservative. The news topic of most interest to Traditionalists is the weather, with 58 percent of them saying they follow weather stories very closely, higher than the percentage in the other two groups (but these groups also followed weather closely).[67]

The Integrators. This group constituted a little less than one-quarter of American news consumers. Integrators follow news across all media. "Avid news consumers," most Integrators followed a variety of topics at greater rates than Traditionalists or Net-Newsers. They were younger than Traditionalists, with a median age of forty-four. Integrators were almost evenly split politically: 26 percent said they were independents, 29 percent were Republicans and 38 percent were Democrats.[68]

The Net-Newsers. This is the smallest group, at 13 percent of news consumers. Almost half say they have a profile on a social network site, 59 percent use the Internet at work and 75 percent said the Internet was typically where they got their news. This group is wealthier, more educated and younger than the others, with a median age of thirty-five. This group is much more at home on the Internet than the other groups. This group has the largest proportion of political independents, with 35 percent, and about one-quarter call themselves liberal.[69]

Integrators spent the most total time with news from all media on a typical day—eighty-eight minutes. They also spent the most time reading newspapers, but that was only sixteen minutes per day. Traditionalists spent fourteen minutes with a newspaper every day and Net-Newsers, just twelve. A majority of the three types of people who followed news said they closely followed national and local news most of the time. (Even 37 percent of the Disengaged said they follow local news closely most of the time.) Far fewer of the three news-consuming groups said they followed international news closely most of the time.[70]

While all of these groups read some news, television attracted a greater percentage of the audience than any other medium, with the exception of the Net-Newsers, who preferred getting news online. (See Table 2) Nonetheless, online news attracted all segments of the audience, even the Disengaged.

Readers Rate Online News

Before the advent of the Internet, reporters rarely knew which stories readers read or what they thought about them unless the readers called or wrote a letter; often, the only readers to do that were angry. The Internet has given reporters and their bosses hard data about which stories readers like because they can measure the number of clicks on each story. This is both a blessing and a curse. Lindsay Peterson, a reporter at *The Tampa Tribune*, like other reporters, observed that she was sometimes disappointed in which stories readers preferred on the newspaper's site: "The stories we put our hearts and souls into don't seem to be getting as many hits as we'd hoped."[71] One of her stories about a wounded soldier from Iraq got 6,000 hits, but another story about a teacher caught sleeping with a student got thousands more. Then there were times when a story that she enjoyed writing, such as one about an eccentric woman traveling from Florida to Texas on horseback, won a massive following online. She was delighted, but surprised: "It's like the viewers are the ones deciding now. It's more democratic, yes, and it's something we need to pay attention to. But it's disturbing and disruptive, too."[72]

For their part, some readers, or their representatives, have expressed anger toward the mainstream media, a vague term that arose to denote the newspapers, television stations and radio stations that had existed before the Internet revolution. Dan Gillmor, a "new media" champion, had labeled news readers "the former audience," and Jay Rosen, a journalism professor at New York University and author of PressThink, a blog about the profession, used the term in a widely circulated online manifesto. It began:

The people formerly known as the audience wish to inform media people of our existence, and of a shift in power that goes with the platform shift you've all heard about....The people formerly known as the audience are those who were on the receiving end of a media system that ran one way, in a broadcasting pattern, with high entry fees and a few firms competing to speak very loudly while the rest of the population listened in isolation from one another—and who today are not in a situation like that at all.[73]

The manifesto argued that big media companies might have connected readers upward, to hear what those in power had to say, but the Internet has connected readers more horizontally, with each other and their communities. The document conceded that many in the audience will still passively read the mainstream media's news stories: "We'll consume them and you can have yourselves a nice little business." But the online audience wanted information and entertainment on its own schedule, Rosen argued, and it wanted news media "to be way better than it is." It would gladly usurp the tools of publishing and broadcasting for its own purposes. It concluded: "You don't own the press, which is now divided into pro and amateur zones. You don't control production on the new platform, which isn't one-way. There's a new balance of power between you and us."[74] As is only appropriate for a new medium, this document was then followed by many reader comments.

Andrew Sullivan, a writer and an editor of *The New Republic* news magazine, also became a powerful online voice promoting an active role of the people formerly known as the audience. Sullivan called blogging the first journalistic model that "harnesses rather than merely exploits the true democratic nature of the Web....This means a writer no longer needs a wealthy proprietor to get his message across to readers. He no longer needs an editor, either. It means a vast amount of drivel will find its way to the Web. But it also means that a writer is finally free of the centuries-old need to suck up to various entities to get an audience."[75]

Reaching out to Readers

As it has empowered the audience, the Internet has also shaken the established media, especially the newspaper business. And newspaper journalists have mourned when readers seemed to have tuned them out and have flinched at readers' anger toward the "mainstream media." Some journalists questioned the argument that they always delivered news top-down and one-way. After all, the first newspaper published in the American colonies in 1690, *Publick Occurrences Both Forreign and Domestick*, was printed on only three of its four pages. The last page was left blank so that citizens could write their own comments and pass it along.[76] Throughout history, even while newspapers grew into big businesses in the nineteenth century and then major global media corporations in the twentieth, the audience could always write letters to the editor—but an editor could also decide not to publish them. The common people did not have the money or the distribution system to reach a large audience of their own until the Internet gave them that power.

To bridge any gulf between the paper and its readers, *The Miami Herald* in 2008 invited readers to talk with reporters, in person. It set up two public meetings and called them "Why We Do What We Do" at a bookstore in Coral Gables, Florida. The journalists showed the people who attended multimedia reports on their coverage of a hurricane in Haiti and of the situation in Cuba, which was preparing for the fiftieth anniversary of its revolution. The journalists invited readers for an in-person conversation about the news. The meetings were held not only to engage the public and explain the value of journalism to them but also to bolster the morale of journalists in the newsroom, which had suffered two rounds of layoffs and was expecting a third. Not only did many readers not comprehend why reporters did what they did, but many reporters also had begun asking themselves the same question.

The *Herald's* sessions with readers attracted more than 300 people, who seemed genuinely curious about the profession of journalism. They asked, "How hard is it to talk to people there?" and "What happens if the government catches your correspondent?" and "How do you decide what photos to put on the front page?" and "Why risk your own lives to tell someone else's tale?" The reporter who wrote about these meetings, Nancy San Martin, a 2006 Nieman fellow, concluded that newspapers of the future would probably rely on fewer professional journalists, but those professionals needed more than ever to make clear to readers why reporters and editors believe so passionately in the value of journalism. "Why do we do what we do?" she asked, explaining, "We do it because it matters."[77]

Table 1. Integrators Spend the Most Time with the News

Average number of minutes spent...	Total	Tradition- alists	Inte- grators	Net- Newsers	Dis- engaged
Watching TV news	31	35	37	23	13
Reading a newspaper	13	14	16	12	5
Listening to news on radio	14	14	21	15	7
Getting news online	8	1	14	28	4
Total	66	64	88	78	29

Source: Biennial news consumption survey released Sunday, August 17, 2008. "Audience Segments in a Changing News Environment; Key News Audiences Now Blend Online and Traditional Sources." Pew Research Center for the People & the Press, a project of the Pew Research Center.

Table 2. Online Newspapers Attract Net-Newsers

News consumption "*yesterday*"	Total %	Tradition-alists %	Inte-grators %	Net-Newsers %	Dis-engaged %
Any News	**81**	**83**	**92**	**86**	**55**
Watched TV news	57	65	66	47	30
Newspaper	34	36	42	35	14
Paper	27	35	30	8	13
Online	4	*	6	17	1
Both paper and online	3	1	6	10	0
Radio news	35	33	46	38	21
News online	29	7	56	75	13
No traditional news	24	18	12	28	51
# of sources					
Two or more sources	48	45	70	58	18
One source	33	38	22	28	36

Source: Biennial news consumption survey released Sunday, August 17, 2008. "Audience Segments in a Changing News Environment; Key News Audiences Now Blend Online and Traditional Sources." Pew Research Center for the People & the Press, a project of the Pew Research Center.

Notes

1. "State of the News Media 2004: Newspapers: Audience," Journalism.org, available at http://www.stateofthemedia.org/2004/narrative_newspapers_audience.asp?cat=3&media=2 (accessed July 6, 2009).
2. "Total Paid Circulation," Newspaper Association of America, available at http://www.naa.org/TrendsandNumbers/Total-Paid-Circulation.aspx (accessed June 14, 2009).
3. Philip Meyer, *The Vanishing Newspaper* (Columbia, Mo.: University of Missouri Press, 2004), 5.
4. "Key News Audiences Now Blend Online and Traditional Sources," Pew Research Center Biennial News Consumption Survey, Pew Research Center for the People and the Press, posted on August 17, 2008, available at http://people-press.org/report/444/news-media (accessed July 4, 2009).
5. Stephanie Clifford, "A Look Ahead at the Money in the Communications Industry," *New York Times*, published on August 4, 2009, B3.
6. Rick Edmonds and the Pew Project for Excellence in Journalism, "The State of the News Media 2009: An Annual Report on American Journalism," available at http://www.stateofthemedia.org/2009/narrative_newspapers_intro.php?cat=0&media=4 (accessed July 7, 2009).

7. Beth Macy, "Hunkering Down," *American Journalism Review* (June/July 2009), 38–43.

8. Jennifer Saba, "Looking on Bright Side," *Editor & Publisher* (March 2009), 6–8.

9. "Newspapers Face a Challenging Calculus: Online Growth, but Print Losses Are Bigger," Pew Research Center for the People and the Press, posted on February 26, 2009, available at http://pewresearch.org/pubs/1133/decline-print-newspapers-increased-online-news (accessed July 3, 2009).

10. Mary Nesbitt, "The Effects of Childhood Exposure to Newspapers on Adult Readership," Readership Institute, Northwestern University, posted on December 2004, available at http://www.readership.org/new_readers/data/childhood.pdf (accessed July 3, 2009).

11. "Key News Audiences Now Blend Online and Traditional Sources," *supra* note 4.

12. Ibid.

13. Nesbitt, *supra* note 10.

14. John Levine, "In Their Own Words: 2004," Newspaper Association of America/American Society Newspaper Editors presentation, Readership Institute, Northwestern University, available at http://www.readership.org/new_readers/newreaders.asp (accessed July 3, 3009).

15. Mary Nesbitt, "Key Newspaper Experiences," Readership Institute, Northwestern University, posted on July 2004, available at http://www.readership.org/new_readers/data/key_experiences.pdf (accessed July 5, 2009).

16. "Key News Audiences Now Blend Online and Traditional Sources," *supra* note 4, at 16.

17. Ibid., 34.

18. Ibid., 36.

19. Ibid., 59.

20. Ibid., 40.

21. Charles E. Clark, "The Newspapers of Provincial America," in John B. Hench, ed., *Three Hundred Years of the American Newspaper* (Worcester, Mass.: American Antiquarian Society, 1991), 383.

22. Ibid., 388.

23. Ibid., 387.

24. Bernard A. Weisberger, *The American Newspaperman* (Chicago: The University of Chicago Press, 1961), 70.

25. Ibid., 74–75.

26. Ibid., 83–86.

27. Gerald J. Baldasty, "The Nineteenth-Century Origins of Modern American Journalism," in John B. Hench, ed., *Three Hundred Years of the American Newspaper* (Worcester, Mass.: American Antiquarian Society, 1991), 412–413.

28. Ted Curtis Smythe, "The Diffusion of the Urban Daily, 1850–1900," *Journalism History* (Summer 2002, Volume 28), 73–84.

29. Ibid.

30. Frank W. Rucker and Herbert Lee Williams, *Newspaper Organization and Management* (Ames, Iowa: Iowa State University Press, 1974), 287.

31. Ibid., 288–290.

32. Jennifer Saba, "Circ Hits Keep Coming," *Editor & Publisher* (May 2009), 15.

33. "The State of the News Media 2004: Newspapers: Audience," The Project for Excellence in Journalism, available at http://www.stateofthemedia.org/2004/narrative_newspapers_audience.asp?cat=3&media=2 (accessed July 30, 2009).

34. Marvin Kalb and Nicholas Kralev, "The Afternoon Newspaper War," *Harvard International Journal of Press/Politics*, (Fall 2000, Volume 5:4), 2–3.

35. Randal A. Beam, "How Newspapers Use Readership Research," *Newspaper Research Journal* (Spring 1995, Volume 16: 2), 28–38.

36. Robert L. Stevenson, "The Disappearing Reader," *Newspaper Research Journal* (Summer 1994), 22–31.

37. Ibid.

38. Keith R. Stamm, "Of What Use Civic Journalism? Do Newspapers Really Make a Difference in Community Participation," in Gregory J. Shepherd and Eric W. Rothenbuhler, eds., *Communication and Community* (Mahwah, N.J./London: Lawrence Erlbaum Associates, 2001), 218, available at http://books.google.com/books?hl=en&lr=&id=vuxqkhDueYMC&oi=fnd&pg=PA217&dq=%22Keith+R.+Stamm%22&ots=gbZrN"Gnm09&sig=M55biop9rUtjdGWE7Em540hmZ08#v=onepage&q=%22Keith%20R.%20Stamm%22&f=false.

39. Keith R. Stamm, Arthur G. Emig and Michael B. Hesse, "The Contribution of Local Media to Community Involvement," *Journalism & Mass Communication Quarterly* (Spring 1997, Volume 74: 1), 97–107.

40. Ibid., 103–104.

41. "News and Editorial Content and Readership of the Daily Newspaper," *News Research Bulletin* No. 5, American Newspaper Publishers Association (Washington, D.C.: 1973).

42. Ibid.

43. Leo Bogart, *Press and Public: Who Reads What, When, Where, and Why in American Newspapers* (Hillsdale, N.J.: Lawrence Erlbaum Associates, 2nd ed., 1989), 286.

44. Ibid., 202.

45. Ibid., 288.

46. Ibid., 294–296.

47. Stevenson, *supra* note 36.

48. Joe Strupp, "Gannett Task Force: Better Keep the Boomers Happy," *Editor & Publisher* (October 2008), 22–23.

49. Mark Fitzgerald, "*RedEye* Wakes a Week Early," *Editor & Publisher* (October 28, 2002), 3.

50. "About *RedEye*," available at http://redeye.chicagotribune.com/about/ (accessed July 6, 2009).

51. Rachel Smolkin, "Too Young to Read?" *American Journalism Review* (October/November 2003), 56.

52. "ABC Releases First Consolidated Media Report for Newspapers," Audit Bureau of Circulations, News Releases available at http://www.accessabc.com/press/press061909.htm (accessed July 6, 2009).

53. Richard Brunelli, "Work in Progress," *Brandweek* (May 18, 2009), special section, 6–9.

54. Kevin Osborne, "*Enquirer* Layoffs Hurt Us All," *CityBeat*, posted on July 15, 2009, available at http://www.citybeat.com/cincinnati/article-18361-enquirer-lay-offs-hurt-us-all.html (accessed August 5, 2009).

55. Patricia S., commenting on "Tribune Co. Profitability Continues to Deteriorate," by Ann Saphir, posted on July 06, 2009, available at http://www.chicagobusiness.com/cgi-bin/news.pl?id=34635 (accessed July 6, 2009).

56. "Key News Audiences Now Blend Online and Traditional Sources," *supra* note 4, at 19.

57. "About AAN," available at http://aan.org/alternative/Aan/ViewPage?oid=2086 (accessed July 5, 2009).

58. Mark Fitzergald and Jennifer Saba, "Who Said Print Is Dead?" *Editor & Publisher* (August 2007), 18–24.

59. Ibid.
60. Frances Cairncross, *The Death of Distance: How the Communications Revolution is Changing Our Lives* (Boston, Mass.: Harvard Business School Press,1997).
61. George Sylvie and Hsiang Iris Chyi, "One Product Two Markets: How geography Differentiates Online Newspaper Audiences," *Journalism & Mass Communication Quarterly* (Autumn 2007), 562–581.
62. "Newspaper Web Site Audience Increases More Than Ten Percent in First Quarter to 73.3 Million Visitors," Newspaper Association of America, posted on April 23, 2009, available at http://www.naa.org/PressCenter/SearchPress Releases/2009/Newspaper-Web-Site-Audience-Increases-More-Than-Ten-Percent.aspx (accessed July 3, 2009).
63. Martin Langeveld, "Online Newspaper Audience Growth: Good News? Not Really," The Nieman Journalism Lab, posted on April 26, 2009, available at http://www.niemanlab.org/2009/04/online-newspaper-audience-growth-good-news-not-really/ (accessed July 3, 2009).
64. Jonathan Rauch, "How to Save Newspapers—and Why," *National Journal* (June 13, 2008), 29–29.
65. Mark Kiemele, "Old Fart Learns New Tricks," in "Letters," *Editor & Publisher* (April 2009), 8.
66. "Key News Audiences Now Blend Online and Traditional Sources," *supra* note 4, at 45.
67. Ibid., 53.
68. Ibid., 46–52.
69. Ibid., 46–52.
70. Ibid., 48.
71. Macy, *supra* note 7.
72. Ibid.
73. Jay Rosen, "The People Formerly Known as the Audience," posted on June 27, 2006, available at http://journalism.nyu.edu/pubzone/weblogs/pressthink/2006/06/27/ppl_frmr.html (accessed July 6, 2009).
74. Ibid.
75. Ian Hargreaves, *Journalism: A Very Short Introduction* (Oxford: Oxford University Press, 2005), 138.
76. Michael Emery, Edwin Emery and Nancy L. Roberts. *The Press and America: An Interpretive History of the Mass Media* (Boston, Mass.: Allyn & Bacon, 2000, 9th ed.), 22.
77. Nancy San Martin, "Engaging the Public in Asking Why We Do What We Do," *Nieman Reports* (Winter 2008), 59–61.

7

Newspaper
Ownership

Newspaper owners can hobnob with the powerful and rub shoulders with the moneyed class. They can express their opinions (one would hope only on the editorial pages) and dispatch them to the population in their region, or beyond. And anyone who has visited the bombastic Hearst Castle, the 165-room palace that newspaper baron William Randolph Hearst built for himself in 1947 atop a rocky hill in San Simeon, California, can see the wealth that newspaper ownership can bestow.

By 2009, however, owning a daily newspaper looked like a chancy venture. Newspapers suffered from competition from the Internet and specialty publications, a continuing loss of audience to other media, the resultant decline in advertising dollars and a worldwide recession that began in December of 2007. Their owners, by and large, were still profitable, but their revenues had plunged.

Advertising had been the primary way most newspapers made money, particularly classified advertising, the ads in small type in the back pages where people could sell goods and services to each other. In 1950, classified advertising accounted for 18 percent of an average newspaper's advertising revenue. By 2000, it made up 40 percent—and that put a large segment of a newspaper's finances at risk. The classified advertising section of a newspaper is susceptible to the business cycle; when the economy dips, people buy fewer ads and so newspaper revenues fall.[1] Add to that the major online competition for advertising revenue from Monster.com, Craigslist and a multitude of other Internet sites, and newspapers faced a huge loss of income. By 2009, many newspapers had laid off or bought out staff, cut the size of their pages, trimmed the number of days they published, declared bankruptcy or simply folded.

Who Owns Newspapers?

A long time ago, individuals and families owned most of the newspapers in America. The year 1910 marked the high point of independent newspaper ownership: 2,140 newspapers were owned by a family or company that owned no other dailies, and only sixty-two were owned by a newspaper group or chain. Independent ownership has been dropping ever since. In 1960, the number of newspapers owned by chains first exceeded the number of papers owned independently, and the number owned by chains just kept growing.[2]

As chains gobbled up newspapers, the number of cities with competing newspapers dwindled. In 1910, almost 60 percent of American cities supported more than one newspaper. By 1971, that number had plummeted to 2 percent.[3]

Money Machines

For much of modern newspaper history, owning a daily newspaper was virtually a license to print money. Since many cities in the country in the last quarter of the twentieth century had only one newspaper, the papers enjoyed a monopoly in their markets. If advertisers wanted to reach a mass audience, they had to buy space in the paper. By the early years of the twenty-first century, a monopoly newspaper in a medium-sized market enjoyed profit margins of 20 percent to 40 percent, compared with the average retail profits of 6 percent or 7 percent.[4] Overall operating profit margins fell to the low teens in 2008,[5] which many businesses would still regard as acceptable, especially during a severe recession. What's more, smaller papers (with circulations of up to 75,000) were more profitable than the newspaper industry as a whole, with profit margins in the high teens.[6] These papers were more likely to have less competition for local advertising dollars and retain something of a monopoly in their geographic area.

Private vs. Public, Independent vs. Group Ownership

Media chains owned most of the daily newspapers people read in America, as media groups went on a buying spree in the last half of the twentieth century. Families that had owned their own newspapers faced high gift and estate taxes if they wanted to pass them on to their heirs or friends, and so many formerly family-owned newspapers sold to public chains, thus making the families another fortune.[7] Between 1960 and 1980, newspaper chains bought more newspapers than ever before, with groups absorbing 587 dailies:[8]

> By 1978, the ten largest newspaper groups (Knight Ridder, Gannett, Newhouse, Tribune Co., Scripps Howard, Dow Jones, Hearst, Times Mirror, Cox and Thomson) had total circulation of 23.8 million, or 38.6 percent of the total market. By 1986, the twelve largest groups accounted for more than 47 percent of U.S. daily circulation.[9]

And by the end of the twentieth century, a group owned more than 80 percent of all American daily newspapers. Looked at another way, newspapers under chain ownership accounted for approximately 70 percent of the daily paid circulation in the country.[10]

In 1963, Dow Jones Co., which published, among other things, *The Wall Street Journal*, went public. Quickly, newspaper chains followed; they sold ownership shares of their companies on the stock market. The money raised by their stock offerings allowed them to invest in new technology, train management—and buy more newspapers.

When newspapers remained owned by private companies or families, just how much money they made remained private as well. The late 1960s marked the first time Wall Street analysts got a close look at newspaper groups' balance sheets, "and Wall Street was delighted with what it saw," wrote Philip Meyer.[11] Citing an analyst's report, Meyer noted that newspapers had collected almost a third of the total advertising dollars from the 1960s to the 1980s, they could pass along increased costs to their customers, and they took in so much money that they did not have to borrow and so avoided interest charges on loans when they wanted to expand.[12] Investors found newspapers attractive because their profits were about twice those of manufacturers.[13]

By 1999 newspaper chains were selling each other newspapers "on a scale never before seen or imagined.…Thomson, Knight Ridder, Cox, Media General, Hollinger, Gannett, Donrey and MediaNews are swapping properties like baseball cards, unloading papers that don't fit their geographic strategies and acquiring ones that do."[14] Consolidated newspaper companies could share printing plants, pool their coverage and cut better deals with advertisers. But consolidation also meant that in twenty-two states, one company owned at least 20 percent of all daily newspapers. And in some states, much more: In Oklahoma, for example, Community Newspaper Holdings Inc. owned 52 percent of the state's dailies; in New Jersey, Gannett owned 37 percent of all dailies.[15]

The money was good. Public newspaper companies enjoyed an average operating profit of 22.2 percent in 1999. The Tribune Co.'s operating profit was much higher—29.2 percent that year—before it bought 48 percent of the Times Mirror Co.,[16] stock that had been owned primarily by the Chandler family.[17]

But fat profits wouldn't last in the face of competition for advertisers and a worsening economy. By the first quarter of 2009, revenue from newspapers' advertisements had dropped 30 percent on average, the largest decline in thirty-eight years.[18] This followed a yearly drop of 17.7 percent in 2008, and declines before that as well.[19]

Investors reacted badly. Between 2005 and 2007, publicly traded newspaper stocks lost 42 percent of their value. Then, in 2008, they lost 83 percent of what was left.[20]

Chain Management

Many journalists grew to despise newspaper chains, especially public chains that answered to Wall Street's demands for growth and profits. They believed that concentrating newspapers into massive media companies, which often owned television and radio stations and later websites, would diminish the number of viewpoints and voices reporting on public affairs. They believed these chains focused too much on the bottom line and on short-term growth to appease stockholders and institutional investors, whereas newspapers have a civic responsibility to cover their local communities, which *costs* money. Finally, they believed that distant owners could not know a community as well as a local owner.

In his book, *The Vanishing Newspaper*, Meyer recounts Wall Street's reaction to the Knight Ridder newspaper chain's winning seven Pulitzer Prizes in 1986. The company's stock fell on the news. The reason, one analyst said, was "you win too many Pulitzer Prizes." He meant that the money spent producing such in-depth, high-quality journalism should have instead padded the bottom line.[21]

In another example, after the Cowles family sold its *Des Moines Register* to the Gannett Co. Inc. chain in 1985, the chain saw more cost than benefit in the paper's statewide coverage. So it cut the newspaper's circulation to remain only in the Des Moines market, abolishing two of the paper's five state news bureaus. The operating margin soared from 10 percent to 25 percent.[22]

While newspaper chains may focus on profit at the expense of journalism, public ownership of newspaper chains is not wholly negative. Some newspapers owned by chains have benefited from investments the chains made in management training and more professional business operations, thus allowing the journalism to flourish. Some research showed that big media corporations "have been more likely to provide autonomy to newsrooms, place more emphasis on quality, and promote diversity more than other companies."[23] *The Houston Chronicle*, which for years had been owned by a trust set up by former owner Jesse H. Jones, was "relatively poorly managed," researchers Robert G. Picard and Aldo van Weezel noted. After it was sold in 1987 to the Hearst Corporation, the paper improved because the chain's "pecuniary interests led to better performance financially and journalistically."[24]

In fact, many studies note a relationship between good journalism and good business, although it is not clear whether high-quality journalism causes a newspaper's business to be good or is its by-product.[25] Yet, the world of newspapering at the start of the twenty-first century had changed so much that what happened in the past might not predict the future anyway.

Knight Ridder

Knight Newspapers and Ridder Publications were two private newspaper chains that went public in 1969. The companies merged in 1974, but large portions of the stock were still held by the Knight and Ridder family members and trustees.[26] For decades, the Knight Ridder chain earned the respect of Wall Street as well as journalists. Its Washington bureau, for example, had become "a formidable journalistic force, emphasizing hard-nosed, fact-based watchdog reporting."[27] Alvah Chapman, who helped to engineer the merger between the two chains and who served as CEO of Knight Ridder Inc., believed publicly owned chains had some strong benefits: [28]

> We expanded our Washington Bureau—doubled the size of the Washington bureau—after we went public [in 1969]. We added our overseas bureaus after we went public. We started Business Monday after we went public. We started the Neighbors sections after we were public....In my 15 years, from 1974 to 1989, Knight Ridder's stock grew 23 percent compound growth rate. We had 15 straight years of increased earnings per share.[29]

The Knight Ridder chain also won thirty-three Pulitzer Prizes under Chapman's leadership.[30] But by 2005, Knight Ridder, like most large chains, had suffered from declining circulation and profits. It would be sold and dismantled within a year.

Gannett

Frank Gannett and some associates bought a half share of one newspaper in 1906 in Elmira, New York, to start what would become one of America's largest media companies. By the time Gannett bought out his partners in 1923, the small chain owned six newspapers in New York State. In 1967 the company went public, and by the end of that decade, Gannett Co. Inc. owned thirty-three dailies, twelve weeklies, six radio and two television stations.[31]

Gannett also bought cable television operations, outdoor advertising plants and the research firm of Louis Harris & Associates. Its consistently profitable ventures were noticed; in a 1986 poll, Wall Street analysts named Gannett the best-managed American publishing company.[32] By 1987 the circulation of Gannett newspapers was greater than that of any other newspaper group in America.[33] Starting in 1999, it branched overseas, purchasing through a subsidiary large regional newspaper companies in Great Britain. By the year 2000, Gannett had sold off its radio, cable, outdoor advertising and Louis Harris companies, but it continued purchasing newspapers. By 2009, Gannett owned eighty-four daily newspapers in the United States, eighteen dailies in the United Kingdom, more than 1,000 non-daily publications throughout the world, a weekly newspaper magazine, twenty-three television stations, commercial printing plants and subsidiaries that did such things as survey research and new media development. Its newspapers and its news service had won forty-five Pulitzer Prizes.[34] Meyer credits Gannett's former CEO and chairman Al Neuharth as being "just the kind of scrappy competitor" the corporation needed to make the newspaper chain grow. Neuharth has also been described as "egomaniacal, stubborn, tyrannical and brilliant. The kind of guy who would title his autobiography *Confessions of an S.O.B.*"[35] He started in the newspaper business at the age of eleven as a paperboy, and later worked for the Associated Press, *The Miami Herald* and *The Detroit Free Press*. He rose to be CEO in 1973 and chairman in 1979,[36] and retired to found the Freedom Forum, a foundation promoting a free press and free speech, as a successor organization to a foundation created by Frank Gannett in 1935.[37]

Neuharth said he remained uninfluenced by Wall Street pressures in 1982, when he launched *USA Today*. Gannett's stock price had fallen, and the company was "ridiculed" for starting a new national newspaper in that era. "So we paid no attention to Wall Street," he said. "Had we, we wouldn't have launched it, [or] we would have folded our tent after the first year."[38]

Neuharth had overseen the chain's purchase of newspapers, concentrating on newspapers in medium-sized cities where they had a monopoly. To avoid the spikes and dips in the bottom line caused by the business cycle, when the economy was in good shape these papers would reinvest earnings in staffing and equipment to restrain profits. When the economic cycle swung low, they postponed investment, cut staff and trimmed the news they delivered to prop up profits. That meant that Gannett's profits rose steadily, which Wall Street appreciated, and the price of its stock soared.[39] But during some of that period, inflation was also high. This meant that profits seemed higher than they actually were in real dollars.[40]

Things Fall Apart

Before the first decade of the twenty-first century was over, the good times were coming to an end for chain ownership. Chains broke apart as advertising revenue continued to decline and stock prices fell.

Knight Ridder had been the second-largest chain in the nation in terms of newspaper circulation and third largest in terms of revenue. But three investors, who owned almost 40 percent of the company's stock, became disillusioned with the company's performance and demanded the chain sell itself.[41] It sold in 2006 for $4.5 billion to another chain, the smaller McClatchy Co., which went $2 billion into debt in the deal. Within months, McClatchy had sold a dozen papers of the former Knight Ridder chain to a variety of new owners.[42] McClatchy also sold off its own largest paper to a private equity company.[43]

In 2008, two public companies split into four: The A.H. Belo Corp., headquartered in Dallas, Texas, owned three newspapers, including *The Dallas Morning News*, while its sister company, the Belo Corp., took the chain's television stations.[44] And the Scripps Howard chain split into two companies:

- Scripps Networks Interactive Inc. included the company's cable networks, such as Home & Garden Television (HGTV), networks such as the Food and DIY Networks and interactive businesses, such as shopping network Shopzilla.
- The E.W. Scripps company included newspapers in fifteen markets, ten broadcast television stations, the Scripps Howard News Service and United Media, which licenses such cartoons as "Peanuts" and "Dilbert."[45]

Splitting apart was intended to appeal to investors, enabling the newly formed companies to spin off money-losing operations, to be "more nimble" in making changes, to reduce expenses[46] and to operate without debt.[47]

New Owners

Rick Edmonds, who tracked the newspaper industry for the Poynter Institute, and researchers at the Project for Excellence in Journalism, reported that when chains started breaking apart in 2006, more private companies and individuals started to step up to buy them. By the end of 2008, private companies and individuals had bought newspapers that accounted for more than 10 percent of the country's total circulation.[48] The long period toward consolidation "was certainly slowing already and showed a little bit of movement in the other direction," Edmonds said in 2009. "I don't pretend to know or say this is the way it will continue. This is a time when certainly public companies do not have the financing or the inclination to want to get more papers."[49]

Private ownership pleased some journalists, who reasoned that these owners, if they lived in the community where the paper published, would be more likely to invest in strong, community-oriented journalism. But the fact that some individuals could purchase newspapers probably was not good news for the industry, because, generally, if a property is valued highly, even a wealthy person would have little chance to buy it.[50] And the investment for some individuals who could buy a daily newspaper proved unlucky. *BusinessWeek* put it this way in 2006: "As one Wall Streeter cracks, newspapers' newest suitors are billionaires trying to become millionaires."[51]

Nevertheless, Edmonds and the Project for Excellence researchers suggested in 2007 "very wealthy individuals are now looking at newspapers as they might look at sports franchises—high-profile enterprises important to their communities, where making lots of money may not be the main point."[52]

Private ownership could also create problems. In California, reporters and editors at the *Santa Barbara News Press* protested against what they believed was interference in news decisions by their local owner, billionaire Wendy McCaw, who bought the paper from The New York Times Co. in 2000. When dozens of reporters and editors quit or were let go, reporters started an effort to unionize, and both sides sued.[53]

Another public newspaper company, the Tribune Company, was bought by a private investor, Sam Zell, in 2007, in a complex deal that technically gave employees ownership of the newspaper but not a lot of control over the company.[54] From the start, Zell, a billionaire real estate mogul, showed that he was not inculcated into newspaper culture: Zell's get-acquainted tour of his properties included several jolting exchanges. He cursed out an *Orlando Sentinel* photographer after she had criticized running "puppy dog" pictures. He told the chain's Washington bureaus that they were balkanized, way overstaffed and producing a large volume of journalism no one cared about. [55]

About six months after buying the company, Zell announced cuts in the number of pages and employees to trim costs. Six months after that, the company filed for Chapter 11 bankruptcy reorganization, leaving the still-profitable newspapers it owned—*The Chicago Tribune*, *The Los Angeles Times* and others—struggling to pay off the $13 billion in debt incurred when Zell bought the company.[56] Interest payments alone cost about $1 billion a year.[57]

Employees of the company, through an employee stock ownership plan (which avoided federal income taxes), technically own the company. But Zell had the right to select two of the company's six company directors, giving him veto power over major decisions. If the company were to fail, employees could lose their retirement benefits, except what they had put into any 401(k) plan before the deal.[58] One *Los Angeles Times* employee told the *New York Times*, "There's a worry that he's betting the employees' retirement."[59] A loss on this investment probably would do little to Zell's own retirement, but, noting the continued decline of newspapers' advertising revenue and readers in 2009 that dragged down many newspapers, the *Economist* called his purchase of The Tribune Co. "a catastrophic commercial mistake."[60] As the summer of 2009 drew to a close, a union representing journalists at another Tribune Co. newspaper, *The Baltimore Sun*, won the right in federal bankruptcy court to see details about company plans to give bonuses of up to $70 million to certain managers despite the company's financial woes.[61]

In Philadelphia, the respected *Philadelphia Inquirer* quickly changed from public to private hands in 2006. The Philadelphia newspapers' website recounted it best, in one blunt sentence: "In the history of *The Inquirer*, the Annenberg era lasted thirty-four years, the Knight Ridder era 36 years, and the McClatchy era about 15 minutes."[62] After the McClatchy newspaper chain had purchased the Knight Ridder chain, it quickly sold a dozen papers. The *Inquirer* and *The Philadelphia Daily News* went to a group of Philadelphia locals, led by public relations entrepreneur Brian P. Tierney. The *Columbia Journalism Review* noted: "The initial reports, after the $562 million deal was struck in May 2006, emphasized the irony of the transaction—that a man who had helped spin, not to mention squelch, newspaper stories was now the most powerful force in Philadelphia journalism."[63]

Tierney's group invested $152 million of its own but took on another $410 million in debt, which the newspapers had to pay off.[64] Tierney, CEO of Philadelphia Media Holdings (PMH), had ideas about improving how the newspapers could sell advertisements, target new publications to niche audiences and change union agreements. But Tierney told a reporter that when he and his partners took over the company, the paper's operations were worse than he had expected.[65] Tierney made moves to reduce expenses, including laying off seventy of the *Inquirer's* newsroom staff.[66] "Tierney is saying smart things about what newspapers could do to thrive. But he also might not need to cut so deeply had he not spent, and borrowed, so much for the papers in the first place," *BusinessWeek* noted.[67]

At first Tierney followed an old-fashioned model of journalism, where the business people are walled off from the journalists. He and his partners even signed an agreement that they would not influence the paper's coverage. But that agreement fell by the wayside, and his newly hired editor said he welcomed Tierney's ideas and leads. "I didn't buy this to put it in a blind trust," Tierney later said. "I'm not here to be a potted plant." And at least one experienced reporter, Art Carey, agreed, noting, "I always thought the idea that he would not interfere with the editorial product was ludicrous. Why would you buy something that you can't shape?"[68]

Despite Tierney's efforts, in early 2009, the two Philadelphia newspapers filed for Chapter 11 bankruptcy restructuring.[69] The added pressures of the large economic downturn that afflicted the world at the end of the first decade of the twenty-first century proved too much for the business, even under local ownership. In addition, Tierney faced criticism from creditors, who asked a judge for an "independent oversight" of the company after Tierney was given a $350,000 bonus and a $232,000 raise at the time the company was lowering its revenue forecast, and two months before it filed for bankruptcy. Tierney rolled back the salary increase after the bankruptcy declaration, according to the newspaper's website, Philly.com.[70]

Under bankruptcy protection, the paper, smaller in staff and pages, continued publishing. *The Inquirer* even won awards for its coverage and had two finalists in the Pulitzer Prize competition in 2009: for a team of reporters' "exhaustive reports on how political interests have eroded the mission of the Environmental Protection Agency and placed the nation's environment in greater jeopardy" and for Inga Saffron's "fascinating and convincing architectural critiques that boldly confront important topics, from urban planning issues to the newest skyscraper."[71]

It also was sued for defamation. The suit alleged that a failed business deal motivated Tierney to publish negative articles about owners of a charter school. The newspaper denied any such motivation for its stories.[72] At this writing, that case is still in court, but it exemplifies one risk of local ownership: The perception that local owners can easily use their publication to punish local adversaries or promote sacred cows.

The worsening economy continued to put pressure on the company. A review of the paper's performance under Tierney's Philadelphia Media Holdings' ownership, published in the *Inquirer's* own pages, noted:

> PMH was the first consortium of local owners to take control of a major newspaper. That type of ownership was supposed to provide relief from Wall Street pressures that forced cutbacks at corporate-owned papers such as the *Los Angeles Times*, the *Chicago Tribune*, and the *Boston Globe*. Instead, economic conditions have proved to be owner-agnostic, damaging to all.[73]

The same article quoted Tierney as saying he was "very hopeful" that the paper would stay in local hands. He added: "I worry about a future where the papers in the near term or long term aren't owned by people who really love them.…This paper's been through the Civil War, the Depression, recessions, economic expansion, world wars—and *The Philadelphia Inquirer* has remained."[74]

Joint Operating Agreements

Some newspaper owners figured out a way to spread their costs around among their competitors. It started in the 1930s, when owners of newspapers that circulated in the same area realized they could reduce costs by sharing such things as their printing plants and advertising departments, while keeping their reporters and editors separate to produce two different newspapers. In 1933, the first such joint operating agreement began in

Albuquerque, New Mexico, when the *Albuquerque Tribune* and the *Albuquerque Journal* joined everything except their editorial departments, the reporters and editors. Between then and 1970, owners set up a total of twenty joint operating agreements (JOAs), between competing newspapers around the country, according to researchers John C. Busterna and Robert G. Picard.[75]

But then in 1965, the federal government sued Tucson newspaper owners on anti-trust grounds. As the case wound its way up to the Supreme Court, newspapers lobbied Congress to pass an exemption to the anti-trust laws, saying they needed the freedom to keep newspapers alive in certain large areas. Congress complied, passing the Newspaper Preservation Act in 1970. These JOAs generally meant that newspapers shared some of their costs but could also split the profits between the owners, who also could divide up their markets and fix prices. Some owners of suburban or weekly papers cried foul, arguing that a JOA between dailies in their area created unfair competition for them. And critics cited "discussions over apparently deliberate efforts by management to cause their newspapers to fail in order to qualify for the antitrust exemption."[76] Busterna and Picard argued that the Newspaper Preservation Act was unnecessary. In any case, nothing stopped the loss of readers and the closings of many newspapers that would follow.

Non-Profit Newspapers

Some entrepreneurs turned to a not-for-profit approach to newspaper ownership.

While non-profit ownership removes the pressure to make ever more money to please shareholders or greedy owners, journalists also worry about the ethical implications of newspapers accepting such funding for reporting. They reason that if a person or group pays for reporting, the news stories could easily become slanted to suit the donor's viewpoint. This is the non-profit variant of the concern about the influence of advertisers at for-profit companies.

At the non-profit, online newspaper, the *New Haven Independent*, although sponsors' names run along the right side of most of the site's pages, the website states clearly: "All financial contributions to the site come with the understanding that contributors will not determine (or have any responsibility for) the articles produced on the site."[77] The editor, Paul Bass, operated the news site with reader donations and grants from institutions and foundations. Foundation grants sponsored coverage of particular topics, such as health care.

Bass had been an investigative reporter for twenty-five years, but he left the *New Haven Advocate* in 2004 to write a book and never returned. At the time, he noted, "Everyone I knew at a conventional newsroom—whether it was newspaper or radio station—was miserable because of what publicly owned corporations were doing to local media."[78] He observed the growth of the "hyperlocal" news sites online, which he pointed out had been called simply "local" before large companies bought and closed competitive newspapers in an area. Discouraged by the corporate model of journalism, Bass drew inspiration from this comment from Daniel Conover on the PressThink blog:

> What if there were a way to treat public interest reporting more like a public service and less like a business? In the current model, newspapers consider their news infrastructure to be a business expense. Their real business is printing and distributing advertising. The capital costs are considerable: big physical plants, expensive presses, newsprint, ink, etc....Could you run something like that as a non-profit? Could you create a board or management structure that emphasizes quality standards and openness over return on investment?[79]

Journalism at non-profit sites, Bass had written, was "defined as a public good," which every community needs for a rich civic life. So he and other journalists established the Online Journalism Project and sought funding for the *Independent*.[80] Bass and his handful of reporters did not even have an office. They met at a coffee shop when they needed to talk.[81] The paper could pay no proofreaders and instead asked readers to tell it if they found errors. The paper has sometimes rewarded the reader who found the most mistakes with a mug and a mug shot on the homepage.[82] Not only did Bass believe that big media's profit margins were things of the past, but he also thought that the competitive model of journalism was dead as well. So each week, the *Independent's* site links to a few stories published by other sites.

Readers particularly liked Bass' vlog, a folksy video editorial called "Compost Bin," in which he typically pulls documents or books out of a bin in what looks like his backyard and delivers his opinion in rapid-fire fashion. "Readers love the vlog because it's goofy and playful. It's certainly not a professional production, but in general readers are open to the amateur side of things," he said.[83] Eleven months after the online paper was started, an invitation to readers to submit their own reviews of art or music drew a miniscule response. Bass reported that he had yet to figure out a way to engage his readers and to sustain his work. His annual budget of $120,000 was composed of 75 percent from foundations for topical reporting, 23 percent from institutional donations, and 2 percent from contributions of readers and others:

> I don't believe one or two or three people can handle all the reporting, editing, comment-posting, e-mailing, fund-raising, bookkeeping, marketing, and community outreach involved in producing a quality daily news site. But trying to raise enough money to substantially increase the budget (like doubling it) would require a major investment of time, which might be unrealistic with our current staffing.[84]

The *Independent* has worked out an arrangement with Christine Stuart, whose "Connecticut News Junkie" blog reports on state capitol news, largely abandoned by other newspapers.[85] House Majority Leader Denise Merrill and other critics believed that newspaper abandonment of statehouse coverage would result in more partisan reports. "You won't have that relatively unbiased medium that could filter this with some knowledge and expertise," she said. "Instead, the public is going to have to sort out what's true and what isn't."[86]

Despite its limitations, the non-profit model, with an experienced professional like Bass at the helm, was successful enough to spawn more non-profit online news sites. In June 2008, with a two-year, $500,000 grant from the John S. and James L. Knight Foundation, the Online Journalism Project, of which Bass is executive director, started the *Valley Independent Sentinel* in the Lower Naugatuck Valley of Connecticut.[87] The Thompson Newspapers chain had closed the only local daily newspaper, the *Ansonia Sentinel*, on Christmas Eve, in 1992.[88] The *News'* two full-time, experienced reporters were to cover the area for the new online venture five days a week. As of the summer of 2009, other non-profit news websites had opened in San Diego, Chicago, Minneapolis, St. Louis and Seattle.[89]

"In the foreseeable future, it seems, there will be two kinds of non-profit newspapers, those which are deliberately so and those which are reluctantly so," wrote *New Yorker* staff writer and a twenty-year veteran of *The Washington Post* Steve Coll. Granted, he said, newspapers such as *The Washington Post* would need "university-sized" endowments,[90] but it could be done.

It had already been done, in fact. One of the oldest, most successful traditional newspapers owned by a non-profit is *The St. Petersburg Times* in Florida. Nelson Poynter, the editor and owner of the newspaper, reviled chain ownership of newspapers, believing that local owners best understood their communities and so best served the public interest. In his will Poynter gave his controlling shares in the for-profit Times Publishing Co., the parent company of the newspaper and magazines *Florida Trend*, *Governing* and *Congressional Quarterly*, to a non-profit, educational journalism institute, The Poynter Institute.[91] Thus, the non-profit Poynter Institute owns the for-profit newspaper. In an opinion piece on Forbes.com, writer Louis Hau noted: "This bears repeating: Poynter gave the paper away. Is this the kind of deal that other would-be media barons have in mind? Here's a wild guess: No."[92]

Be that as it may, the *Times* flourished for decades under this non-profit system. The paper's fine journalism won eight Pulitzers, including two in 2009,[93] its reporters earned healthy salaries and the newspaper enjoyed an extensive and loyal readership. But being non-profit did not protect the newspaper from economic forces at work in the real world: Nelson Poynter may have controlled the most shares of the newspaper, but he had nieces who owned 200 shares. Poynter himself and his successor at the *Times* tried repeatedly to buy those shares, but were unsuccessful. Then, in 1988 Texas billionaire Robert M. Bass bought them, gaining control over 40 percent of the company. In a *Times* letter to readers, former chairman and CEO Andrew Barnes explained Bass' plans:

> He wanted somehow to parlay his stake into ownership of the whole paper and have us send him more money in the meantime. Those of us running the paper fought back. Our loyalty was to the newspaper and its communities, and to the school, not to a financier's greater wealth.[94]

The Times Publishing Company took on debt and bought back *Times* stock from Bass for $56 million, taking on debt to do so.[95] The publishing company finally paid off the debt at the end of 1999.[96]

But by the start of the new century, the economy and decline in advertising hurt the non-profit *Times*. It froze wages and shrunk its pages and its staff, mostly through attrition and early retirement packages.[97] In 2009 it sold the *Congressional Quarterly*[98] and announced it would sell *Governing* magazine.[99] Yet, throughout the economic downturn, the newspaper published strong journalism. That dedication to quality journalism comes not from how the ownership is set up but from the people who decide the news policy.

Two other family-owned newspapers planned to turn themselves over to a not-for-profit foundation to preserve local ownership: In 2002 H. Brandt Ayers and his sister, Elise Ayers Sanguinetti, announced they would, over time, transfer ownership of their daily, *The Anniston Star*, to a trust that would operate the paper and help pay to run a graduate program in community journalism with the University of Alabama. Students would learn journalism at the *Star* itself, and the paper's editor would teach at the university. The Knight Foundation would contribute $1.5 million to the venture. Ayers said he would pass up the $50 million or so he could earn by selling his shares to do so.[100] Turning over his holdings in the publishing company, he said, would instead preserve its tradition of investing in serious journalism, which included fighting for desegregation and exposing pollution and government corruption.[101]

Perhaps the oldest successful newspaper operated by a non-profit entity in the country operates in Connecticut: In 1939, Theodore Bodenwein left his newspaper, *The Day*, of New London, to The Day Trust. Bodenwein had worried that when he died, the paper, which had been a Republican Party organ in the nineteenth century, would be bought by a chain or ignored by his heirs. Today, the trust oversees the newspaper and the Bodenwein Public Benevolent Foundation. The money the newspaper earns goes to the foundation, which every Christmas season gives some of it away as grants to charities, civic groups and local governments. The newspaper beat back a lawsuit by the son of the owner and the Internal Revenue Service, languished for about twenty years, but then modernized in the 1960s. Between 1971 and 2003, the trust reported it had donated more than $6.5 million to local groups.[102]

Editor-Owned Small Newspapers

Since the early days of the country, editors have owned their own newspapers. For many journalists, owning their own paper remains their dream. Because journalists typically do not make much money, if they achieve the dream, their papers would consequently be small.

After working for more than thirty years as a reporter and editor at newspapers in the Northeast, Jim Kevlin learned that "weekly newspapers were the only growing niche" in newspaper journalism.[103] So he and his wife, M.J., bought the *Freeman's Journal*, a 200-year-old weekly in Cooperstown, N.Y., on May 30, 2006. "Jagged lightning flashed, thunder rolled…Was someone trying to tell us something?" he later wrote of the day he took over the paper.[104]

In its first two years, however, disaster did not strike. Kevlin's four full-time and four half-time reporters focused on intensely local stories, including the silly, such as a citizen who was asking $3,000 for a freeze-dried grapefruit signed by baseball outfielder Sammy Sosa, and the serious, such as the community's resistance to the construction of seventy-five windmills in the area. Kevlin figured that mid-sized daily papers were trying to charge $15 to $20 an inch for advertising, which was probably far too expensive for many of the local, small businesses to afford. So he planned to charge between $7 and $9 an inch. He installed new computers and cameras, he and his staff delivered some papers themselves and he kept the staff small.

Kevlin also got a chance to practice journalism idealistically as well and wrote about freeing himself from the "corrosive union that's developed between journalism and marketing." He recalled that at his first job as a reporter in 1973, he wrote a story about an oil distributor whose storage tank was polluting a local river. The distributor was a major advertiser, however, and the paper refused to publish the piece. More than thirty years later, when an advertiser for his *Freeman's Journal* wanted to influence news stories, Kevlin told him no. The decision cost the little paper $2,000, he figured, but even though he then knew how much freedom cost, he concluded, "It's been worth every nickel." Circulation grew from 1,800 to 2,500, the paper turned a profit and Kevlin figured that it would take only five years to pay off the note he had taken out to buy the paper.[105]

Does Ownership Matter?

According to newspaper economic research published in 2008, publicly traded corporations owned about 40 percent of all newspapers. Employee ownership and foundation ownership accounted for less than 1 percent of dailies. The rest were privately owned by individuals, families, partnerships or private corporations.[106] No one form of ownership has proven itself best for journalism. The dedication and perseverance of the people who direct newspapers' businesses remain critical. These owners also need imagination, and probably luck, to continue in the newspaper business.

Ownership does matter. Newspapers are businesses, and their proprietors need to keep an eye on the bottom line. But newspapers also provide a service to their readers. Some newspaper owners have focused too much on one aspect or the other, and a bad economy has impeded the goals of even the noblest owner. Nonetheless, owners with dedication, resolve and character have kept newspapers afloat throughout this country's history and will continue to do so.

While the largest daily newspapers and many public newspaper chains suffered huge losses, an important fact to remember is that, on the whole, newspapers remained profitable in 2008. The big losses of large chains obscured some smaller success stories, and the bottom line of companies that owned even profitable newspapers suffered after some owners took on huge debts. John Morton, a former newspaper reporter and consultant who analyzes newspapers and other media properties, noted that small newspapers, which presumably enjoyed closer ties with their communities and less competition for advertising dollars, appeared to be performing better than larger ones. "Overall, the beleaguered newspaper industry's financial health has been weakened but remains healthy by most measures," he concluded.[107]

We believe newspapers will endure, most likely under many different types of ownership and in many different types of formats. Since the recession at the end of the decade caused as much as half of the advertising declines,[108] some newspapers will likely rebound with the economy. Nevertheless, the huge profit margins newspaper owners once enjoyed were lost with their monopolies. But newspapers can still make money, which means that journalists can still earn a living doing the work that they love. Philip Meyer put it this way:

> Imagine an economic environment in which newspapers earn the normal retail margin of 6 or 7 percent of revenues. As long as there are entrepreneurs willing to produce a socially useful product at that margin—and trust me, there will be—society will be served as well as it is now.[109]

Notes

1. Philip Meyer, *The Vanishing Newspaper* (Columbia, Mo.: University of Missouri Press, 2004), 37–38.
2. Mary A. Anderson, "Ranks of Independent Newspapers Continue to Fade," *Presstime* (August 1987), 16–23.

3. Suzanne M. Kirchhoff, "The U.S. Newspaper Industry in Transition," Congressional Research Service, posted on July 8, 2009, available at http://www.fas.org/sgp/crs/misc/R40700.pdf (accessed July 31, 2009).

4. Philip Meyer, "The Wrong Way to Make Money," in Charles M. Madigan, ed., *The Collapse of the Great American Newspaper* (Chicago, Ill.: Ivan R. Dee, 2007), 73.

5. Project for Excellence in Journalism and Rick Edmonds, "Newspapers: Economics," *State of the News Media 2009*, available at http://www.stateofthe-media.org/2009/narrative_newspapers_economics.php?media=4&cat=3 (accessed July 10, 2009).

6. Ibid.

7. Ibid., 357.

8. Stephen L. Vaughn, *Encyclopedia of American Journalism* (New York: Taylor & Francis Group, LLC, 2008), 356. Accessed as ebook at http://books.google.com/books?id=W08IY50MpX4C&lpg=PA357&ots=NK8Q_N9XA5&dq=own-ership%20independent%20newspapers%20%22independent%20newspa-pers%22&pg=PA356 (accessed July 24, 2009).

9. Ibid., 357.

10. Ibid., 354.

11. Meyer, *supra* note 4, at 74.

12. Ibid., 74.

13. Robert G. Picard, "Institutional Ownership of Publicly Traded U.S. Newspaper Companies," *Journal of Media Economics* (1994, Volume 7), 49–65.

14. Jack Bass, "Newspaper Monopoly," *American Journalism Review* (July/August 1999), 64–78.

15. Ibid.

16. "Tribune, Times Mirror deal," CNN, posted on March 13, 2000, available at http://money.cnn.com/2000/03/13/deals/tribune/ (accessed August 1, 2009).

17. John Morton, "Who Will Be Next?," *American Journalism Review* (April 2000), 72.

18. Greg Bensinger, "Newspaper Ads Drop 30% in 1st Quarter," *Bloomberg News*, posted on June 2, 2009, available at http://www.detnews.com/article/20090602/BIZ/906020346 (accessed June 15, 2009).

19. "Advertising Expenditures," Newspaper Association of America, available at http://www.naa.org/TrendsandNumbers/Advertising-Expenditures.aspx (accessed July 24, 2009).

20. Project for Excellence in Journalism and Rick Edmonds, "Newspapers: Introduction," *State of the News Media 2009*, available at http://www.stateofthe-media.org/2009/narrative_newspapers_intro.php?media=4 (accessed July 10, 2009).

21. Meyer, *supra* note 1, at 6.

22. Ibid., 12.

23. Robert G. Picard and Aldo van Weezel, "Capital and Control: Consequences of Different Forms of Newspaper Ownership," *The International Journal on Media Management* (2008, Volume 10:1), 22–31.

24. Ibid.

25. Meyer, *supra* note 1, at 1–2.

26. Davis Merritt, *Knightfall: Knight Ridder and How the Erosion of Newspaper Journalism Is Putting Democracy at Risk* (New York: AMACOM, March 2005), 57–58.

27. Charles Layton, "White Knights," *American Journalism Review* (April/May 2006), 38–45.

28. Ibid.

29. Meyer, *supra* note 1, at 184–185.

30. Robert D. McFadden, "Alvah H. Chapman Jr., Civic-Minded Leader of Knight Ridder, Dies at 87," available at http://www.nytimes.com/2008/12/28/business/media/28chapman.html?_r=1&pagewanted=1 (accessed July 23, 2009).

31. "A Brief Company History, Gannett Co. Inc.," posted on May 2009, available at http://www.gannett.com/about/history.htm (accessed July 14, 2009).

32. Ibid.

33. Anderson, *supra* note 2.

34. "A Brief Company History," *supra* note 31.

35. Lauren Janis, "A $1 Billion Gamble, A New Newspaper," *Columbia Journalism Review* (November/December 2001), 93.

36. "A Brief Company History," *supra* note 31.

37. "Who We Are," Freedom Forum, posted on November 26, 2007, available at http://www.freedomforum.org/templates/document.asp?documentID=4020 (accessed July 25, 2009).

38. Meyer, *supra* note 1, at 184.

39. Meyer, *supra* note 4, at 76–77.

40. Ibid., 78.

41. Project for Excellence in Journalism and Rick Edmonds, "Newspapers: Ownership," *State of the News Media 2007*, available at http://www.stateofthemedia.org/2007/narrative_newspapers_ownership.asp?cat=4&media=3 (accessed July 23, 2009).

42. Ibid.

43. Ibid.

44. Associated Press, "Belo Corp. to Split Newspapers off from Its TV Business," *New York Times*, published on October 2, 2007, available at www.nytimes.com/2007/10/02/business/media/02belo.html (accessed July 11, 2009).

45. "Scripps Reports Second Quarter Results," E.W. Scripps Co. posted on July 24, 2008 available at http://pressreleases.scripps.com/release/1058 (accessed July 13, 2009).

46. "Belo to Create Separate Television and Newspaper Businesses," posted on October 1, 2007, available at http://finance.paidcontent.org/paidcontent?GUID=3343748&Page=MediaViewer&Ticker=BLC (accessed August 1, 2009).

47. Project for Excellence in Journalism and Rick Edmonds, "Newspapers: Ownership," *State of the News Media 2009*, available at http://www.stateofthemedia.org/2009/narrative_newspapers_ownership.php?media=4&cat=5 (accessed July 23, 2009).

48. Ibid.

49. Rick Edmonds, Media Business Analyst, The Poynter Institute, interview by Mary Carmen Cupito, July 27, 2009.

50. Mark Fitzgerald and Jennifer Saba, "Going Local," *Editor & Publisher* (November 2006, Volume 139), 36–43.

51. Jon Fine, "The New Sport of Billionaires," *BusinessWeek*, December 25, 2006, 26.

52. Project for Excellence in Journalism and Rick Edmonds, "Newspapers: Ownership," *State of the News Media 2007*, available at http://www.stateofthemedia.org/2007/narrative_newspapers_ownership.asp?cat=4&media=3 (accessed July 30, 2009).

53. Sharon Waxman, "U.S. Seeks Rehiring of Reporters Fired in Newspaper Labor Fight," published on March 19, 2007, available at http://www.nytimes.com/

2007/03/19/business/media/19barbara.html?_r=1&ref=business&oref=slogin (accessed July 23, 2009).

54. Ryan Chittum, "The Grave Dancer: Sam Zell and *The Tribune*'s Fate," *Columbia Journalism Review* (March/April 2008), 34–35; Project for Excellence in Journalism and Rick Edmonds, "Newspapers: Introduction," *State of the News Media 2009*, available at http://www.stateofthemedia.org/2009/narrative_news-papers_intro.php?media=4 (accessed July 23, 2009)

55. Project for Excellence in Journalism and Rick Edmonds, "Newspapers: Ownership," *State of the News Media 2009*, available at http://www.stateofthe-media.org/2009/narrative_newspapers_ownership.php?media=4&cat=5 (accessed July 23, 2009).

56. Ibid.

57. Chittum, *supra* note 54.

58. Phil Rosenthal and Michael Oneal, "Tribune Co. Files for Bankruptcy Protection" *Chicago Tribune*, posted on December 9, 2008, available at http://archives.chicagotribune.com/2008/dec/09/business/chi-081208tribune-bankruptcy (accessed July 23, 2009).

59. Floyd Norris, "Zell Gets Veto Power at *Tribune*," *New York Times*, published on April 6, 2007, available at http://www.nytimes.com/2007/04/06/business/media/06tribune.html (accessed July 23, 2009).

60. "All the News That's Free to Print," Economist.com, posted on July 21, 2009, available at http://www.economist.com/businessfinance/displaystory.cfm?story_id=14072274 (accessed July 23, 2009).

61. Randall Chase, "Newspaper Union to See Tribune Bonus Information," Associated Press, posted on August 12, 2009, available at http://abcnews.go.com/Business/wireStory?id=8302249 (accessed August 12, 2009).

62. "Local Owners, Longterm View," Philly.com, posted on May 31, 2009, available at http://www.philly.com/inquirer/world_us/46460352.html (accessed July 13, 2009).

63. Julia M. Klein, "Brian Tierney's Grand Experiment: Fitting Philly Pigs for Wigs," *Columbia Journalism Review* (July/August 2007), 28–32.

64. Mark Fitzgerald, "Philly Newspapers' Parent Company Follows It into Bankruptcy Court," posted on June 15, 2009, available at http://www.editorandpublisher.com/eandp/search/article_display.jsp?vnu_content_id=1003984383 (accessed July 10, 2009).

65. Fitzgerald and Saba, *supra* note 50.

66. Klein, *supra* note 63.

67. Jon Fine, *supra* note 51.

68. Klein, *supra* note 63.

69. "Local Owners, Longterm View," *supra* note 62.

70. Daily News Staff Report, "Creditors Seek 'Oversight' of Philadelphia Newspapers, LLC," Philly.com, posted on April 11, 2009, available at http://www.philly.com/philly/hp/news_update/42840812.html (accessed July 13, 2009).

71. "Columbia University Announces 93rd Pulitzer Prizes in Journalism, Letters, Drama and Music," posted on April 20, 2009, available at http://www.pulitzer.org/files/PressRelease2009PulitzerPrizes.pdf (accessed July 14, 2009).

72. Dan Hardy, "Charter School Appeals to Block Release of Records," posted on June 11, 2009, available at http://www.openrecordspa.org/news_files/9f7b8d79b9233df670ae22345a256cd8–199.html (accessed July 24, 2009).

73. "Local Owners, Longterm View," *supra* note 62.

74. Ibid.

75. John C. Busterna and Robert G. Picard, *Joint Operating Agreements: The Newspaper Preservation Act and Its Application* (Norwood, N.J.: Ablex Publishing, 1993), 4.

76. Ibid.

77. "About the *New Haven Independent*," *New Haven Independent*, available at http://www.newhavenindependent.org/about_us.php (accessed July 13, 2009).

78. "Virtual Declaration of *Independent*," *Business New Haven* posted on June 12, 2006, available at http://www.conntact.com/article_page.lasso?id=40023 (accessed July 13, 2009).

79. Paul Bass, "Liberation! Guest Writer Paul Bass on Creating the *New Haven Independent*," PressThink, posted on August 8, 2006, available at http://journalism.nyu.edu/pubzone/weblogs/pressthink/2006/08/08/pl_bass.html (accessed July 13, 2009).

80. "Virtual Declaration of *Independent*," *supra* note 78.

81. John Burke, "The *New Haven Independent*: Community-dedicated, Hyperlocal, Online Reporting," The Editors Weblog, posted on November 20, 2006, available at http://www.editorsweblog.org/analysis/2006/11/the_new_haven_independent_communitydedic.php (accessed July 13, 2009).

82. Bass, *supra* note 79.

83. Burke, *supra* note 81.

84. Bass, *supra* note 79.

85. Rob Gurwitt, "Death and Life in the Pressroom," *Governing*, posted on January 2009, available at http://www.governing.com/article/death-and-life-pressroom (accessed July 13, 2009).

86. Ibid.

87. Doug Hardy, "Next for news? Introducing the *Valley Independent Sentinel*," CT Newsjunki.com, posted on June 19, 2009, available at http://www.ctnewsjunkie.com/general_news/next_for_news_introducing_the.php (accessed August 11, 2009).

88. Rick Green, "Naugatuck Valley Going Online to Get Its News," Courant.com, posted on April 28, 2009, available at http://www.courant.com/news/local/columnists/hc-valley-independent-sentinelapr28-column,0,3556445.column (accessed July 13, 2009).

89. Ibid.

90. Steve Coll, "Nonprofit Newspapers," *The New Yorker* posted on January 28, 2009, available at http://www.newyorker.com/online/blogs/stevecoll/2009/01/nonprofit-newsp.html (accessed July 13, 2009).

91. Louis Hau, "Why Newspapers Pray to St. Petersburg," Forbes.com, posted on December 4, 2006, available at http://www.forbes.com/2006/12/01/newspapers-poynter-st-petersberg-tech-media_cx_lh_1204stpete.html (accessed July 9, 2009).

92. Ibid.

93. Stephen Nohlgren, "*St. Petersburg Times'* PolitiFact, Lane DeGregory Win 2009 Pulitzer Prizes," posted on April 21, 2009, available at http://www.tampabay.com/features/media/article993724.ece (accessed August 4, 2009).

94. Andrew Barnes, "Who Owns the *St. Petersburg Times*? Why It Matters to Readers," Poynter Online, posted on January 11, 2000, available at http://www.poynter.org/dg.lts/id.4100/content.content_view.htm (accessed July 9, 2009).

95. Hau, *supra* note 91.

96. Barnes, *supra* note 94.

97. *"Times* will Reduce Staff, Freeze Pay," Tampabay.com, posted on May 28, 2008, available at http://www.tampabay.com/news/business/article528577.ece (accessed August 4, 2009); *"St. Pete Times* Employees Told No Layoffs Coming after Strong Response to Early Retirement Offer," Tampabay.com, posted on August 18, 2008, available at http://blogs.tampabay.com/media/2008/08/st-pete-times-s.html (accessed July 12, 2009).

98. Richard Perez-Pena, "In Washington, Roll Call is Buying *Congressional Quarterly,*" *The New York Times*, published on July 21, 2009, available at http://www.nytimes.com/2009/07/22/business/media/22mag.html (accessed July 16, 2009).

99. "Times Publishing to Sell *Governing* Magazine," *Tampa Bay Business Journal*, posted on July 29, 2009, available at http://www.bizjournals.com/tampabay/stories/2009/07/27/daily51.html (accessed August 11, 2009).

100. Felicity Barringer, "Alabama Paper Plans to Go Nonprofit," *The New York Times*, posted on December 16, 2002, available at http://www.nytimes.com/2002/12/16/us/alabama-paper-plans-to-go-nonprofit.html (accessed July 30, 2009).

101. David Folkenflik, "Small Paper Uses Profits to Train New Reporters," NPR.org, posted on May 2, 2006, available at http://www.npr.org/templates/story/story.php?storyId=5373738 (accessed July 14, 2009).

102. Gregory N. Stone, "About Us," theday.com, posted on January 20, 2003, available at http://www.theday.com/theday/aboutus.aspx (accessed July 14, 2009).

103. Jim Kevlin, "Liberation Journalism," *American Journalism Review* (April/May 2008), 40–45.

104. Ibid.

105. Ibid.

106. Picard and van Weezel, *supra* note 23.

107. John Morton, "It Could Be Worse," *American Journalism Review* (December 2008/January 2009), 52.

108. Project for Excellence in Journalism and Rick Edmonds, *supra* note 5.

109. Meyer, *supra* note 4, at 78.

8

Newspaper Ethics

Members of the Society of Professional Journalists believe that public enlightenment is the forerunner of justice and the foundation of democracy. The duty of the journalist is to further those ends by seeking truth and providing a fair and comprehensive account of events and issues. Conscientious journalists from all media and specialties strive to serve the public with thoroughness and honesty. Professional integrity is the cornerstone of a journalist's credibility. Members of the Society share a dedication to ethical behavior and adopt this code to declare the Society's principles and standards of practice.[1]

–Preamble, Code of Ethics of the Society of Professional Journalists

The First Amendment to the Constitution is not the only guide for reporters and editors practicing journalism. As explained above, journalists are engaged in *public enlightenment*, informing the public, which is the *foundation of democracy* and *the forerunner of justice*. This is not just another way to earn a living; journalism is public service that is indispensable to freedom and the ability of the people to govern themselves.

For all of journalism's many failings—and "many" really signifies far too numerous to list—the work of those who report on the activities of government, the conditions of society and the debates on civic issues is elevated to service because the democratic form of government of the United States could not continue without it. The unparalleled service and sacrifice of the men and women of the various branches of the U.S. military are essential to the maintenance of freedom. But the service of men and women who report on public affairs is also essential to the maintenance of a government that serves the people rather than enslaves them.

If journalists are going to fulfill the mission the code spells out—*seek truth and provide a fair and comprehensive account of events and issues*—their work must be trusted by those who depend on the information provided. *Professional integrity is the cornerstone of a journalist's credibility.* That is the reason that acts bankrupt of professional integrity are so egregious; they undermine journalism's mission, which undermines the ability of citizens to participate in their self-government, which undermines the very cornerstone of this country. Neither making up news nor deliberately distorting information is a minor misstep because both are an assault upon the foundations of freedom.

The Credibility Gap Becomes a Canyon

Journalism, including newspapers, finds itself at a crossroads, in large part because the public has lost faith in journalists. "A canyon of disbelief and distrust has developed between the public and the news media," media lawyer Bruce Sanford wrote a decade ago. The canyon "has widened at an accelerating rate during the last decade. Its darkness frightens the media. It threatens not just the communication industry's enviable financial power but its special role in ordering American journalism."[2]

Sanford's gloomy statement is not based on perception alone. More than 1,000 studies of public opinion about the media conducted in the twenty years before 2006 found "ample evidence to suggest that Americans at large no longer trust, if they ever did, the American media."[3] The Gallup survey in 2007 found 9 percent of Americans said they had a great deal of trust and confidence in the mass media to report the news "fully, accurately and fairly," and 38 percent more said they had a "fair amount" of trust. In 1976, 72 percent of Americans said they had a great deal or fair amount of trust in the news media.[4]

Journalists have not turned a deaf ear to the public outcry against them. The American Society of Newspaper Editors conducted a major study as part of its million-dollar Journalism Credibility Project.[5] The survey found the public believed (1) journalists make too many factual errors and spelling or grammar mistakes; (2) fail to respect and understand their communities; (3) the bias of journalists affects what they cover and how they cover it, and that advertisers and powerful people manipulate the press; (4) newspapers spend too much time and devote too much of the news hole to covering sensational stories, and (5) the media are too quick to invade the privacy of individuals.[6]

A survey in 2000 found 48 percent would require journalists to disclose their political leanings while 45 percent would not; 48 percent said the press makes conditions in this country seem worse while 45 percent said better; 42 said media outlets should be licensed like hospitals while 36 percent said they should not; and 41 percent said journalists should be licensed like doctors, while 50 percent said they should not.[7]

More than one journalism ethicist has said that journalism has never been more ethical. "Paradoxically, the media are accused of every sin at a time when they have never been better."[8] So why this conjunction of two contradictory conditions: Journalists have never been more ethical, yet the public has never trusted them less?

The Role of the Audience

One answer lies with the public. A 2000 survey concluded the public has to share responsibility because of its confusion of news with non-news programming, such as "America's Most Wanted," on television. The survey also uncovered the public's hypocrisy; while decrying the lengths reporters will go to uncover a news story, the respondents acknowledge they drink in that kind of news. "What Americans said they want in news and how they will actually behave are entirely different," the pollster concluded.[9]

The Role of Technology

Another answer lies with rapidly changing technology. For several hundred years, newspapers had the mass communication field pretty much to themselves. They competed against each other to report news first. But the twentieth century brought competition from radio, then television, then cable television and finally the Internet. News consumers now had access to the news of the day from multiple sources. The audience suddenly could easily compare media reports and find fault with those that omitted facts or provided incorrect information.

And the pressure to be first with the news too often outreached the need to be accurate. That pressure to be first also led many media outlets to report that another outlet was reporting information without first verifying its accuracy.

The classic example of this development was the story of President Bill Clinton and his involvement with White House intern Monica Lewinsky that led to his impeachment by the House of Representatives in 1998. *Newsweek* reporter Michael Isikoff had written the story, but his editor decided to delay publication a week so that Isikoff could work to confirm more of the information. Hours after that decision, Matt Drudge posted on his website, The Drudge Report, that the magazine had killed a story involving the president:

> **"NEWSWEEK KILLS STORY ON WHITE HOUSE INTERN: BLOCKBUSTER REPORT: 23-YEAR OLD, FORMER WHITE HOUSE INTERN, SEX RELATIONSHIP WITH PRESIDENT."**[10]
>
> At the last minute, at 6 P.M. on Saturday evening, NEWSWEEK magazine killed a story that was destined to shake official Washington to its foundation: A White House intern carried on a sexual affair with the President of the United States! The DRUDGE REPORT has learned that reporter Michael Isikoff developed the story of his career, only to have it spiked by top NEWSWEEK suits hours before publication. A young woman, 23, sexually involved with the love of her life, the President of the United States, since she was a 21-year-old intern at the White House. She was a frequent visitor to a small study just off the Oval Office where she claims to have indulged the president's sexual preference. Reports of the relationship spread in White House quarters and she was moved to a job at the Pentagon, where she worked until last month.

And so, without ever conducting any of the reporting needed to confirm the facts of this blockbuster story, Drudge, based on a source at *Newsweek*, took the outline of Isikoff's story public late Saturday, and it spread from outlet to outlet. On Sunday, it was discussed briefly on *This Week*, the ABC News program, during the weekly roundtable. On Monday, that discussion was mentioned in a *Washington Post* story. It was discussed that evening on a cable program. Reporters, tracking the scent from the Drudge Report, nailed down most of the story, and American Broadcasting Company (ABC) News, *The Washington Post* and *The Los Angeles Times* all broke their versions of the story on Wednesday. Isikoff appeared on National Broadcasting Company (NBC) news programs that day and *Newsweek*, trying to recover its lost story and damaged prestige, posted on its website the story it had withheld from publication.[11]

The ethical repercussions were severe; a carefully reported story was scooped by someone who did no reporting. The lesson to newspaper journalists was clear: The Internet was the Wild West of journalism, and the old rules did not apply. Shoot fast or be shot. "Drudge peddled unconfirmed information—what might be called gossip; Isikoff tried, as a responsible reporter, to publish news," wrote veteran journalist and commentator Marvin Kalb. "Over a period of many months, Isikoff had carefully cultivated his sources, combed through hundreds of pages of election rules and regulations, refused to cross ethical lines and listen to incriminating tape recordings and pursued this story when there were few leads and little encouragement. Isikoff prided himself on being a product of the old school of journalism (however in the current environment that needs to be defined), but he had been scooped by the new school and quickly learned that he had to adapt in order to survive."[12]

The Role of Public Attention

One other factor explains why the media have never been more loathed while at the same time they have never been more reliable. The controversies and sins of journalism are easily visible to anyone who is interested in looking for them even for a moment.

One such factor is known as "The Romenesko Effect."[13] Jim Romenesko, a senior online reporter at the Poynter Institute, has brought media controversies to public attention almost instantly since 1999.[14] His online column, subtitled "Your daily fix of media industry news, commentary, and memos," serves as "an ad hoc, post-publication, peer review mechanism for the journalistic profession. It also contributes to journalistic transparency. No newsroom memo or in-house letter of any consequence circulates inside a newspaper for very long before being posted on 'Romenesko Memos' or 'Romenesko Misc.'"[15] Distributed daily via the Internet, news of the latest plagiarism accusation or ethical omission zips from coast to coast at the speed of light. "What's new," according to one commentator, "is the way the Romenesko megaphone distributes the news of these offenses, allowing journalists to box their peers' ears while the subject is still green in memory."[16]

Other online sites also serve as clearinghouses for journalism news and journalism's sins. They include The Daily Briefing by the Project for Excellence in Journalism,[17] Mediabistro.com[18] with its "Morning Newsfeed" and blogs, I Want Media[19] with its emphasis on the business of news, and CJRDaily,[20] a site born from *Columbia Journalism Review*.[21] Other groups, both conservative and liberal, provide online news criticism. Some of the larger newspapers often employ an ombudsman, a staff member assigned to listen to and evaluate reader complaints.

But bloggers who now have access to the public through the Internet also play a major role in holding the media accountable. The best-known example involved bloggers challenging the veracity of the "60 Minutes" report on documents that Dan Rather said raised questions about the military service of George W. Bush. A blogger using the screen name of "Buckhead" wrote on the conservative blog Free Republic that the memos Rather reported on seemed to have been prepared on office equipment that did not exist in 1972, the year the memos were purportedly written. The "60 Minutes" story quickly unraveled, and Rather, the CBS News anchor, later apologized for the use of the bogus memos. CBS President Andrew Heyward appointed a committee to investigate the story.[22] Soon, Rather announced he would be stepping down from the anchor's desk after the 2004 presidential election, a position he had held for twenty-four years.[23] When the committee returned its 224-page report, CBS fired three executives and a producer.[24]

Bill Powers, media critic at *National Journal*, talked about the impact of bloggers on journalism ethics in a 2006 interview:

> Suddenly there are about 10 million more media critics than there were ten years ago. I actually think there are a lot of bloggers who are so good at it that I sort of wish they would be picked up by mainstream media outlets and do both.[25]

The confusion of news versus infotainment, the increased pressure to be first even if it means not being accurate, the nearly instantaneous widespread publicity afforded media mistakes in a communication world saturated with around-the-clock news from many sources, and the opportunity for anyone with a keyboard and a modem to become a media critic have combined to lower the public's trust of the news media even though journalists may never have been more trustworthy.

Codes of Ethics

The era when journalists were not as ethical produced cries of outrage over the practices of those engaged in reporting and publishing a newspaper. Those corrupt practices led to development of codes of ethics and heightened attention to how journalists practice their profession.

The state press association of Kansas developed in 1910 the first American code, a code that applied to both editors and publishers. By 1924, more than half a dozen daily newspapers had created their own codes of ethics.[26] The American Society of Newspaper Editors adopted the Canons of Journalism in 1923 at its first meeting, just after embarrassing revelations about the role of some journalists in the Teapot Dome Scandal under the administration of President Warren G. Harding. American Society of Newspaper Editors (ASNE) three years later censured and temporarily suspended from its membership the editor of the *Denver Post*.[27] Frederick Bonfils, a scam artist who used dubious methods to grow his newspaper, had accepted a bribe to sit on the evidence he had of the administration's involvement, and *The Post* never published another story about it.[28]

The Society of Professional Journalists, then known as Sigma Delta Chi, adopted the ASNE code in 1926. The concern over ethics in journalism also resulted in the publication of four books on journalism ethics and four articles published in *Journalism Quarterly* in that decade. But from the 1930s to the 1970s, journalism ethics received little attention. Since the 1970s, one reviewer said that journalism has been occupied "with its own ethics movement." The number of media ethics courses has tripled.[29] The SPJ code underwent a major revision in 1973 and again in 1996.

Many believe the renewed interest in ethics during the 1970s resulted from the Watergate break-in, which culminated in the resignation of President Nixon. Journalism played a central role in the unraveling of the scandal, although Congress and the courts were instrumental as well.[30]

Two kinds of ethics codes exist today. Several professional organizations have developed codes, which are advisory, suggesting the standards necessary to provide a credible report of the news. Neither the Society of Professional Journalists nor the American Society of Newspaper Editors is likely to revoke a membership as a result of a violation of the organization's code of ethics. These codes lack the muscle and the will to truly hold an ethical violator accountable.[31] The Society of Professional Journalists has discussed whether it should hold members accountable. "The majority has felt that establishing a quasi-judicial system, such as those found in some other professions, would inevitably lead to actions by governments, courts or their proxies that would restrict the rights to free speech and free press guaranteed by the First Amendment to the U.S. Constitution."[32] SPJ has decided "the best enforcement is in publicizing, explaining and applying those principles and weighing alternatives, as individuals, as journalists and as an organization, in the form of comment and opinion, without issuing definitive, quasi-legal judgments that might be put to improper use."[33]

But many newspaper publishers also have ethical statements, and most of them require employees to sign a statement that they have read the code and pledge to follow it. Media owners can be aggressive in enforcing their own ethical and professional codes. For example, running for political office will almost certainly mean that a journalist loses his or her reporting or editing job. Dating a news source such as the mayor can cost you your primary assignment. Plagiarism can get you suspended or fired.[34]

How Effective Are Codes of Ethics?

Statements like the ethics code of the Society of Professional Journalists give journalists and journalism students a guide for the ethical issues they encounter and will encounter along the course of their career. However, no code can anticipate every nuance or provide guidance for every issue. Ethical issues are not always clear-cut; what would be unthinkable at some large newspapers may not even be questioned at smaller newspapers where everyone in town knows the editor. Ethical issues are not always the choice between something that is right versus something that is wrong; often journalists face issues that have conflicting values that force the journalist to choose between following one ethical guideline at the expense of another.

Despite the widespread presence and reliance upon codes of ethics, ethical violations continue. Critics argue they are too formal, they are too general, and they don't deal with all the important dilemmas journalists encounter. Through the decades, codes have been criticized as providing legal ammunition for libel plaintiffs.[35] The bottom line is that codes of ethics don't ensure good journalism, as some of the most egregious violations have occurred in the past decade, long after adoption of codes became widespread.

But those who defend the use of codes of ethics reply that codes articulate to the public what journalists and newsrooms stand for; they make journalists aware of the ethical dilemmas they may face and provide principles to address them; codes encourage consistency in how dilemmas are faced; they increase public and professional accountability and ultimately a code allows the public to hold journalists accountable.

The rest of this chapter will describe the SPJ Code of Ethics and cite some of the ethical violations that have occurred over the years as a way of providing a roadmap for future practice.

The SPJ code is divided into four principles:

Seek Truth and Report It

This is by far the longest section of the code, filling almost half of the one-page version. These are among the elements:

Journalists should test the accuracy of information from all sources.

Unfortunately, journalists do not always test information or seek it from all sources. No worse example of this exists than a story that broke in March 2006.

Duke University lacrosse players, required to remain on campus for practice, held a team party while their fellow students were away on spring break. Unbeknownst to some of the attendees, the team captains hired two strippers for entertainment at a party that otherwise was described as "sedate." All but one of the lacrosse team players were white; the strippers were black.[36]

One of the strippers later told police that she had been raped by two, three, five or twenty white men in the bathroom of the house.[37] Despite the dearth of credible evidence—DNA test results implicated none of the lacrosse players, the woman who said she had been raped had told conflicting stories, and a substantiated alibi that should have cleared one of the three suspects—the prosecutor persuaded a grand jury to indict three of the players on rape charges. Ultimately the charges were dropped and the three declared innocent by the state's attorney general; the prosecutor resigned and was disbarred.

But the lives of three young men were disrupted and scarred; other members of the team were vilified and painted as drunken sons of privilege;

the Duke lacrosse coach—who over sixteen years had built a championship program—was fired, and the team's season was canceled. The families of the three players spent untold thousands to defend their sons.

The media's role in this episode is one of the most shameful in the history of American journalism. Kelly McBride, who writes about media ethics for the Poynter Institute, described what happened as the media learned about the story: "Commentators and pundits on television, in print, on the radio and, of course, on the Internet then magnified an already distorted reality by shouting over each other. In their attempt to shed light, they lit a fire of public scorn."[38]

Several cable television personalities particularly disgraced themselves by their stampede to judgment and by their incendiary comments. (CNN's Nancy Grace: "I'm so glad they didn't miss a lacrosse game over a little thing like gang rape!")[39]

But newspapers did not distinguish themselves either, and they come in for criticism in some of the six books that have been written on this terrible episode.[40] The *Herald-Sun*, the newspaper in Durham, was one of them. "The *Herald-Sun*'s coverage was dependably biased," according to one of the books that reviewed the case. The newspaper is faulted for quoting one lawyer who supported prosecutor Mike Nifong's handling of the accusations while ignoring a more-respected Duke law professor who was highly critical. Editor Bob Ashley, in a column four months later, endorsed a suggestion by a *Washington Post* columnist that a type of insanity infected the media covering the case.[41] The newspaper also had ignored complaints about police misconduct and the hostility toward students among members of the neighborhood where the party took place.

Ashley told *American Journalism Review* his reporters took prosecutor Nifong at his word. "We weren't prepared for what turned out to be the enormously nonexistent case of the district attorney. It was a veteran prosecutor. He'd been here for a while. We kept arguing we needed to wait and see." That is not the stance of a newspaper prepared to serve as the community's check on power run amok. And clearly, Nifong was more interested in his re-election effort than ensuring that justice was done.

Ashley said his paper "always noted there was a presumption of innocence in a case like this. Given the context and the context of what we knew at the time, we were fair. We were opinionated, but we were fair."

But the newspaper's editorial only a few days after the story broke doesn't sound fair. While it did at least pay lip service near the end to the presumption of innocence as a basis for American justice ("the crimes...if they occurred; suspects in our free society are granted the presumption of innocence"), the newspaper added a shrill voice to the clamor that was beginning in Durham, two days after a demonstration in front of the house where the party had been held. The rest of the editorial hardly seemed worded to give the lacrosse players any benefit of the doubt:

> There's no question the student-athletes were probably guilty of all the usual offenses—underage drinking, loud partying, obnoxious behavior. But the allegations of rape bring the students' arrogant frat-boy culture to a whole new, sickening level....[42]

Daniel Okrent, who by then had stepped down as public editor (ombudsman) of *The New York Times*, in a speech on April 13, 2006, less than three weeks after the story broke in the Charlotte *News & Observer*, said *The Times*, which published nearly two dozen stories in the first two weeks, had turned the story into a national event. "Had *The Times* not pounded the story so much in the first several weeks—if they had reported the charges, run the story on A11 and dropped it—it wouldn't have become a national event." He said *The Times'* treatment put the story on the cover of *Newsweek* magazine and at the beginning of the evening newscasts.[43]

Reporters looking for follow-up stories on the Duke campus, according to one person who was there, searched out people who were ready to convict the lacrosse players without benefit of a trial. "It's like these fringe lunatics who were around the campus around Durham, that's who the media went after," according to Debbie Savarino, a Duke fundraiser and daughter of Duke's most famous coach, basketball coach Mike Krzyzewski. "If you had an intelligent, knowledgeable, calm opinion of the whole situation, you were not to be interviewed," said Savarino, a close friend of the wife of the lacrosse coach, who was fired in the university administration's rush to minimize the public relations disaster that was sweeping across the university.

The post-mortems on many of the participants in the debacle—the justice system, the university administration, the faculty, the neighbors and journalists—do not treat anyone well. The players will be compensated for their life-shattering ordeal through the lawsuits that they filed. But everyone lost a great deal.

Journalists should avoid stereotyping by race, gender, age, religion, ethnicity, geography, sexual orientation, disability, physical appearance or social status.

Many of the journalists who covered the Duke lacrosse case violated another principle of the SPJ Code of Ethics. Okrent, the former public editor of *The New York Times*, summed it up in his comments to *American Journalism Review*: "It was too delicious a story. It conformed too well to too many preconceived notions of too many in the press: white over black, rich over poor, athletes over non-athletes, men over women, educated over non-educated. Wow. That's a package of sins that really fit the preconceptions of a lot of us."[44]

The *American Journalism Review* report found that the usual story line depicted "an elite, largely white university colliding with the working-class, racially mixed city that surrounds it. The privileged nature of Duke's students, particularly its athletes, was frequently invoked."[45]

In outlining the consequences the prosecutor experienced, the *AJR* report said, "the media deserve a public reckoning, too, a remonstrance for coverage that—albeit with admirable exceptions—all too eagerly embraced the inflammatory statements of a prosecutor in the midst of a tough election campaign. Fueled by Nifong, the media quickly latched onto a narrative too seductive to check: rich, wild, white jocks had brutalized a working class, black mother of two.[46]

Test the accuracy of information from all sources and exercise care to avoid inadvertent error.

> *A dozen miners trapped 12,000 feet into a mountainside since early Monday were found alive Tuesday night just hours after rescuers found the body of a 13th man, who died in an explosion in an adjacent coal mine that was sealed off in early December.*[47]

That's the lead on a *Washington Post* story from January 2004. The problem with the lead, and similar stories in newspapers around the country, is that it is terribly, terribly wrong. The optimism that produced this story or ones like it across the country was thoroughly misguided. All but one of the miners trapped in Slago, West Virginia, were gone.

How did the nation's newspapers make such a dreadful mistake? *Columbia Journalism Review* examined the stories and offered an answer:

> A close reading of the articles themselves tells the tale of how journalists bungled the story: In most, there are no sources at all for the information; in some, the sources are the rumors spread by frantic family members. Those sorts of sources are hardly a solid basis for headlines screaming, "They're Alive!"...But what is equally obvious is that reporters at the scene did not do enough to verify the truth of what they were being told by happy family members. They then produced articles...that almost unbelievably failed to offer any sources.[48]

Howard Kurtz, who covers the media for *The Washington Post*, took an even stronger stance. "The fault lies with the journalists for not instinctively understanding that early, fragmentary information in times of crisis is often wrong. You don't broadcast or publish until it's absolutely nailed down, or at least you hedge the report six ways to Sunday. This was, quite simply, a media debacle, born of news organizations' feverish need to breathlessly report each development 30 seconds ahead of their competitors."

CJR asked the questions many readers probably were asking. Is this the way reporters function in a high-pressure crisis? Do they always report information without sources or with bad sources?

Breaking news stories do test the professionalism and skill of reporters, especially as they are facing deadlines and competing to be first. A newspaper story is an account of the situation as the reporter was able to put it together in a limited time. The next edition will have more information, amplifying and even correcting previous reports. What makes the Internet so exciting for journalists is that a breaking news story can be updated almost minute by minute. But as the mine disaster that became a terrible journalistic blunder shows, being right is always more important than being first.

Journalists should never plagiarize.

If someone breaks into a house and removes a high definition television, the law defines it as burglary and the burglar can go to jail. But if a journalist lifts paragraphs from another reporter's story and fails to acknowledge the source, it is plagiarism, the theft of someone's work. Some who have plagiarized have lost their jobs, while others have not. The plagiarists are not always rookies or lazy practitioners.

For example, Maureen Dowd, a columnist for *The New York Times* who won the Pulitzer Prize for commentary in 1999, acknowledged in 2009 plagiarizing a statement in her column. She failed to attribute a statement that had originated on a political website.[49]

Jack Kelley, a reporter for *USA Today*, was investigated by his own newspaper after reporters became suspicious of his work. He resigned before the newspaper's investigation was completed after those involved in checking his work said he lied to them. The report was breathtaking:

> Investigation found "strong evidence that Kelley fabricated substantial portions of at least eight major stories, lifted nearly two dozen quotes or other material from competing publications, lied in speeches he gave for the newspaper and conspired to mislead those investigating his work....But an extensive examination of about 100 of the 720 stories uncovered evidence that found Kelley's journalistic sins were sweeping and substantial. The evidence strongly contradicted Kelley's published accounts that he spent a night with Egyptian terrorists in 1997; met a vigilante Jewish settler named Avi Shapiro in 2001; watched a Pakistani student unfold a picture of the Sears Tower and say, "This one is mine," in 2001; visited a suspected terrorist crossing-point on the Pakistan-Afghanistan border in 2002; interviewed the daughter of an Iraqi general in 2003; or went on a high-speed hunt for Osama bin Laden in 2003.[50]

The classic cases of plagiarism and its sister sin of fabrication involve two of the nation's most respected and influential newspapers, *The Washington Post* and *The New York Times*.

The story of Janet Cooke and her perversion of the truth is well documented and has been told and retold. Most journalism ethics books make her the poster child for cheating journalists. Cooke won the Pulitzer Prize for feature writing in 1981, but *The Post* returned the prize and fired Cooke when it learned the story was fabricated. It had been a shocking story:

> Jimmy is 8 years old and a third-generation heroin addict, a precocious little boy with sandy hair, velvety brown eyes and needle marks freckling the baby-smooth skin of his brown arms....Jimmy's is a world of hard drugs, fast money and the good life he believes both can bring. Every day, junkies casually buy heroin from Ron, his mother's live-in-lover, in the dining room of Jimmy's home. They "cook" it in the kitchen and "fire up" in the bedrooms. And every day, Ron or someone else fires up Jimmy, plunging a needle into his bony arm, sending the fourth grader into a hypnotic nod.[51]

Washingtonians were outraged by the story. The mayor ordered that the boy be found and rescued from this drug-dependent life. The District of Columbia police chief threatened to subpoena Cooke and her editors if they refused to reveal his identity. Winning the Pulitzer Prize was her undoing. The *Toledo Blade*, where Cooke had worked previously, was preparing to write a story about a local woman making good, but it found her Pulitzer biography did not match the newspaper's records. The Toledo editors believed she was a graduate of The University of Toledo, but the Pulitzer Committee believed she was an honor graduate of Vassar. Confronted with this contradiction and other questions about her reporting, Cooke admitted to her editor "Jimmy" didn't exist and was a composite of the accounts social workers had given her.[52]

The announcement sent tremors through the journalism world. A more recent headline-grabbing episode involved Jayson Blair, a twenty-seven-year-old reporter for *The New York Times*. In a four-page investigative report, the *Times* told its readers that it found fabrications, inaccuracies, plagiarism and other serious errors in at least thirty-six of the seventy-three articles he had written for the newspaper during a six-month period.

In the wake of his dismissal, the top editors of the *New York Times*—Executive Editor Howell Raines and Managing Editor Gerald Boyd—resigned in June 2003. Under their leadership fourteen months earlier, the *Times* had won a record seven Pulitzers, all but one for its coverage of the terrorist attacks on September 11, 2001.[53]

Plagiarism and fabrication are two of the most discussed topics by media critics. The Janet Cooke and Jayson Blair episodes are almost legends because they have been repeated so many times. But a report to the American Society of Newspaper Editors based on a 2005 survey of editors found plagiarism and fabrications are among the ethical issues least discussed in newsrooms.[54]

Still, editors saw the revelation of Jayson Blair's fraudulent behavior as a wake-up call. "Our credibility, what newspapers hold most dear, was under attack," Vicki Gowler, editor of the *St. Paul Pioneer Press* and chair of the ASNE ethics and values committee, wrote in a special report for the organization that focused on ethics.[55]

"We now cherish credibility and are doing wonderful things to protect it. This is a wonderful by-product." Ben Marrison, editor of the *Columbus Dispatch*, said in the 2003 report.[56]

Journalists should admit mistakes and correct them promptly.

A Los Angeles Times *article about a DVD anthology titled "Animated Soviet Propaganda" stated that famed Russian animator Boris Yefimov, who was interviewed by the anthology's producers, had died. Yefimov, who turned 106 in September, is alive.*[57]

Running a correction after prematurely killing someone off has to be one of the most embarrassing moments possible for a newspaper. Indeed, the great American novelist and journalist, Samuel Clemens, or Mark Twain, was a victim of the early obituary. When a reporter found Clemens in London, he said, "The report of my death was an exaggeration."[58] Other premature "victims" have included the historian Arthur Schlesinger Jr., comedian Bob Hope, retired U.S. Senator Jesse Helms, baseball Hall of Famer Joe DiMaggio and character actor Abe Vigoda.[59]

Mistakes erode the public's confidence in newspapers and what they report. The directors of the Pew Research Center's Project for Excellence in Journalism wrote that accuracy is "the foundation upon which everything else builds: Context, interpretation, debate, and all of public communication. If the foundation is faulty, everything else is flawed."[60]

Accuracy has long been a problem in journalism. The obituary of legendary television broadcaster Walter Cronkite, who personified media credibility, in the *New York Times* contained six reporter errors and a seventh mistake added by an editor.[61] The discovery of another error required a second correction. A recent academic study of fourteen newspapers reported that sources found errors in 61 percent of the stories, but studies over seventy years have consistently found many stories contain errors.[62]

The Journalism Credibility Project conducted by the American Society of Newspaper Editors a decade ago found in a survey that 35 percent of readers said they found spelling or grammar mistakes in their newspaper more than once a week—and that was before the downsizing began that has reduced the ranks of newspaper copy editors.[63] Those surveyed said that errors they find in newspapers were the primary reason they find newspapers less credible. But what the survey also found is that readers who noticed that the newspaper regularly corrected mistakes "felt better" about their newspaper's accuracy.[64]

Craig Silverman, who writes a column on mistakes and corrections for *Columbia Journalism Review* and the "Regret the Error" blog, argues that most errors go uncorrected:

Many readers think the press is unlikely to correct an error, and so they don't bother to follow up. Some believe a correction is pointless and ineffectual anyway; others simply don't know how to go about getting one. Sources also decline to request corrections when they don't believe an error is consequential. As a result, if a media outlet doesn't notice a mistake on its own, the error will remain uncorrected and, frequently, will be accessible online and in archives and databases forever.[65]

Silverman wrote that once a story is published, reporters and editors move on to the next story; with few exceptions, they don't go looking for errors to correct. They rely on the public and their sources to report errors.

A study of 631 corrections published in seventy newspapers in 2005 found that 83 percent were objective, misinformation; the remaining 17 percent were subjective—misquotes, plagiarism, omissions, wrong assumptions and wrong suggestions. The study found that few (twenty-four) included an apology and few disclosed a reason for the mistake.[66]

Researchers contacted sources in 400 newspaper stories of twenty-two newspapers over a two-year period. They found that one in ten of the 2,700 sources who said the story contained an error had reported it to the newspaper.[67] In fact, a study of 1,220 errors identified by news sources in ten newspapers found that less than 2 percent were corrected.[68]

Still, readers say that corrections are important. Newspapers seem to have gotten the message. For example, on August 21, 2009, the *New York Times* listed on Page 2A and on its web site eight corrections from stories it had reported and another from an Associated Press story it had published. The corrections column concludes with this invitation:

> *The Times welcomes comments and suggestions, or complaints about errors that warrant correction. Messages on news coverage can be e-mailed to nyt-news@nytimes.com or left toll-free at 1–888-NYT-NEWS (1–888–698–6397). Comments on editorials may be e-mailed to letters@nytimes.com or faxed to (212) 556–3622.*[69]

A comparison study of the corrections published by *The Times* and the *Washington Post* in 1997 and 2007 found *The Times* published more than twice as many in 2007 while *The Post* published slightly more that year.[70] Research makes it clear that even though newspapers are doing a better job of correcting mistakes, they still have a long road to accuracy.

Journalists should distinguish news from advertising and shun hybrids that blur the lines between the two.

Everyone associated with journalism recognizes that these are perilous times for the industry as publishers everywhere search for a business model that will support the efforts of those who keep the public informed and help keep the governments accountable for their decisions. As part of the effort to survive and create new revenue, newspapers are experimenting and rightly so. But some of those experiments have crossed the ethical divide.

One effort that went awry blurred the lines between news content and advertisements. The front page of the *Los Angeles Times* on April 9, 2009, featured a five-column ad across the bottom of the page for the premiere of NBC's "Southland" program. What it also featured in the lower left-hand corner was an ad disguised as a news story promoting the show. While the ad was set in a different typeface and the NBC peacock logo and "advertisement" ran above the headline—distinguishing marks to be sure—the ad was laid out like any other news story. *TVweek.com* called it a "faux story."[71]

Front-page advertisements have been embraced by a number of newspapers in the past few years, a practice resurrected from the nineteenth century. The practice itself is not unethical. As long as advertising dollars do not influence editorial content or front page news judgment, it is hard to see how an ad purchased for the front page of the newspaper is any more troublesome than an ad placed on page six or on the back page.

The *Times'* ad blurred the line because it was a definite attempt to grab readers' attention without making the clear distinction the "story" was a paid advertisement and not news.

The *Times* acknowledged as much. "The delivery of news and information is a rapidly changing business, and the *Los Angeles Times* is continuously testing innovative approaches," it said in a statement. "That includes creating unique marketing opportunities for our advertising partners, and today's NBC 'Southland' ad was designed to stretch traditional boundaries."

The *Times* followed that up with a four-page advertisement for a movie in a Sunday section that the *New York Times* said was laid out like a news section. NBC and Paramount Pictures both said the newspaper brought the ad ideas to them. The journalists responsible for the news content of the *Los Angeles Times* objected to the NBC ad, according to Reuters, reporting that one hundred employees signed a petition protesting the ad the day before it ran.

"The NBC ad may have provided some quick cash, but it has caused incalculable damage to this institution," the petition said. "This action violates a 128-year pact with our readers that the front page is reserved for the most meaningful stories of the day. Plac(ing) a fake news article on A-1 makes a mockery of our integrity and journalistic standards."

One respected media critic told the *New York Times* she agreed. "You dress an ad up to look like editorial content precisely because you think it will make it more valuable," said Geneva Overholser, director of the school of journalism at the University of Southern California's Annenberg School for Communication. "Fundamentally, that's an act of deception."

Journalists should be free of obligation to any interest other than the public's right to know.

Journalists treasure their credibility above all else. If readers do not perceive reporters as credible sources of information, their newspapers are seriously threatened. Why would someone depend on a newspaper for news he didn't trust? One ethicist explained this situation like this: "(W)hen decisions about news judgments are influenced by factors outside the bounds of professional perceptions of newsworthiness or are shaped by something other than the journalistic commitment to the broad public interest, we say that journalistic independence has been compromised."[72]

Because a major role of journalism is to serve as a watchdog on government and government officials, most journalists consciously avoid any involvement with the government. The exceptions raise questions.

On the Government Payroll

The federal government spent $500 million between the mid-1980s and 2006 to fund radio and television stations with programming to promote the creation of democracy in Cuba. Radio Martí began broadcasting in 1985 and TV Martí in 1990.[73] An American diplomat angered Cuban officials by distributing short-wave radios capable of picking up Radio Martí, while the four-hour, six-nights-a-week broadcast of the television station has been routinely jammed.[74]

The stations received more attention than usual in 2006 when the publisher of the *Miami Herald* and *El Nuevo Herald*, the *Herald's* Spanish-language version, fired three reporters at the *El Nuevo Herald*, when it was revealed they had been receiving regular payments from the federal government for their work with the stations aimed at Cuba.

According to a story published by the *Miami Herald* on September 8, 2006, one *El Nuevo Herald* journalist who reported on Cuba and wrote an opinion column had been paid almost $175,000 since 2001 to host Radio Marti and TV Marti shows. A staff reporter who covered the Cuban exile community and politics received almost $15,000 between 2001 and 2006. A freelance reporter who wrote about Cuban culture received about $71,000 for work for the Cuban stations, all money paid by the federal government.[75]

The *Miami Herald* reviewed articles by the trio of *El Nuevo Herald* journalists and reported no instance in which the reporters disclosed they had received payments.[76] In a front-page letter to readers nine days later, Jesús Diaz Jr., publisher of the *Miami Herald* and *El Nuevo Herald*, said he approved the dismissal of the three journalists because, "I am deeply committed to the separation between government and a free press. Further, our employees violated our conflict-of-interest rules. All of our journalists acknowledge and agree to adhere to our policies, which include this statement:

> We demonstrate our principles by operating with fairness, accuracy and independence, and by avoiding conflicts of interest, as well as the appearance of conflicts of interest. Our news operations will be diligent in their pursuit of the truth, without regard to special interests."[77]

The dismissals created an uproar in the Cuban community in South Florida. The publisher resigned the next month, telling readers "the events of the past three weeks have created an environment that no longer allows me to lead our newspapers in a manner most beneficial for our newspapers, our readers and our community." However, he reinstated the reporters, acknowledging he had since learned other reporters also had received money from the stations, and announced the newspaper had clarified its ethical statement and promised rigorous enforcement of its policy on conflicts of interest and outside employment and media appearances.[78]

In a commentary on the ethics involved in the situation, Jane Kirtley, director of the Silha Center for the Study of Media Ethics and Law, said, "A government watchdog cannot accept government money." She argued that accepting money from the government for journalistic work is "an irreconcilable conflict of interest. Government permeates everything journalists do, and everything they report on, so no one in the news business is exempt. End of story."[79]

Beyond the Codes of Ethics

The SPJ Code of Ethics covers most of the same issues covered in other journalism codes. And no chapter on journalism ethics could begin to cover all the issues, the sins of commission and omission of the practitioners. Journalists do make mistakes in judgment, get careless in their reporting, leap to conclusions, skip steps of fact checking in the rush to be first, and sometimes, either to get ahead and make a name for themselves or fatten their bank account, violate the code of ethics.

The critics, and they obviously are numerous, launch legitimate attacks. Sometimes they don't understand what and why journalists do what they do. Sometimes they don't agree with what journalists write and attack because they are sure the journalists are biased. And some scholars think the entire discussion is off-target. The focus should be on issues involving corporate ownership, the way newsrooms go about covering their communities and even the way newsrooms are organized.

A decade ago, in introducing this topic, Jeremy Iggers said the issues are bigger than journalism and its ethics.

> Moreover, newspapers are experiencing the fallout of a larger crisis in the culture, a period of cultural upheaval that is sometimes described as the end of the modern era. There is a growing acceptance of the idea that reality is socially constructed and that the competing versions of reality presented to us via the news media are not and indeed cannot be unbiased representations of reality. Faith in facts has given way to an understanding that facts don't interpret themselves and to a distrust of all sources of authority, including newspapers and the experts whose authority they transmit.[80]

Indeed, the assault on journalism ethics is not simply the failure of journalists to follow the principles outlined in a code, even one last updated a dozen years ago. Journalists today are under unbelievable pressure to do the work they once did with many more colleagues and resources. They are up against politicians who are more likely to seek re-election than solutions. They face the power and wrath of special interest groups that have redesigned their spin machines and mobilization efforts to near-perfect levels. Add to that the bloggers, who are capable of not only pointing out the mistake journalists make, which is a good thing, but also of impugning the motives and dismissing the good work they do.

And journalists are the victims of their own methods. One journalistic lapse is recapped a thousand times and magnified beyond its context. Ten thousand correct ethical decisions merit not even a paragraph in the daily account.

SPJ Code of Ethics

Preamble

Members of the Society of Professional Journalists believe that public enlightenment is the forerunner of justice and the foundation of democracy. The duty of the journalist is to further those ends by seeking truth and providing a fair and comprehensive account of events and issues. Conscientious journalists from all media and specialties strive to serve the public with thoroughness and honesty. Professional integrity is the cornerstone of a journalist's credibility. Members of the Society share a dedication to ethical behavior and adopt this code to declare the Society's principles and standards of practice.

Seek Truth and Report It

Journalists should be honest, fair and courageous in gathering, reporting and interpreting information. Journalists should:

§ Test the accuracy of information from all sources and exercise care to avoid inadvertent error. Deliberate distortion is never permissible.

§ Diligently seek out subjects of news stories to give them the opportunity to respond to allegations of wrongdoing.

§ Identify sources whenever feasible. The public is entitled to as much information as possible on sources' reliability.

§ Always question sources' motives before promising anonymity. Clarify conditions attached to any promise made in exchange for information. Keep promises.

§ Make certain that headlines, news teases and promotional material, photos, video, audio, graphics, sound bites and quotations do not misrepresent. They should not oversimplify or highlight incidents out of context.

§ Never distort the content of news photos or video. Image enhancement for technical clarity is always permissible. Label montages and photo illustrations.

§ Avoid misleading re-enactments or staged news events. If re-enactment is necessary to tell a story, label it.

§ Avoid undercover or other surreptitious methods of gathering information except when traditional open methods will not yield information vital to the public. Use of such methods should be explained as part of the story

§ Never plagiarize.

§ Tell the story of the diversity and magnitude of the human experience boldly, even when it is unpopular to do so.

§ Examine their own cultural values and avoid imposing those values on others.

§ Avoid stereotyping by race, gender, age, religion, ethnicity, geography, sexual orientation, disability, physical appearance or social status.

§ Support the open exchange of views, even views they find repugnant.

§ Give voice to the voiceless; official and unofficial sources of information can be equally valid.

§ Distinguish between advocacy and news reporting. Analysis and commentary should be labeled and not misrepresent fact or context.

§ Distinguish news from advertising and shun hybrids that blur the lines between the two.

§ Recognize a special obligation to ensure that the public's business is conducted in the open and that government records are open to inspection.

Minimize Harm

Ethical journalists treat sources, subjects and colleagues as human beings deserving of respect. Journalists should:

§ Show compassion for those who may be affected adversely by news coverage. Use special sensitivity when dealing with children and inexperienced sources or subjects.

§ Be sensitive when seeking or using interviews or photographs of those affected by tragedy or grief.

§ Recognize that gathering and reporting information may cause harm or discomfort. Pursuit of the news is not a license for arrogance.

§ Recognize that private people have a greater right to control information about themselves than do public officials and others who seek power, influence or attention. Only an overriding public need can justify intrusion into anyone's privacy.

§ Show good taste. Avoid pandering to lurid curiosity.

§ Be cautious about identifying juvenile suspects or victims of sex crimes.

§ Be judicious about naming criminal suspects before the formal filing of charges.

§ Balance a criminal suspect's fair trial rights with the public's right to be informed.

Act Independently

Journalists should be free of obligation to any interest other than the public's right to know. Journalists should:

§ Avoid conflicts of interest, real or perceived.

§ Remain free of associations and activities that may compromise integrity or damage credibility.

§ Refuse gifts, favors, fees, free travel and special treatment, and shun secondary employment, political involvement, public office and service in community organizations if they compromise journalistic integrity.

§ Disclose unavoidable conflicts.

§ Be vigilant and courageous about holding those with power accountable.

§ Deny favored treatment to advertisers and special interests and resist their pressure to influence news coverage.

§ Be wary of sources offering information for favors or money; avoid bidding for news.

Be Accountable

Journalists are accountable to their readers, listeners, viewers and each other. Journalists should:

§ Clarify and explain news coverage and invite dialogue with the public over journalistic conduct.

§ Encourage the public to voice grievances against the news media.

§ Admit mistakes and correct them promptly.

§ Expose unethical practices of journalists and the news media.

§ Abide by the same high standards to which they hold others.

The SPJ Code of Ethics is voluntarily embraced by thousands of writers, editors and other news professionals. The present version of the code was adopted by the 1996 SPJ National Convention, after months of study and debate among the Society's members. Sigma Delta Chi's first Code of Ethics was borrowed from the American Society of Newspaper Editors in 1926. In 1973, Sigma Delta Chi wrote its own code, which was revised in 1984, 1987 and 1996.

Notes

1. SPJ Code of Ethics, available at http://www.spj.org/ethics.
2. Bruce W. Sanford, *Don't Shoot the Messenger: How Our Growing Hatred of the Media Threatens Free Speech for All of Us* (New York: The Free Press, 1999), 11.
3. Tom Cooper, "Between the Summits: What Americans Think About Media Ethics," *Journal of Mass Media Ethics* (2008, Volume 23), 1.
4. Frank Newport, "Republicans Deeply Distrustful of News Media, Democrats Much More Positive," *Gallup News Service*, posted on October 8, 2007, available at http://www.gallup.com/poll/101677/Republicans-Remain-Deeply-Distrustful-News-Media.aspx. (accessed November 21, 2009).
5. Herbert N. Foerstel, *From Watergate to Monicagate: Ten Controversies in Modern Journalism and Media* (Westport, Conn.: Greenwood Press, 2001), 6.
6. *Examining Our Credibility, 1999*, American Society of Newspaper Editors. Summary available online at http://204.8.120.192/index.cfm?ID=2632 (Last accessed November 22, 2009).
7. The survey was conducted for publication in the magazine *Brill's Content*, a media watchdog journal. The results are reported by Foerstel, *supra* note 5, at 7–8.
8. Claude-Jean Bertrand, *Media Ethics and Accountability Systems* (New Brunswick, N.J.: Transaction Publishers, 2000), 2.
9. See note 7.
10. Matt Drudge, "Newsweek Kills Story on White House Intern: Blockbuster Report: 23-year Old, Former White House Intern, Sex Relationship with President," *The Drudge Report*, posted on January 17, 1998, available at http://www.drudgereportarchives.com/data/2002/01/17/20020117_175502_ml.htm (accessed August 5, 2009).
11. Marvin Kalb, "The Rise of the 'New News:' A Case Study of Two Root Causes of the Modern Scandal Coverage," *Discussion Paper D-34*, October 1998. The Joan Shorenstein Center on the Press, Politics and Public Policy: Harvard University.
12. Ibid.
13. Jack Shafer, "The Romenesko Effect: How a One-man Web Site is Improving Journalism," *Slate*, posted on Monday, April 18, 2005, available at http://www.slate.com/id/2116903 (Last accessed, November 22, 2009).
14. Available at http://www.poynter.org/column.asp?id=45 (accessed November 22, 2009).
15. Shafer, supra note 13.
16. Ibid.
17. Available at http://www.journalism.org/dailybriefings. Last accessed, November 22, 2009
18. Available at http://www.mediabistro.com. (Last accessed November 22, 2009).
19. Available at http://iwantmedia.com. (Last accessed November 22, 2009).
20. Available at http://www.cjr.org, (Last accessed November 22, 2009).
21. Mark Jurkowitz, "The Romenesko Effect: How a Media Web Site Is Changing the Face—and Pace—of Media Culture," *The Boston Phoenix*, posted on August 26, 2005, available at http://www.bostonphoenix.com/boston/news_features/dont_quote_me/multi-page/documents/04927098.asp (accessed November 22, 2009).
22. David Bauder, "CBS Says It Cannot Vouch for Authenticity of Bush Documents," *Las Vegas* (Nevada) *Sun*, September 20, 2004, A8. See also K.C. Howard,

"Filmmaker Tells 'Slacker Friends' to Get Out, Vote," *Las Vegas* (Nevada) *Review-Journal*, October 16, 2004, A9.

23. Howard Kurtz, "Dan Rather to Step Down at CBS: Anchor's Decision Comes Amid Probe of Flawed Bush Report," *The Washington Post*, November 24, 2004, A01.

24. Howard Kurtz, "CBS Fires 4 Staffers in Wake of Probe; Panel Faults Rather for His Defense of Bush Guard Story," *The Washington Post*, January 11, 2005, A01.

25. "Journalist Q&A: William Powers, National Journal," *PR Week*, August 28, 2006, 12.

26. Bertrand, *supra* note 8, at 44.

27. Philip Meyer, *Ethical Journalism* (White Plains, N.Y.: Longman Press, 1987), 18.

28. Laton McCartney, *The Teapot Dome Scandal: How Big Oil Bought the Harding White House and Tried to Steal the Country* (New York: Random House, 2009), 122–141.

29. Edmund B. Lambeth, "Public Journalism as Cultural Change," in Edmund B. Lambeth, Philip E. Meyer and Esther Thorson, *Assessing Public Journalism* (Columbia, Mo.: University of Missouri Press, 1998), 233. Cited in Renita Coleman and Lee Wilkins, "The Moral Development of Journalists: A Comparison with Other Professions and a Model for Predicting High Quality Ethical Reasoning," *Journalism and Mass Communication Quarterly*, Autumn 2004 (81:3), 511.

30. Douglas Anderson, "How Managing Editors View and Deal with Ethical Issues," *Journalism Quarterly* (Summer/Autumn 87, Volume 64: 2), 341.

31. Ibid.

32. *"Why Doesn't SPJ Enforce Its Code of Ethics?,"* available at http://www.spj.org/ethicsfaq.asp (accessed November 22, 2009).

33. Ibid.

34. For a list of ethics codes of journalism organizations and companies, see http://www.journalism.org/resources/ethics_codes.

35. Bob Steele, "Genuinely Torn," in "What Are Editors Doing about Ethics?" *The American Editor* (November/December 2003), 10–12.

36. R. B. Parrish, *The Duke Lacrosse Case*, (self-published, 2009), 11.

37. Ibid., 23–24.

38. Kelly McBride, "Winners and Losers in the Duke Lacrosse Story," Poynteronline, posted on April 11, 2007, available at http://www.poynter.org/column.asp?id=67&aid=121262 (accessed November 22, 2009).

39. Rachel Smolkin, "Justice Delayed," *American Journalism Review*, August/September 2007.

40. Nader Baydoun and R. Stephanie Good, *A Rush to Injustice: How Power, Prejudice, Racism, and Political Correctness Overshadowed Truth and Justice in the Duke Lacrosse Case* (Nashville, Tenn.: Thomas Nelson, 2007); Paul Montgomery, *Party Like a Lacrosse Star* (self-published, 2007); R. B. Parrish, *The Duke Lacrosse Case* (self-published, 2009), Michael L. Siegel, *Race to Injustice: Lessons Learned from the Duke Lacrosse Rape Case* (Durham, N.C.: Carolina Academic Press, 2009); Stuart Taylor Jr. and KC Johnson, *Until Proven Innocent* (New York: St. Martin's Press, 2007); Don Yager, *It's Not About the Truth* (New York: Simon & Schuster, 2007).

41. "Outrage at Duke Lacrosse Players," *The Herald-Sun*, March 28, 2006, A8.

42. Bob Ashley, "Has the Lacrosse Case Induced Insanity?" *The* (Durham, N.C.) *Herald-Sun*, July 23, 2006, A9

43. Yager, *supra* note 40, at 148.

44. Smolkin, *supra* note 39.

45. Ibid.

46. Ibid.

47. Ann Scott Tyson, "12 Found Alive in W.Va. Coal Mine—Body of 13th Man Was Discovered in Adjacent Area," *Washington Post*, January 4, 2006, A1.

48. Gal Beckerman, "How the Press Got the Slago Story Wrong," *Columbia Journalism Review*, Jan. 4, 2006, www.cjr.org/behind_the_news/how_the_press_got_the_sago_sto.php

49. Maureen Dowd, "Cheney, Master of Pain," *New York Times*, posted on May 16, 2009, available at http://www.nytimes.com/2009/05/17/opinion/17dowd.html?_r=1&scp=10&sq=Maureen%20Dowd&st=cse. See also Belinda Luscombe, "Is Maureen Dowd Guilty of Plagiarism?," *Time Magazine*, May 18, 2009, available at http://www.time.com/time/arts/article/0,8599,1899530,00.html.

50. Blake Morrison, "Ex-USA TODAY Reporter Faked Major Stories," *USA Today*, March 19, 2004, 1A.

51. Janet Cooke, "Jimmy's World: 8-year-old Heroin Addict Lives for a Fix," *The Washington Post*, September 28, 1980, A1.

52. Ron F. Smith, *Ethics in Journalism* (Malden, Md.: Blackwell Publishing, 2008, 6th ed.), 99–100.

53. Jacques Steinberg, "Times' 2 Top Editors Resign after Furor on Writer's Fraud," *New York Times*, June 6, 2003, A1.

54. Gabriel Dance, "None of This Is Made Up: Fabrication and Plagiarism," in Philip Meyer, ed., *Newspaper Ethics in the New Century*, (Reston, Va.: ASNE, 2006), 93–95.

55. Vicki Gowler, "Survey says…," in "What Are Editors Doing about Ethics?", *supra* note 35, at 5.

56. Brian Tolley, "Beyond Facts," in "What Are Editors Doing about Ethics?", *supra* note 35, at 16.

57. "Entertainment, Television, Culture," *Los Angeles Times*, February 7, 2007.

58. Craig Silverman, *Regret the Error* (New York: Union Square Press, 2007), 170–171.

59. Ibid., 174–177.

60. Bill Kovach and Tom Rosenstiel, *The Elements of Journalism* (New York: Three Rivers Press, 2001), 43.

61. Craig Silverman, "Wrong, Wrong, Wrong, Wrong, Wrong, Wrong," *Columbia Journalism Review*, posted on July 24, 2009, http://www.cjr.org/regret_the_error/wrong_wrong_wrong_wrong_wrong.php.

62. Scott R. Maier, "Accuracy Matters: A Cross-market Assessment of Newspaper Error and Credibility," *Journalism and Mass Communication Quarterly* (August 2005, Volume 82:3), 533–551.

63. The number of *The Washington Post* copy editors in 2005 was seventy-five, and that number had been reduced to forty-three by mid-2008. Craig Silverman, "The Copy Editing Equation," *Columbia Journalism Review*, posted on July 10, 2009, http://www.cjr.org/regret_the_error/the_copy_editing_equation.php.

64. "Examining Our Credibility: Building Reader Trust," American Society of Newspaper Editors, April 2000.

65. Silverman, *supra* note 57, 226.

66. Michael Bugeja and Jane Patterson, "How Complete Are Newspaper Corrections?: An Analysis of the 2005 "Regret the Error" Compilation," *Media Ethics Online*, (Spring 2007, Volume 18:2), 7, 20–25 available at http://media.www.mediaethicsmagazine.com/media/storage/paper655/news/2007/07/01/AnalysesCommentary/How-Complete.Are.Newspaper.Corrections.An.Analysis.Of.The.2005.regret.The.Error-2923347.shtml.

67. Scott R. Maier, "Setting the Record Straight: When The Press Errs, Do Corrections Follow?" *Journalism Practice* (January 2007, Volume 1:1), 33–43.

68. Scott Maier, "Tip of the Iceberg: Published Corrections Represent Less than Two Percent of Factual Errors in Newspapers." Paper presented at the annual meeting of the Association for Education in Journalism and Mass Communication (Washington, D.C., August 8, 2007) available at http://www.allacademic.com/meta/p203767_index.html.

69. "Corrections," *The New York Times*, posted on August 21, 2009, available at http://www.nytimes.com/ref/pageoneplus/corrections.html.

70. Neil Nemeth and Craig Sanders, "We Regret the Error: Changes in Correction of Error Practices of the *New York Times* and the *Washington Post*," Paper presented August 2008 at the annual meeting of the Association for Education in Journalism and Mass Communication, Marriott Downtown, Chicago, Ill., available online at http://www.allacademic.com/meta/p271990_index.html.

71. Josef Adalian, "NBC's 'Southland' Pushes Ad Limits in L.A. Times," *TVweek.com*, posted on April 9, 2009, available at http://www.tvweek.com/news/2009/04/nbcs_southland_pushes_ad_limit.php.

72. Patrick Lee Plaisance, *Media Ethics: Key Principles for Responsible Practice* (Thousand Oaks, Calif.: Sage, 2009), 153.

73. Laura Wides-Munoz, "Radio and TV Marti Beef up Broadcasting to Promote Change in Cuba." *Associated Press*, August 10, 2006.

74. Christopher Marquis, "Bush Plans to Tighten Sanctions on Cuba, Not Ease Them," *New York Times*, Wednesday, May 15, 2002.

75. Oscar Corrall, "10 Miami Journalists Take U.S. Pay," *Miami Herald*, September 8, 2006, 1A.

76. Ibid.

77. Jesus Diaz Jr., "A Free Press Can Require Painful Choices," *Miami Herald*, September 17, 2006, 1A.

78. Jesus Diaz Jr., "A Letter to Readers from Jesús Díaz," *Miami Herald*, October 3, 2006, 1A.

79. Jane E. Kirtley, "Objecting to Parasites, Whatever Their Price," *Journal of Mass Media Ethics* (2008, Volume 23: 2), 169–172,

80. Jeremy Iggers, *Good News, Bad News*, (Boulder, Colo.: Westview Press, 1999), 4.

9

Newspapers and the Law

To the untrained ear, the words of the First Amendment sound absolute: Congress shall make no law…abridging the freedom of speech or of the press. But the Supreme Court has never said that freedom of the press is unlimited or that newspapers have an absolute right to publish whatever they choose.

Legal scholars and justices of the Supreme Court have struggled to understand what members of the First Congress meant when they drafted the proposed Bill of Rights and sent it to the states for ratification. The records of the Constitutional Convention held during the summer of 1787 are sketchy, but they do reveal that a bill of rights was not discussed until the final days of the convention. George Mason, one of Virginia's most influential delegates, announced that he would "sooner chop off his right hand than put it to the Constitution as it now stands," in part because it lacked a bill of rights. He refused to sign the completed draft of the Constitution at the end of the convention.[1]

The biggest obstacle to ratification of the document was its lack of guaranteed rights for citizens. James Madison, who persuaded a majority of delegates from Virginia to rat-ify the Constitution, pledged to introduce a bill of rights if he was elected to serve in the First Congress. He won the election, and on June 8, 1789, Madison took to the floor of the House of Representatives for several hours and outlined his proposal, which required support from two-thirds of the members of the House before it could be forwarded to the Senate. His proposal called for 19 amendments, many of them similar to those adopted by his home state of Virginia, and a new preamble to the Constitution affirming that the country was committed to the principle that "all power is vested in, and consequently derived from the people. That government is instituted and ought to be exercised for the benefit of the people; which consists in the enjoyment of life and liberty, with the right of acquiring and using property, and generally of pursuing and obtaining happiness and safety."[2]

But Madison's proposed amendments were modified in the House during eleven days of debate beginning August 13 and then drastically rewritten in the Senate before they were transmitted to the states.[3] Because the Senate met in closed session in those days and no records were kept of its debates, history has left no clear account of what the Senate debated, making it hard for judges and scholars to know what they intended to protect with the First Amendment's free press clause.[4] The freedom of the press clause originally written by Madison—"The people shall not be deprived of their right to speak, to write or to publish their sentiments; and the freedom of the press, as one of the great bulwarks of liberty, shall be inviolable"— would have limited the power of both state and federal governments.[5] But the Senate altered the wording so that the version submitted for ratification by the states—"Congress shall make no law respecting an establishment of religion, or prohibiting the free exercise thereof; or abridging the freedom of speech, or of the press; or the right of the people peaceably to assemble, and to petition the government for a redress of grievances."—protected those freedoms from the power only of the federal government. It was not until 1925 that the Supreme Court held that a clause in the Fourteenth Amendment, ratified in 1868 after the end of the Civil War, applied to efforts by state government to abridge speech and the press.[6]

"The brevity of the First Amendment belies its complexity," two well-respected First Amendment advocates have written. "The words themselves seem unambiguously to prohibit Congress from censoring or controlling newsgathering activities and media content."[7]

But from their earliest debates about the meaning and range of protection guaranteed the press by the Bill of Rights, the justices of the Supreme Court—with a few exceptions—have held that freedom of speech and freedom of the press were never intended as absolute rights; the words "Congress shall make no law" were not to be interpreted literally. Justice Henry Billings Brown declared in a 7–1 decision in 1897 that the First Amendment "does not protect the publication of libels, blasphemous or indecent articles, or other publications injurious to public morals or private reputation."[8]

Justice Louis Brandeis, one of the Court's earliest supporters of free speech rights for those who criticized the government, also saw limits to the First Amendment:

Although the rights of free speech and assembly are fundamental, they are not in their nature absolute. Their exercise is subject to restriction, if the particular restriction proposed is required in order to protect the state from destruction or from serious injury, political, economic or moral.[9]

Those words of the First Amendment, *Congress shall make no law…abridging freedom of the press,* make journalism the only profession given special protection by the Constitution of the United States. While that protection is not absolute and must be balanced with other interests, it still gives its practitioners privileges that enable them to report the news and serve as a watchdog of the government and the governors.

This chapter will survey the legal issues that most directly affect newspaper journalists:

- Can the government stop a newspaper from printing information?
- Does the First Amendment offer newspapers any protection from libel lawsuits?
- Can judges prevent journalists from covering courts?
- Can prosecutors force journalists to identify their sources?

But the migration of newspaper content to Internet websites has introduced more issues. In the Telecommunications Act of 1996, Congress provided immunity for Internet service providers from defamation lawsuits for content they did not create, meaning that if a defamatory remark is posted on a newspaper's website by someone commenting on a story, the poster is responsible and not the newspaper.

A college student filed a defamation lawsuit in June 2009 and asked the court to order the newspaper to reveal the identity of a commenter who, she said, libeled her. The student bought a dress at a mall and returned the next day wearing it. She was asked to leave the mall because she was told the dress was too short. *The Richmond (Ky.) Register* wrote about the incident, and a comment on the story posted on the newspaper's website said the real reason she was asked to leave was that she exposed herself to a mother and her two children. Her suit is not the first time a newspaper has fought a subpoena for the identity of those who have written comments on its website. Like other issues involving the Internet, the courts have yet to clarify the legal issues surrounding the identity of those sources.[10]

Prior Restraint: Can the Government Stop a Newspaper from Printing Information?

A Nassau County, New York, legislator was arrested in May 2009 on federal charges of tax evasion. Photojournalists took a picture of Thomas Corbin wearing handcuffs after his arrest. Corbin filed a motion in U.S. District Court asking the judge to bar a newspaper and a television station from continuing to use the picture, arguing that it would make it difficult for him to get a fair trial. The judge ruled against Corbin.[11]

A federal judge in Denver in May 2009 denied a request for a restraining order to stop *The Pueblo Chieftain* and a reporter from publishing information obtained from a court hearing in a lawsuit related to accusations of the sexual abuse of high school students. The suit was filed to settle a dispute between a Catholic group and an insurer about who must pay the costs related to the sexual abuse lawsuits.[12]

In both of these cases, the judges declined to issue prior restraint orders, thus denying public officials in these circumstances the power to stop individuals from disseminating information. Prior restraint is defined as any system that gives public officials the power to deny someone a forum in advance of its actual expression.[13] In other words, prior restraint is an act by the government that prohibits someone from expressing an opinion or thought, either in writing, in speaking or in action. Examples would include shutting down a newspaper or its website, seizing copies of a newspaper before they can be distributed to readers or denying an individual (usually someone with unpopular views) the opportunity to write, deliver a speech or otherwise communicate information or opinions. Both of the cases cited—prohibiting a newspaper from publishing a picture or reporting information it had learned—are examples of prior restraint.

However, history is replete with examples of prior restraint, and the practice is not extinct, even under the First Amendment's guarantee of freedom of the press. For example, in April 2005, a federal district judge in Boston ordered a newspaper reporter who sat in on a hearing in a drug case, a hearing that was open to the public and the press, not to publish information he learned during that hearing. The "protected" information was that the defendant, accused of running a drug ring for eight years involving thousands of tons of marijuana, was cooperating with prosecutors. Even though the hearing was not closed, when a defense attorney learned that one of the spectators was a reporter, he notified the judge who issued the gag order. The newspaper objected, but the judge left the order in place until it expired a week later.[14]

Governments have used three different prior restraint approaches to muzzle the press. One was licensing printers, requiring those who owned a printing press to obtain a license from the government to allow the printer to legally publish material. Anyone who published material the government decided was critical of it or of its policies was in danger of losing the license. Anyone who tried to publish without a license was dealt with severely. This practice continued in the American colonies up to 1730.[15]

One of the victims of British licensing practices, practices that were brought to America, was Benjamin Harris. His *Publick Occurrences Both Forreign and Domestick* is considered by many the first newspaper published in the Colonies, although it published but once. Harris refused to get a license for printing his newspaper, which the law required. Two of his "stories"—one a rumor about the king of France who was said "to lie with his son's wife" and another about Mohawk Indians, miserable "salvages," who had taken hostage some colonists and killed them during a border war—provoked the colonial council to order that the licenseless Harris stop publishing. And that was the end of America's first newspaper.[16]

A second approach has been censorship. Writers and newspapers were required to submit their work to officials who checked it before it was published. One example was in Prussia, where a young Karl Marx—who was then a democrat rather than a socialist—edited a newspaper. Because the Prussian government did not like what he wrote, he had to submit everything to a censor, who read every word.[17] Eventually, the government shut his newspaper down and drove him to France.

A third approach was taxation, taxing newspapers out of existence. In 1712, the British parliament passed the Stamp Act, which put a tax on each copy of a newspaper. The purpose was to reduce the circulation of opposition newspapers, but printers soon found loopholes in the law.[18] In 1765, the British imposed a new stamp act on the colonies, primarily to help pay the cost of stationing troops in the new world. That angered the colonial spirit and fanned the flame of liberty.[19]

A powerful Louisiana official tried to revive the practice in 1934, when he convinced the legislature to pass a tax on newspapers, magazines and other periodicals with a circulation of more than 20,000 copies per week. The Supreme Court ruled the tax unconstitutional, saying it was enacted for "the plain purpose of penalizing the publishers and curtailing the circulation of a selected group of newspapers."[20] The intent of the law was to silence newspapers in the state that were critical of U.S. Sen. Huey Long's policies. Since these newspapers were the larger newspapers, the tax was applied to them in an attempt to either shut them down or convince them that opposing Long was too expensive.

Another method of silencing a newspaper is violence. It was risky business to publish views that ran counter to those of others who might be moved to inflict a beating on the editor, smash the printing press or just burn the building down. That happened frequently during the days leading up to the Revolutionary War, during the war, during the bitter political feud between the Federalists and Republicans at the end of the eighteenth century and during the Civil War. Such violence flared up against abolitionist newspapers and against newspapers that opposed the labor union movement after the Civil War.

The state of Minnesota tried another approach to prior restraint. It passed what is known as the Minnesota gag law, which allowed a judge to ban a newspaper found to be a public nuisance for printing criticism of public officials that the judge considered "obscene, lewd and lascivious" or "malicious, defamatory and scandalous."[21] The first test of the law arose when a judge put the *Saturday Press* out of business after public officials in Minneapolis became irate over repeated published charges that they were corrupt and in collusion with criminal elements responsible for prostitution and alcohol sales during the Prohibition era.[22]

The Supreme Court took up the issue in 1931, invalidating for the first time a state law because it violated the First Amendment rights of a newspaper.[23] In *Near v. Minnesota*, Chief Justice Charles Evans Hughes wrote for a 5–4 majority that such a gag law was prior restraint forbidden by the First Amendment. "In determining the extent of the constitutional protection, it has been generally, if not universally, considered that it is the chief purpose of the guaranty to prevent previous restraints upon publication."[24] In other words, if the First Amendment meant anything in 1931, it was that the government could not stop the publication of news or criticism of the government without some overriding interest, such as national security. The decision vindicated the publisher and discouraged other legislatures from passing similar gag laws. And as one scholar wrote, "Since the 1931 release of the Supreme Court's opinion in *Near v. Minnesota*, the doctrine of prior restraint has been an essential element of First Amendment jurisprudence."[25]

The next year, the *Saturday Press* reappeared. On the front page, publisher Jay Near proclaimed: "The only paper in the United States with a United States Supreme Court record of being right; the only paper that dared fight for freedom of the press and won!"[26]

Another method of prior restraint the government has used is a restraining order banning a newspaper from publishing news. That issue arose during the Vietnam War. The war in Southeast Asia became increasingly unpopular as more and more body bags returned to the United States. Robert McNamara, secretary of defense under Presidents John Kennedy and Lyndon Johnson, ordered his staff to begin collecting documents and writing a history of American involvement in Vietnam. The result of McNamara's order, which wasn't completed until early 1969 after the end of the Johnson administration, was a work of 47 volumes and more than 7,000 pages.

The work, known as the *Pentagon Papers*, might have remained classified for decades were it not for Daniel Ellsberg, who had worked first for the Rand Corp., a civilian research institute that did work for the Air Force, then as a contractor for the Defense Department and in the Pentagon during the McNamara era. Because he was an expert on U.S. defense, he was asked to prepare options for the Vietnam War by Henry Kissinger, national security adviser to President Nixon. As part of his research, Ellsberg was allowed to read the Pentagon Papers. As he became increasingly disillusioned by the country's Vietnam policy, he decided he could influence the war by making the documents public. For several weeks during the fall of 1969, Ellsberg would take volumes late at night from the safe of a Defense Department contractor and make copies of them, then return the originals the next morning.[27]

He tried to persuade Sen. William Fulbright, an opponent of the war and the chairman of the Foreign Relations Committee, to make the papers public, but Fulbright refused.[28] Then he turned to Sen. Eugene McCarthy, an anti-war Democrat who ran unsuccessfully for his party's presidential nomination in 1968, but McCarthy also refused to release them.[29] So Ellsberg gave a copy to Neil Sheehan, a Washington correspondent for *The New York Times* in March 1971. Four reporters for *The Times* reviewed the material secretly for three months in a three-room suite on the eleventh floor of the New York Hilton Hotel, protected by a security guard when no one was there. With the assistance of three copy editors and other support staff, they prepared a 10-part series; the first installment was published on Sunday, June 13, 1971.[30]

After the second installment was in print, Attorney General John Mitchell sent a telegram asking *The Times* to stop. When *The Times* refused and published its third installment, the Justice Department went to court.[31] A federal district judge in New York issued a temporary order restraining *The Times* from publishing further until a hearing. This was the first time in the history of the United States that a federal judge had imposed prior restraint on the basis of national security concerns.[32] The date was June 15, 1971.

With *The Times* under a federal court order, Ellsberg turned over another copy of the *Pentagon Papers* to Ben Bagdikian, assistant managing editor of *The Washington Post*, which had been clamoring for a copy since *The Times* had begun publishing.[33] *The Post* published its first article on Friday, June 18. Attorney General Mitchell asked *The Post* to stop, but executive editor Ben Bradlee refused.[34] This time, when Mitchell went to court, he did not win an immediate restraining order. After appeals of both cases to the U.S. Court of Appeals, the cases ended up before the Supreme Court. In an extraordinary step, the Supreme Court held a hearing on Saturday, June 26, 1971.

The government argued that the newspapers had published material that violated the Espionage Act and that the president had a constitutional duty to conduct foreign affairs and the responsibility to classify documents. This was an unauthorized disclosure of classified documents and publishing the material, the government contended, would cause irreparable harm to the nation and the ability of the government to conduct foreign affairs.

Attorneys for the newspapers replied that the government classified material whenever it didn't want people to learn something embarrassing or controversial. They also argued the government's restraining orders were a violation of the First Amendment. Four days later, the Court announced a 6–3 decision, ruling the government failed to establish that publication of the stories would produce irreparable harm.[35] Quoting a 1963 decision, the Court said, "Any system of prior restraints of expression comes to this Court bearing a heavy presumption against its constitutional validity."[36]

That basic doctrine of prior restraint has existed for more than three-quarters of a century now. Even when government secrecy expanded during the War on Terrorism, the Bush administration did not go to court to try to stop a newspaper from publishing a story. But *The New York Times* did receive substantial criticism from President George W. Bush, Vice President Dick Cheney and others over a 2006 story that pulled back the curtain on a secret program initiated not long after the September 11, 2001, attacks. Counterterrorism officials attempted to trace transactions of people suspected of having ties to Al Qaeda by reviewing records from the nerve center of the global banking industry, a Belgian cooperative that routed about $6 trillion daily between banks, brokerages, stock exchanges and other institutions. *The Times* report said the program was viewed by the administration as a vital tool, and it had helped in the capture of the most wanted Al Qaeda figure in Southeast Asia.[37]

Whether the administration figured it had gleaned all the information it could from the program or recognized it would have a difficult time making a case, it never sought to invoke prior restraint to preserve the program.

Libel: How Much Protection Does the First Amendment Offer the Press from Defamation Lawsuits?

Libel, the publication or broadcast of false information that damages a person's reputation, can prove expensive for a newspaper. The *Kane County Chronicle* lost a $7 million judgment to the Illinois chief justice, which was reduced to $3 million in a settlement agreement in 2007.[38] *The Cincinnati Enquirer* turned over $14 million to Chiquita Brands International, the banana company, before the firm even filed a libel lawsuit after a series of stories on the company's business practices.[39]

The most important Supreme Court case related to libel, *New York Times v. Sullivan*, began, not with a hard-hitting investigative piece about a politician who had padded his pocket at the public's expense or had demanded money for a vote but with an advertisement.[40] "Heed Their Rising Voices" was a plea for financial contributions for the defense of Dr. Martin Luther King Jr.[41] The civil rights leader had been indicted by an Alabama grand jury that charged he had committed perjury in 1958 while signing his tax return.[42] The indictment followed King's endorsement of the sit-in movement that started at a Woolworth's lunch counter in Montgomery. *The Times* received about $4,800 to run the ad.[43]

The New York Times sold 394 copies in Alabama in 1960. One of the thirty-five copies sold in the state capital came to the attention of the editor of *The Montgomery Advertiser*.[44] He brought it to the attention of his readers by writing an editorial criticizing the "crude slanders" against the city.[45] The next day city Commissioner L. B. Sullivan, whose responsibilities included oversight of the police department, wrote a letter demanding a retraction from *The Times*.

The advertisement did contain some errors. As *The Journal* story pointed out, black student leaders were expelled from Alabama State College after leading a sit-down strike at the courthouse grill. The ad said the expulsion followed the students singing "My Country 'Tis of Thee" on the capitol steps, when they actually had been singing the national anthem.[46] Another error concerned the statement that a dining hall had been padlocked "in an attempt to starve (the students) into submission" when they refused to register to protest the expulsion of the student leaders. The college did not padlock the hall, and registration for the spring semester nearly equaled registration for the previous fall semester.[47]

The Times responded to Sullivan's letter, asking why he felt his reputation had been damaged by the ad. He answered with a lawsuit, filed April 19, 1960, claiming he had been libeled by the ad. He also sued four Alabama ministers whose names were listed among those endorsing the ad's plea for contributions to Dr. King's defense fund. Other lawsuits filed by Alabama officials quickly followed. The newspaper was facing legal claims of $3 million.[48]

An all-white jury returned a verdict of $500,000 for Commissioner Sullivan after deliberating two hours and twenty minutes.[49] In August 1962, the Alabama Supreme Court upheld the jury's award. Herbert Wechsler, a professor at Columbia Law School who by then had argued a dozen cases before the Supreme Court, was approached to handle the appeal. Wechsler said he realized that in order to persuade the Supreme Court to review this decision he had to convince the court that the rules of libel in Alabama, which were similar to the libel statutes and case law in most states, violated the First Amendment guarantee of freedom of the press.[50]

In his petition to the Supreme Court, Wechsler, quoting a 1937 opinion of Chief Justice Charles Evans Hughes, argued that the libel awards by Alabama juries could stifle the "free political discussion" that was "the security of the Republic, the very foundation of government."[51] Within a month, the Supreme Court had accepted the case and heard oral arguments on January 6 and 7, 1964. The Court's unanimous decision reversing the Alabama court was announced on March 9. It remains a landmark in the development of the First Amendment.

Justice William Brennan Jr. first held that the *New York Times* ad differed from a typical commercial advertisement, which historically had little or no First Amendment protection. He said the "Heed Their Rising Voices" ad "communicated information, expressed opinion, recited grievances, protested claimed abuses, and sought financial support on behalf of a movement whose existence and objectives are matters of the highest public interest and concern."[52]

Then he addressed a most important point related to freedom of speech:

To what extent does the First Amendment protect citizens who criticize their government and their governors? Brennan declared that the Court had considered "this case against the background of a profound national commitment to the principle that debate on public issues should be uninhibited, robust and wide-open, and that it may well include vehement, caustic and sometimes unpleasantly sharp attacks on government and public officials...."[53] In doing so, he cited a 1932 opinion of Judge Learned Hand of the U.S. Court of Appeals, who had written that the First Amendment "presupposed that right conclusions are more likely to be gathered out of a multitude of tongues, than through any kind of authoritative selection."[54]

After stipulating that in the heat of debate, mistakes, like those in the *Times* ad, are going to be made, Brennan came to the remaining key issue: Does the First Amendment protect false information at some level? His answer was yes, and in language that would greatly strengthen the protection offered by the First Amendment, he wrote that "requiring critics of official conduct to guarantee the truth of all (their) factual assertions—and to do so on pain of libel judgments virtually unlimited in amount—leads to a comparable self-censorship."[55]

Justice Brennan then laid down the actual malice rule for libel lawsuits: "The constitutional guarantees (of the First and Fourteenth Amendments) require, we think, a federal rule that prohibits a public official from recovering damages for a defamatory falsehood relating to his official conduct unless he proves that the statement was made with 'actual malice'—that is, with knowledge that it was false or with reckless disregard of whether it was false or not."[56]

The Supreme Court had erected an important barrier to protect the press from libel lawsuits brought by public officials, which otherwise could have proven financially devastating. Those who hold important government positions would no longer be able to collect damages from journalists for criticizing them or their performance in office, unless the reporter knew the information published or broadcast was not true or the reporter should have known it was not true.

Three years later, that barrier was extended to include public figures and people who inject themselves into a public controversy hoping to influence public opinion.[57] In 1974, the Supreme Court ruled that states could set their own libel standards for private persons to prove in a lawsuit. Most of the states have chosen negligence, a much less difficult standard to prove than actual malice.[58]

Libel lawsuits actually are on the decline, and media defendants win more often than they used to, according to an organization that tracks lawsuits against the media.[59] But those lawsuits that are filed can prove costly, in terms of legal fees, time spent preparing for court, judgments and reputations of the reporters involved.

A lawsuit can result from aggressive reporting or careless reporting, the big story or the everyday story, a story about the mayor or an ordinary person. It is possible to do everything right and still be sued, although it is unlikely. Sound reporting practices, however, are the best hedge against losing a libel lawsuit.

Those good practices require reporters to have several sources for a story. Those sources must be reliable, people who are in a position to know the information the reporter seeks and who have a sound reputation. Reporters should avoid relying solely on people who have an ax to grind, have been convicted of crimes, have had mental problems or are known to lie. Reporters should check and double-check all the facts in the story because false information is a requirement for a libel lawsuit filed against a newspaper. Reporters should utilize public documents for information whenever they exist, and they should never rely on their memory but on their notes and previously published stories. Newspapers should give anyone criticized or accused of a crime in a story an opportunity to respond. Reporters should be careful to put stories in context, explaining the bigger picture that may give the readers a better idea of the significance of what has happened.

Attributing information is important, but if the information is false and damages someone's reputation, attribution will not always prevent a lawsuit. Avoid using words like "unprofessional" or "unscrupulous" because they can prove extremely damaging to a reputation. The word "allegedly" does not mitigate the damage of a false statement.

Free Press/Fair Trial: Do Reporters Have a Constitutional Right to Cover the Courts?

The Right to Attend Criminal Trials

Veteran *Louisville Courier-Journal* reporter Tom Loftus drove to the federal courthouse in Frankfort, Ky., on May 13, 2009, to attend a preliminary hearing in one of the most important political corruption cases in Kentucky over the past two decades. The former chief of the state's Transportation Cabinet, an appointee of the governor, had been indicted on charges he had leaked significant information about pending road construction contracts worth $130 million to a major highway contractor in return for $67,000.

But Loftus never heard any of the arguments about the six motions on the hearing docket that day. Federal marshals informed him that the hearing was closed by order of the federal magistrate presiding at the hearing.[60] It was closed despite the fact that two of the state's most powerful elected officials—the governor and the president of the state Senate—were on the witness list for the trial;[61] despite the fact that one of the defendants, a high-ranking state official, was accused of accepting a bribe; despite the fact that prosecutors argued that a bribe may have influenced the award of state road contracts worth millions of dollars of tax money[62] and despite the fact the First Amendment has been interpreted by courts to require that court-rooms be open to the public and the press.

Judges face a dilemma. While the First Amendment guarantees freedom of the press, the Sixth Amendment guarantees a fair and public trial to a defendant in criminal trials. Judges are required to protect the right of the defendant and the right of the press, sometimes in the face of pretrial pub-licity that is clearly prejudicial. While reporters are seeking to learn every-thing they can about a defendant and his actions, prosecutors are preparing their case for trial and the defense attorney is trying to be sure potential jurors are not reading and hearing news reports that will influence their deci-sion on the defendant's guilt or innocence.

The Kentucky road story was first reported on April 8, 2008, when the head of the transportation department in the new gubernatorial adminis-tration acknowledged that the FBI had sought information about the bid process for state road contracts.[63] From that point until June 2009, when the trial was scheduled to begin, the *Courier-Journal* published more than 50 stories about the case, the pretrial rulings and questions about the evi-dence.[64] In response, the judge ordered the trial be moved from the state capital, where many of the residents are state employees, to the northern part of the state, almost 95 miles, to help ensure the defendants would receive a fair trial.[65]

Attorneys for the *Courier-Journal* and the *Lexington Herald-Leader* filed motions to protest the magistrate's decision to close the May 13 hearing. The federal judge scheduled to preside over the corruption trial said the magistrate's decision had been correct but ordered a transcript of the hear-ing be prepared for the newspapers, certainly contradictory orders.[66]

The Supreme Court of the United States has said that courts should be open to the public and the press. In December 1975, the manager of the Holly Court Motel in Ashland, Virginia, was found stabbed to death in her apartment adjoining the motel office. The wallet of John P. Stevenson of Baltimore was found near the body, and he had been seen at the motel with his brother-in-law, who had a room adjoining the victim's apartment. Stevenson was arrested and in July 1976, he was found guilty and sen-tenced to 10 years in prison. The state Supreme Court, however, reversed his conviction and ordered a new trial, ruling that the defendant's bloody shirt should not have been admitted as evidence.[67] Stevenson's second and third trials were declared mistrials because of problems involving jurors. At the beginning of the fourth trial in September 1978, the defense asked the judge to clear the public and the press from the courtroom to ensure that there was no collusion among witnesses about their testimony. The prose-cution didn't object, and the judge ordered all spectators and reporters removed from the courtroom. The judge later that day denied an objection of the newspaper. The next day, before a courtroom empty of reporters or ordinary citizens, the judge granted a defense motion to dismiss the murder charge.[68]

The Supreme Court, in response to the question whether the right of the public and press to attend criminal trials is guaranteed under the U.S. Constitution, answered "yes" by a vote of 7–1. Chief Justice Warren Burger, writing for the majority, noted that criminal trials dating back to thirteenth-century England had been open to anyone who chose to attend. "From these early times, although great changes in courts and procedure took place, one thing remained constant: the public character of the trial at which guilt or innocence was decided."[69] The Court had addressed the issue even more emphatically in 1948:

> We have been unable to find a single instance of a criminal trial conducted [in closed chambers] in any federal, state, or municipal court during the history of this country. Nor have we found any record of even one such secret criminal trial in England since abolition of the Court of Star Chamber in 1641, and whether that court ever convicted people secretly is in dispute....This nation's accepted practice of guaranteeing a public trial to an accused has its roots in our English common law heritage. The exact date of its origin is obscure, but it likely evolved long before the settlement of our land as an accompaniment of the ancient institution of jury trial.[70]

In Burger's 1980 opinion, he explained why courtrooms should remain open to the public: witnesses will more likely tell the truth, fearing someone will hear a lie and expose it. An open judicial process provides a therapeutic purpose, creating "an outlet for community concern, hostility and emotion." No "community catharsis can occur if justice is" conducted in secret. "People in an open society do not demand infallibility from their institutions, but it is difficult for them to accept what they are prohibited from observing. When a criminal trial is conducted in the open, there is at least an opportunity both for understanding the system in general and its workings in a particular case."[71] He also recognized that journalists attend courts as surrogates for the public.[72]

In 1982, the Supreme Court ruled unconstitutional a state law that allowed for automatic closure of a rape or sexual assault case during the testimony of minors. The Court said that judges must decide the issue on a case-by-case basis.[73] Some courts also have closed the courtroom during the testimony of an undercover police officer if revealing the officer's identity would be dangerous.[74]

Supreme Court decisions have clearly established that criminal trials must be open to the public and the press. While lower federal and state courts have ruled that civil courts also must be open to the public, the Supreme Court has never addressed the issue.[75]

What should a reporter do when a judge moves to close the courtroom? The reporter should politely ask the court to be recognized or ask to speak to the judge privately. If the judge recognizes the reporter, he should identify himself and his employer and ask the judge to call a recess until the newspaper can contact its attorney. (Reporters should go to court knowing the newspaper's policy on openness and knowing the name of the newspaper's attorney.) If the judge declines to recognize the reporter or denies her request for a recess, the reporter should leave the courtroom and call her editor immediately. Reporters should always be respectful of the judiciary, even if the judge rules against an open courtroom. Judges hold the power of contempt, even if they rule wrongly. In either case, the newspaper or its attorney should ask the judge to hold a hearing on the newspaper's request to reopen the court to the public and the press. If the newspaper does not have an attorney, some state press organizations offer legal assistance. The Reporters Committee for Freedom of the Press makes available its Legal Defense Hotline, 1–800–336–4243.[76]

The Right to Attend Preliminary Hearings

If criminal trials must be open to the public and the press, must all parts of the proceeding also be open? Since a Supreme Court decision in 1986, courtrooms have presumptively been open, and a party that seeks to close it must convince the judge that a good reason exists to close the proceedings.[77] If the request is made, the Court must conduct a hearing on the request and ask whether the closure would be "essential to preserve higher values" and "narrowly tailored to serve that interest."[78]

This includes preliminary hearings, hearings on bail, *voir dire* (questioning members of the jury pool to select a jury panel), and sentencing hearings.

The Right to Report on Court Proceedings

The Supreme Court also has declared that judges who try to stop reporters or newspapers from printing information revealed in court or in court documents are violating the First Amendment guarantee of freedom of the press. In October 1975, six members of a Nebraska family were murdered. The deaths attracted substantial media attention, and the judge entered an order prohibiting reporters who attended a preliminary hearing from publishing anything they learned at the hearing until a jury had been chosen for the trial and sequestered. The Supreme Court in 1976 ruled that the judge, while attempting to protect the Sixth Amendment rights of the defendant, had violated the First Amendment rights of the press.[79]

To ensure a fair trial for the accused without trampling the rights of the press, the Court said in a previous decision that judges could take alternative steps including moving the trial to another location where the publicity is less intense; postponing the trial to allow the publicity to subside;

questioning potential jurors carefully to ensure they are capable of making a decision uncolored by pretrial publicity; giving clear instructions to the jury that emphasize their responsibility to decide the verdict only on the basis of evidence and testimony presented; and sequestering the jurors to try to ensure they are not exposed to more news reports.[80]

The Issue of Juvenile Hearings

While courts in the United States are presumptively open to the public and the press, hearings involving children and teenagers often are not. The Supreme Court has never ruled that court procedures involving juveniles must be open to the public and the press.[81] Only New Hampshire bans everyone except affected parties from the courtroom. Most states have laws that allow the court to be open only on petition of the juvenile, allow the judge to admit interested parties or allow the judge to admit the public and the press.[82]

The states established juvenile justice systems centered on the belief that juvenile delinquents could be rehabilitated. To encourage rehabilitation and to limit the possibility that a young person would be stigmatized throughout life by a childhood mistake, states designed their systems to protect delinquency proceedings and juvenile records from the public and the press.[83] As proof of the success of this policy, supporters point to Adlai Stevenson, the former governor of Illinois, presidential candidate and ambassador to the United Nations who as a child fatally shot a playmate with what he thought was an unloaded gun.[84]

But public attitudes have been shifting as juvenile crime rates have increased and as more juveniles have committed heinous crimes. In cases where a juvenile is accused of a crime that is considered a felony, court records and proceedings are now public in Idaho, Indiana, Iowa, Maine, Maryland, Minnesota, Missouri, Utah and Virginia.[85] Under the federal juvenile Delinquency Act, judges have the discretion to open hearings of defendants under 21 years old charged with violating a federal law.[86]

The Supreme Court has ruled that a state law barring the media from publishing the name of a juvenile accused of a crime is unconstitutional. When a 14-year-old shot and killed another junior high school student in 1978 in St. Albans, West Virginia, reporters for newspapers in Charleston learned the identity of the victim and the assailant from witnesses. Both newspapers eventually published the name and were indicted for violating the state law. The Supreme Court ruled that state punishment for the publication of lawfully obtained truthful information can seldom be constitutional.[87]

Reporters should check with their state press associations or their newspapers' attorney about laws and court rules in their states concerning access to juvenile courts. Many require a reporter to file a petition seeking access well in advance of the hearing.

Reporter's Privilege: Can Prosecutors Force Journalists to Identify Their Sources?

Arguably the most memorable scene from the most memorable movie about the most memorable political scandal in the United States occurred in a dimly lit garage in the nation's capital. For three decades, the man with the glowing cigarette, his face obscured by the shadows, was known simply as "Deep Throat." He was a key source in assisting *Washington Post* reporters Carl Bernstein and Bob Woodward as they painstakingly unraveled the Watergate cover-up that ultimately toppled the only American president forced to resign. In writing about their source thirty years later, Woodward and Bernstein said Deep Throat "confirmed the breadth of questionable and illegal activities by [the Committee for the Re-election of the President] and the White House and their possible significance, and he carefully steered us in important directions, supporting the theme we were discovering in our reporting: namely that the Watergate burglary was not an isolated event but part of a sweeping pattern of illegal, undercover activities aimed at perceived Nixon enemies...."[88]

Deep Throat was W. Mark Felt, who in 1973 was the acting associate director of the FBI, then the second-highest position in the bureau. He walked out of the shadows in May 2005, revealing his role in the Watergate investigation three years before his death at age 95.[89] He was almost certainly the most famous anonymous source in the history of American journalism, but thousands of others have provided tips, copies of documents and other information that enabled reporters to pull back the curtain on some government secrets and expose wrongdoing.

Their motives are their own. Some fear losing their jobs, their careers or even their lives. Some don't want to be embarrassed by being at the center of a controversy. Some want to get even. Some are driven by a sense of justice. Some want to see their bosses brought down because of the way they treat others. Some want to expose the waste of tax dollars or blow the whistle on fraud without losing their jobs. Whatever the reason, they provide information that enables reporters to expose government secrets, much of it information that would not be available in any other way.

Most reporters use confidential sources, but many say they use them sparingly, according to a survey conducted by the Freedom Forum's First Amendment Center in conjunction with Investigative Reporters and Editors and the Radio Television Digital News Association. Fifty-nine percent of the 711 journalists who completed an online survey in December 2004 said confidential sources were the basis for about ten percent of the stories they had written or broadcast in their careers. However, 86 percent of those journalists said the use of confidential sources was essential to their ability to report some news stories. One of ten said they had never used a confidential source.[90]

Anonymous sources, however, present problems. Many journalists believe that anonymous sources undermine the credibility of the story. "Reporters really recognize, as do editors, that when you can name sources, you have a much more authoritative first draft of history than you do with one larded with anonymous sources," said Jill Abramson, the managing editor for news at *The New York Times*.[91]

In the nation's capital, however, quoting unnamed sources is more of a rule than an exception. Consider this example recorded by Clark Hoyt, public editor of *The New York Times:*

> ...President Obama recently...joined senior members of his administration who were arguing with The Times's David Brooks about one of his columns. In Brooks's next column, about this meeting, the most senior of all officials simply became one of "four senior members of the administration." His cover was blown later. I asked Brooks if he had asked the president to go on the record. He said he had not, because "I thought in those informal circumstances it would be wrong to quote him by name."[92]

Imagine having a debate with the president of the United States over a policy and referring to him in a subsequent column as a "senior member of the administration." But in Washington, in the rough and tumble of national politics, government sources are often reluctant to provide information unless they are guaranteed varying degrees of anonymity.[93] And as Brooks's column illustrates, even veteran journalists accustomed to the national stage have bought into this practice. Ben Bradlee, former executive editor of the *Washington Post*, criticizes the press for its reliance on anonymous sources, even though the Watergate stories that ran while he was editor used many of them. "Why, then, do we go along so complacently with withholding the identity of public officials?" After acknowledging that he did not know, he continued, "I do know that by doing so, we shamelessly do other people's bidding: We knowingly let ourselves be used....In short, we demean our profession."[94]

The legal problem comes when a reporter publishes a story that is based on an anonymous informant, and the story either attracts the attention of a prosecutor who believes a crime has been committed or those named in the story believe they have been libeled. The reporter receives a subpoena to appear before a grand jury and testify as to what she knows about what she wrote in the story and to identify the anonymous source so that the grand jurors can listen to what that person knows about the commission of a crime. Or in the case of a libel lawsuit, the plaintiff's attorney demands the identity of the source and, if the reporter refuses to reveal it, asks a judge to order the reporter to identify the source.

In a 2001 survey conducted by the Reporters Committee for Freedom of the Press, 319 media outlets reported receiving a total of 823 subpoenas.[95] The U.S. Justice Department said in 2001 that during the previous decade it had issued subpoenas for eighty-eight journalists. Of that number, seventeen demanded the identity of confidential sources while others sought notes, unpublished materials or testimony to verify material that had been published or broadcast. Citing the need for grand jury secrecy, the department declined to say whether any confidential sources had been disclosed.[96] Between 2001 and 2006, the Justice Department said the attorney general approved requests for 65 subpoenas.[97]

The fight between journalists and government over sources originated as early as the colonial period. Printers provided confidentiality to many contributors and published letters that were anonymous or submitted under a pseudonym. Some of them even resisted demands from the government to reveal the sources' names. They argued that journalism ethics and their own livelihood required them to avoid revealing the identity of confidential sources. The public interest in good government also required journalists to protect those sources because some stories could be told only if reporters promised confidentiality to those who had information about government corruption.[98]

The Supreme Court of the United States has considered the question of whether the First Amendment provides a privilege for reporters that allows them to protect their sources. In 1972, taking up the cases of three reporters who had been ordered separately to appear before grand juries and identify their sources, the justices ruled 5–4 that the First Amendment does not exempt journalists from the requirement that citizens must testify before a grand jury.[99]

This case should never have been the one to test this important constitutional principle. Prosecutors sought the testimony of reporters who either had witnessed a crime or were believed by prosecutors to have witnessed a crime. Thus the case was mostly unrepresentative of those in which reporters offer confidentiality to their sources.

But rather than answer the question of whether the First Amendment provides a privilege that would exempt reporters from testifying before a grand jury, the Court's decision simply ignited the debate. Judges have since held that the Supreme Court decision dealt only with grand jury subpoenas and endorsed reporter's privilege in other proceedings.[100]

But in the past ten years, journalists have been locked up or threatened with jail for not revealing their sources in legal proceedings. A Texas freelance journalist, Vanessa Leggett, spent 168 days in jail in 2001 when she refused to turn over notes from an interview to a federal prosecutor.[101] A Pulitzer Prize winner, *New York Times* reporter Judith Miller, spent eighty-five days in jail when she refused to identify a source she never used in a story.[102] One of the most extraordinary cases involved a former federal worker who sued the FBI after investigators leaked information that accused him of providing classified information to the Chinese government. When five reporters refused to identify their sources, a judge found them in contempt. Their media employers—ABC, the Associated Press, *The Los Angeles*

Times, *The New York Times* and *The Washington Post*—participated in a $1.7 million settlement in 2006 to eliminate the possibility the reporters would go to jail for contempt or be forced to identify their sources.[103] *San Francisco Chronicle* reporters Lance Williams and Mark Fainaru-Wada were found in contempt for refusing to explain how they obtained a copy of grand jury testimony. Their reporting revealed the widespread use of steroids in baseball. Nevertheless, they likely would have gone to jail if the defense attorney who leaked it had not been identified.[104] But the record for jail time belongs to Josh Wolf, a video blogger, who spent 226 days in jail for refusing to turn over a video of a demonstration by anarchists.[105]

Thirty-seven states and the District of Columbia have enacted some degree of protection for journalists in the form of state shield laws.[106] The first was passed by Maryland in 1896 and the most recent was enacted by Texas in May 2009. They vary in the degree of protection they offer journalists and how they define a journalist.[107] Twelve of the remaining 13 states—Wyoming is the exception—offer some shield protection either in their state constitution or through a state court ruling. Despite repeated attempts, Congress has not passed a shield law that would protect journalists in the federal court system, but as 2009 closed, the House of Representatives had passed such legislation and the Senate Judiciary Committee had sent a similar bill to the floor for a vote.

Recognizing the possible consequences of taking information off the record, reporters should assess the situation carefully before agreeing to do so. They should know the policy of their newspaper and follow it closely because taking information off the record can have unintended consequences. It is wise to consult with an editor before making any agreements. Be clear with the source what you are agreeing to; does this mean the information cannot be used at all, can be used only if someone else confirms it or can be used as long as the source is not identified? Understand the source's motive before making any agreement. Does this source have important information? Does this source have an ulterior motive? Does this source seem to be trying to use the newspaper for his or her own purposes?

Notes

1. Richard Labunski, *James Madison and the Struggle for the Bill of Rights* (New York: Oxford University Press, 2006), 10–12.
2. Ibid., 192–199.
3. Ibid., 217–235.
4. Ibid., 235–236.
5. Ibid., 266.
6. *Gitlow v. New York*, 268 U.S. 652, 666 (1925). "For present purposes we may and do assume that freedom of speech and of the press—which are protected by the First Amendment from abridgment by Congress—are among the fundamental

personal rights and 'liberties' protected by the due process clause of the Fourteenth Amendment from impairment by the States."

7. Bruce W. Sanford and Jane E. Kirtley, "The First Amendment Tradition and Its Critics" in Geneva Overholser and Kathleen Hall Jamieson, *The Press* (New York: Oxford University Press, 2005), 263.

8. *Robertson v. Baldwin*, 165 U.S. 275, 281 (1897).

9. *Whitney v. California*, 274 U.S. 357, 375–77 (1927) (*Brandeis, J., concurring*).

10. Jason Riley, "EKU Student Sues over Anonymous Post," *Courier-Journal* (Louisville), June 28, 2009.

11. Robert E. Kessler, "Suit by Corbin against *Newsday*, News12 thrown out," *Newsday* (New York), posted on May 28, 2009, available at http://www.news-day.com/news/local/politics/ny-pocorb3012820418may29,0,4216260.story (accessed November 20, 2009).

12. "Colorado Judge Refuses to Gag Press in Sex Abuse Case," Reporters Committee for Freedom of the Press, posted on May 19, 2009, available at http://www.rcfp.org/newsitems/index.php?i=10761 (accessed November 20, 2009).

13. Henry Campbell Black, *Black's Law Dictionary* (St. Paul, Minn.: West Group, 1990), 1194.

14. Joseph R. LaPlante, "S-T challenges gag order in drug case, "*Standard Times* (New Bedford, Mass.), posted on April 5, 2005, available at http://archive.south-coasttoday.com/daily/04–05/04–06–05/a01l0066.htm (accessed November 20, 2009).

15. William David Sloan, ed., *The Media in America* (Northport, Ala.: Vision Press, 2008), 39–40.

16. Eric Burns, *Famous Scribblers* (New York: PublicAffairs, 2006) 30–33.

17. J. Herbert Altschull, *From Milton to McLuhan: The Ideas Behind Journalism* (White Plains, N.Y.: Longman, 1990), 176–177.

18. Paul Starr, "*The Creation of the Media: Political Origins of Modern Communications*" (New York: Basic Books, 2004), 38.

19. Ibid., 65–67.

20. *Grosjean v. American Press Co.*, 297 U.S. 233 (1936).

21. The Minnesota Gag Law provided "whenever any such nuisance is committed or exists, the county attorney of any county where any such periodical is published or circulated...may maintain an action in the district court of the county in the name of the state to enjoin perpetually the persons committing or maintaining any such nuisance from further committing or maintaining it. Upon such evidence as the court shall deem sufficient, a temporary injunction may be granted." Mason's Minnesota Statutes, 1927 §§ 10123–1 to 10123–3.

22. This story is told in Fred W. Friendly, *Minnesota Rag* (New York: Vintage Press, 1981).

23. *Near v. Minnesota*, 283 U.S. 697 (1931).

24. *Near*, 714.

25. Marin Scordato, "Distinction Without a Difference: A Reappraisal of the Doctrine of Prior Restraint," *North Carolina Law Review* (1989, Volume 68), 1, 2.

26. Friendly, *supra* note 22, at 163.

27. David Rudenstine, *The Day the Presses Stopped* (Berkeley, Calif.: University of California Press, 1996), 33–42.

28. Ibid., 43.

29. Ibid., 45.

30. Sanford J. Ungar, *The Papers and the Papers* (New York: Columbia University Press, 1972, 1989), 14.

31. Ibid., 120–122.

32. Rudenstine, *supra* note 27, at 2.

33. Ibid., 130–142.

34. Ibid., 185.

35. *New York Times v. United States*, 403 U.S. 713, 714 (1971)

36. *Bantam Books, Inc.* v. *Sullivan*, 372 U.S. 58, 70, (1963)

37. Eric Lichtblau and James Risen, "Bank Data Sifted in Secret by U.S. to Block Terror," *New York Times*, June 23, 2006.

38. Dan Rozek and Eric Herman, "Justice gets $3 mil., apology: Newspaper settles Supreme Court chief's lawsuit," *The Chicago Sun-Times*, October 12, 2007.

39. Dan Horn, "Enquirer Paid Chiquita $14 Million in Settlement, Magazine Reports," *The Cincinnati Enquirer*, January 24, 2001.

40. *New York Times Co. v. Sullivan*, 376 U.S. 254 (1964).

41. The ad appeared in the *New York Times* on March 29, 1960.

42. At his trial during the last week of May, Dr. King was acquitted. The state could produce no evidence for its charge that he had committed perjury. Anthony Lewis, *Make No Law: The Sullivan Case and the First Amendment* (New York: Vintage Books, 1991), 27.

43. Rodney A. Smolla, *Suing the Press: Libel, The Media & Power* (New York: Oxford University Press, 1986), 30.

44. Ibid.

45. Lewis, *supra* note 41, at 10–11.

46. During the trial, other errors were noted. The students were expelled not in connection with singing on the state capitol steps but after seeking service at the lunch counter at the Montgomery County Court House. Also, Dr. King had been arrested four times, not seven, as the ad said.

47. Lewis, *supra* note 41, at 10–11.

48. Ibid., 12–15. Justice Black wrote that the Columbia Broadcasting System also had been sued for libel; five suits sought judgments that totaled $1.7 million. *New York Times v. Sullivan*, 376 U.S. 254, 295 (1964) (*Black, J, concurring*).

49. The two black jurors in the pool had been struck by attorneys for Commissioner Sullivan. During the trial, Judge Jones referred to the white attorneys for Sullivan as Mr. Nachman and Mr. Embry, but he called the black attorneys for the black ministers Lawyer Gray and Lawyer Crawford. At the outset of the trial, Judge Jones announced the seating in the courtroom would not be integrated. Lewis, *supra* note 41, at 27.

50. Ibid., 106–108.

51. *DeJonge v. Oregon*, 299 U.S. 353, 365 (1937).

52. *New York Times v. Sullivan*, 376 U.S. 254, 266 (1964).

53. *New York Times*, at 270.

54. *New York Times*, citing *United States v. Associated Press*, 52 F.Supp. 362, 372 (S.D.N.Y., 1943).

55. *New York Times*, at 266.

56. *New York Times*, at 270.

57. *Curtis Publishing v. Butts*, 388 U.S. 130, (1967).

58. *Gertz v. Robert Welch*, 418 U.S. 333 (1974.)

59. Media Law Resource Center @ *www.medialaw.org*.

60. *United States v. Leonard Lawson, Charles William Nighbert, Brian Russell Billings*, 3:08-CR-21-DCR, (E.D. Ky.) Courier-Journal's motion to intervene.

61. Tom Loftus, "Beshear Testimony Sought in Bribe Case," *Courier-Journal* (Louisville), May 20, 2009; "Senator Expected to be Called as Trial Witness," *Courier-Journal* (Louisville), May 23, 2009.

62. Tom Loftus and Stephenie Steitzer, "Lawson, Nighbert Indicted," *Courier-Journal* (Louisville), September 4 , 2008.

63. Tom Loftus, "FBI Studies Road Bids under Fletcher," *Courier-Journal* (Louisville), April 9, 2008.

64. The judge subsequently postponed the trial and recused himself after he discovered he had a conflict of interest dating to his days as an attorney in private practice. Tom Loftus, "Trial in Bid-rigging Case Is Postponed," *Courier-Journal* (Louisville), June 10, 2009.

65. Tom Loftus, "Judge Moves Highway Bidding Trial to Covington," *Courier-Journal* (Louisville), March 3, 2008. The new judge scheduled the trial for Lexington.

66. Stephenie Steitzer, "Judge Unseals Transcript of Closed Hearing," *Courier-Journal* (Louisville), May 29, 2009.

67. *John Paul Stevenson v. Commonwealth of Virginia*, 218 Va. 462 (1977).

68. *Richmond Newspapers v. Virginia*, 448 U.S. 555 (1980).

69. *Richmond Newspapers*, at 566.

70. *In re Oliver*, 333 U.S. 257, 266 (1948).

71. *Richmond Newspapers*, at 572.

72. *Richmond Newspapers*, at 573.

73. *Globe Newspaper Co. v. Norfolk County Superior Court*, 457 U.S. 596 (1982).

74. *New York v. Rivera*, 656 N.Y.S. 2d 884 (1997).

75. *Prolicker Industries v. Cohen*, 733 F.2d 1059 (1984); *NBC Subsidiary v. Superior Court*, 980 P. 2d 337 (1999).

76. The Reporters Committee for Freedom of the Press @ www.rcfp.org/about.html#hotline.

77. *Press-Enterprise v. Riverside Superior Court*, 478 U.S. 1 (1986).

78. *Press-Enterprise v. Riverside Superior Court*, 464 U.S. 501, 510 (1984).

79. *Nebraska Press Association v. Judge Stuart*, 427 U.S. 539 (1976).

80. *Sheppard v. Maxwell*, 384 U.S. 333, 361 (1966).

81. In *In re Gault*, 387 U.S. 1, 25 (1967), the United States Supreme Court stated, "There is no reason why, consistently with due process, a State cannot continue, if it deems it appropriate, to provide and to improve provision for the confidentiality of records of police contacts and court action relating to juveniles."

82. "Media Access to Juvenile Justice: Should Freedom of the Press Be Limited to Promote Rehabilitation of Youthful Offenders?" *Temple Law Review* (Winter 1995, Volume 68), 1897.

83. Danielle R. Oddo, "Removing Confidentiality Protections and the 'Get Tough' Rhetoric," *Boston College Third World Law Journal* (Winter 1998, Volume 18), 105.

84. Ibid.

85. Reporters Committee for Freedom of the Press, "Access to Juvenile Courts," available at http://www.rcfp.org/juvcts/index.html#a (accessed November 20, 2009).

86. Ibid.

87. *Smith v. Daily Mail Publishing Co.*, 443 U.S. 97 (1979).

88. Bob Woodward, *The Secret Man* (New York: Simon & Schuster, 2005), 7.

89. David Von Drehle, "FBI's No. 2 Was 'Deep Throat,'" *Washington Post*, June 1, 2005, A1.

90. First Amendment Center, *Survey Suggests Journalists Use Confidential Sources Sparingly*, press release March 17, 2005, available at http://www.fac.org/news.aspx?id=14988 (accessed November 20, 2009).

91. Clark Hoyt, "Those Persistent Anonymous Sources," *The New York Times*, March 21, 2009.

92. Ibid.

93. Michael Sheehy, "Foreign News Sources More Likely to Include Unnamed Sources," *Newspaper Research Journal* (Summer 2008, Volume 29: 3), 24–25.

94. John R. Bender, Lucinda D. Davenport, Michael W. Drager & Fred Fedler, *Reporting for the Media* (New York: Oxford University Press, 2009, 9th ed.), 256.

95. Reporters Committee for Freedom of the Press, *Agents of Discovery: A Report on the Incidence of Subpoenas Served on the News Media in 2001*, 4 (2003). It is possible, however, that the numbers are understated because of lack of response. In 1999, 440 news organizations that responded to a similar survey for the Reporters Committee reported receiving 1,326 subpoenas.

96. Adam Liptak and Peter T. Kilborn, "2 Journalists Subpoenaed over Source of Disclosure," *New York Times*, May 23, 2004, at A22.

97. *Shields and Subpoenas: The reporter's privilege in federal courts*, Reporters Committee for Freedom of the Press, available at www.rcfp.org/shields_and_subpoenas.html#number (accessed November 20, 2009).

98. A. David Gordon, "Protection of News Sources: The History and Legal Status of the Newsman's Privilege" (PhD diss. University of Wisconsin, 1971), 440.

99. *Branzburg v. Hayes*, 408 U.S. 665 (1972).

100. Anthony Fargo, "Analyzing Federal Shield Law Proposals: What Congress Can Learn from the States," *Communications Law & Policy* (Winter 2006, Volume 11), 35, 39.

101. Ross E. Milloy, "Writer Who Was Jailed In Notes Dispute Is Freed," *New York Times*, January 5, 2002, at A8.

102. Adam Liptak, "Reporter Jailed After Refusing to Name Source," *New York Times*, July 6, 2005, at A1.

103. Adam Liptak, "News Media Pay in Scientist Suit," *New York Times*, June 3, 2006, at A1.

104. Jesse McKinley, "Reporters Avoid Jail in Balco Case," *New York Times*, February 15, 2007, at D2.

105. Jesse McKinley, "8-Month Jail Term Ends as Maker of Video Turns Over a Copy," *New York Times*, April 4, 2007, at A9.

106. Ahnalese Rushman, "Texas becomes 37th state to enact a shiled law," *News Media & the Law* (Spring 2009, Vol. 33: 2), at 26

107. Laurence B. Alexander & Leah G. Cooper, "Words That Shield: A Textual Analysis of the Journalist's Privilege," *Newspaper Research Journal* (1997, Volume 18), 51.

10

The Newspaper
Meets the Internet

Deborah S. Chung*

The days of only reading a newspaper, watching the evening news on television or listening to National Public Radio's Morning Edition are quickly fading. The media environment today is a complicated system of information sources on a multi-media platform. While the traditional forms of media—the newspaper, the radio and the television—relied on a single mode of information delivery, today's media environment invites, or even requires, the news audience to use multiple informational channels.

Today's news audiences, however, are turning to the Internet as their primary source of information, where they find the opportunity to use visual, audio and text-based informational sources altogether. They can even interact with the news. Thus the presentation of news has become unquestionably more complex.

This process of merging media, the process of multi-platform publishing or cross-platform consolidation in news delivery, is referred to as convergence. But the process requires more than taking news stories from one medium and copying them to another. It entails taking a newspaper story and adapting it for the Internet and adding interactive features so that readers can participate in experiencing the story. On some platforms the print story will be married with video interviews or footage from the event. It may be wedded not with one picture but with a gallery of pictures and sound.

All of this can and has produced clashes of traditional newsroom cultures: the blurring of lines between photographers, videographers and reporters; the demand for multi-skilled journalists who can report, write and shoot photographs and video; and the cooperation between television stations and newspapers, once rivals in gathering and reporting the news.

While the emergence of various new technological tools has taken center stage in such discussions, convergence is not merely about technology. This chapter explores definitions of convergence, its emergence and significance, its practices and its reception and its implications for the future.

What Is Convergence?

In his book *Convergent Journalism: The Fundamentals of Multimedia Reporting*, Stephen Quinn examines the emergence of convergence as a new form of storytelling.[1] But he notes that the concept is hard to define. He conducted numerous in-depth interviews with forward-thinking media professionals in successfully converged newsrooms and held discussions with leading academics about their visions for the future of journalism. He discovered that the definition of convergence varied from "country to country, company to company and culture to culture."[2] In his view, convergence may be seen as the process of telling news stories through multiple media platforms to communicate the story through the most appropriate medium through cooperation and collaboration to better serve the public interest. His focus is on the latter. Ultimately, it is about doing better journalism in the digital news media environment.

Janet Kolodzy, a faculty member at Emerson College, said it best: "When it comes to journalism, convergence means a new way of thinking about the news, producing the news, and delivering the news, using all media to their fullest potential to reach a diverse and increasingly distracted public."[3] She underscored that convergence refocused journalism to its core mission of informing the public about its world in the best way possible—in a multiple media way.

Full convergence is not merely about sharing staff, creating partnerships or sharing content. Full convergence refers to a radical change in mindset and approach. It is about working together to create the most meaningful journalism for the audience. Kerry Northrup, former director of Newsplex, a facility for professionals and academics at the University of South Carolina dedicated to studying and learning about new media, said convergence is important because it offers new ways for audiences to absorb and experience news and is not just about journalists creating new ways to present stories.[4]

Why the Emergence of Convergence?

Since the mid-1990s news organizations around the globe have been trying to make media collaborations work.[5] While no single factor can be pinned down as "causing" convergence, it can largely be attributed to the integration of the Internet in the daily lives of individuals around the world.

In 2004, Jane Singer, a professor at the University of Iowa's School of Journalism, said the process of convergence in the United States is due in part to the deregulatory environment in Washington and the resulting growth in media companies owning multiple other media outlets.[6] Such deregulation and the subsequent concentration of economic and political power to a select few media giants have raised concern about the absence of diversity in the content of the audiences' daily informational diet. However, Singer cautioned that convergence is not the same thing as deregulation or consolidation. Rather, it refers to cooperation among various media outlets, namely print and television and online journalists, to work together to deliver a product to as many audiences as possible.[7]

Technology and the Internet

The Internet allows various media forms to merge and offers audiences numerous ways to consume news. It has also changed the way audiences think about news. The audience no longer needs to wait for tomorrow's newspaper to read about current events. The audience no longer needs to wait in front of the television to visually experience a breaking news story. The audience no longer needs to listen to stories being broadcast to them from news block to news block on the radio to learn about information of their particular interests. In other words, the Internet allows audiences to actively experience news when they want it and how they want it. News websites offer up-to-the-minute information, customized news stories and multimedia downloads. Viewers can watch the six o'clock news whenever they wish, or they can watch or listen to a broadcast multiple times.

Since the advent of journalism, technology has played a critical role in the profession. From Gutenberg's printing press and the development of photography to radio and television, technological transformations have advanced journalism practice and at the same time challenged existing journalism conventions.[8] Newspapers, for example, which have been losing readership for decades,[9] have migrated online hoping to regain their audience through the interactive lure of the medium.[10]

In this regard, technology is key in the evolution of news. The penetration of broadband in particular has had a significant impact. High-speed Internet has dramatically changed the way people consume media. A 2005 Yahoo Inc. and Mediaedge:cia report found that consumers went online for deeper content, entertainment and communication capabilities. The report also found that broadband users viewed twice as many pages per month compared with consumers with dial-up connections.[11] A 2009 Pew report found a 15 percent growth rate in broadband usage from a year earlier despite the rise in cost for the service. As of April 2009, 63 percent of the population had broadband Internet access, with increased broadband adoption among older people, rural people, low-income people and people with high school diplomas. Mobile technologies are also changing the way people receive and share news as more users receive news through mobile devices.[12]

Evolving Information-Seeking Behaviors

While technology is a key player in the emergence of the global convergence phenomenon of news industries, the changing patterns of those seeking information have also contributed heavily.

The western world is witnessing staggering amounts of general media consumption and the growth of various types of media. The 2004 Communications Industry Forecast showed that in the United States, the average consumer spent 3,475 hours of the 8,760 hours in a year using all forms of media, including recorded music, video games, home video and yellow pages.[13] According to North American Technographics Benchmark Surveys, in 2004, in a typical week, people spent two hours reading magazines, four hours reading newspapers, eight hours listening to radio, about seven hours using the Internet and about thirteen hours watching television.[14] In 2005, Ball State University's Middletown Media project tracked the media use habits of 350 individuals. It found people spent about 30 percent of their waking day with media that was not work-related, while they spent 20.8 percent of their day on work activity.

The project researchers reported the following overall amounts of media minutes per user per day based on the 5,000 hours of observations recorded:

- Television: 240.9 minutes
- Any computer use: 135.8 minutes
- All Internet: 93.4 minutes
- Radio: 80.0 minutes
- Music [includes MP3 players]: 65.1 minutes
- Phone, includes cell phones: 42.2 minutes
- All print media: 32.8 minutes
- All video [VCR and DVD]: 32.6 minutes
- Newspapers: 12.2 minutes
- Game console: 11.6 minutes[15]

More recent figures indicate that time spent with media is growing. The amount of time U.S. Internet users spend watching video has increased a whopping 40 percent.[16] According to a report, online viewers tuned in to 273.1 minutes of video online in November 2008 compared with 195 minutes in November 2007. The number of online videos also increased 34 percent. That represents 12.7 billion videos, which is also an increase from 9.5 billion in November 2007.[17]

Another factor contributing to convergence is the increase in consumers using multiple forms of media simultaneously. People are engaging in a high degree of multimedia multitasking.[18] A study of simultaneous media consumption released in 2004 by The Media Center at the American Press Institute revealed:

- 74.2 percent of media consumers regularly or occasionally watch TV and read the newspaper at the same time.
- 66.2 percent of media consumers regularly or occasionally watch TV while going online.
- People listen to the radio (52.1 percent), watch TV (61.8 percent) and read the newspaper (20.2 percent) while they wait for downloads from the Internet.[19]

Ball State University's Middletown Media project in 2005 also stressed the importance of concurrent media exposure and its implications for journalists and advertisers as it is becoming increasingly important to consider not only which medium to use in presenting news but also how much time and attention will be given by news audiences.[20]

Personalization and Fragmentation

The multiple uses of media and the significant amounts of media consumption overall also led to personalization of news. Consumers could and did actively seek what they found interesting and even tailored news reports to their liking. Many news websites today offer e-newsletters or news alerts. Audiences can subscribe to RSS feeds, also known as "Really Simple Syndication" or "Rich Site Summary," a format for delivering updated or changing news content. They can also share news through social bookmarking sites that allow users to store, organize and share Web resources, such as Delicious, and through social networking sites, such as Facebook. Ultimately, news consumers derive an increased sense of control and bypass layers of information that used to be communicated in a top-down, one-way fashion.

While such personalization of news seems appealing, it also has implications for the mass media. It fragments an audience that was once a mass. Countless information sources exist offline and online, and more channels appear by the minute. For example, people are watching more television, but the proliferation of channels suggests that viewership per channel will keep decreasing.[21] With the exponential growth of new content being created for the Internet, news consumers will continue to be divided into smaller and smaller audience segments.

Three Types of Convergence

Scholars have conceptualized convergence in various ways, but it is helpful to discuss three main types of media convergence: technical convergence, economic convergence and regulatory convergence.[22] Technical convergence refers to the merging of media. It is the process of slowly collapsing technologies due to the growing influence of digital electronics. In other words, newspaper stories now appear on the Internet alongside broadcast content delivered through video files available on the newspaper site. Economic convergence refers to operating with multiple and integrated media platforms as well as sharing content across those platforms. Regulatory convergence refers to the joining of separate industries into one single legal regulatory framework, or a more limited deregulatory action, allowing organizations to engage in economic or technological convergence.[23]

Convergence cannot be attributed to a single phenomenon or to technology alone. However, technological development amplifies changes within society, the economy, politics and culture. Technology, embedded in society, has made profound changes to the way existing processes work, changing newsroom infrastructures and newsroom dynamics in every way possible.

Changing Practices and Changing Curricula

New Tools, New Skills

The tools of the news trade are rapidly changing, and skills necessary in the media environment are constantly in transition. Recognizing these changes and the implications of such changes for journalism education and the journalism profession, some scholars have called for the introduction of innovative, integrated journalism curricula where students are taught the basic principles, practices and standards of news reporting, cutting across all media venues.[24] Some predicted that when students graduate from journalism institutions they will be working in careers that have not even fully emerged, using technology and employing skills not yet invented.[25]

Many journalism managers and instructors concur that journalists today must develop new skills. They must learn to be web savvy, to write for various media, to be skilled in producing audio reports or shooting and editing a basic video, to maintain a blog and to create an online slideshow with sound.

Web-based publishing is flourishing, with many newspaper organizations using the Internet as their primary platform for publishing. In such a multimedia, converged, online media environment, many individuals starting their journalistic careers have worked with the Internet in a variety of capacities. An annual survey of journalism and mass communication graduates found that of those who had jobs in the communications field, about 56 percent said they were writing and editing for the Web.[26] Eighty-two percent reported they spent some time each week using the Web for research. Thirty-eight percent used the Web for promotion; about 32 percent reported managing web operations and another 31 percent said they produced photos or graphics for the Web. About 28 percent reported spending some time each week to create and use blogs, and about 25 percent reported creating web advertising.[27]

However, another study reports that journalism students reported not feeling prepared with technology-related skills though they responded that they felt prepared utilizing listening, writing and oral communication skills at their jobs after graduation.[28]

Journalism educators have made efforts to respond to such expectations in the industry and the lack of preparation in the classrooms by integrating online and convergence courses into their curricula. A study found that seven in ten programs included at least one course designed to teach online or Web-based journalism skills. In addition, three-quarters of journalism and mass communication institutions reported including instruction in Web layout and design, writing for the Web, using the Web in reporting and using still photographs on the Web.[29]

Journalists must not only learn and understand traditional core values and principles, but they must also be equipped with new media skills to tell more compelling stories. The level of expectation is higher, and the skills set is more specialized. This requires an even deeper commitment and passion for the profession. Journalists must develop a good grasp of the pulse of society and the trends that are moving the world along. At the same time, they are expected to use solid news judgment in telling stories creatively.

Traditional Principles and Values

The core journalism skills of good writing and editing, fact checking for accuracy and fair and balanced coverage remain constants. While the form in which news is delivered and received is in flux, the content being communicated has not changed. Good writing and reporting are essential skills for every journalist. Quality journalism and credibility are still key. A recent study found that newspaper editors still value basic journalism skills as most important when hiring new staff members.[30] Efficient writing and interviewing skills, striving for objectivity, developing sources and writing effective leads topped the list of skills or experiences editors believed journalism educators should concentrate on when preparing journalism students. Computer-assisted and online reporting skills plus the ability to write for online also rose in importance from their ranking in a 1990 study, although they lagged behind the traditional skills in terms of importance.[31]

There is considerable support for these findings. One reporter found both editors and news professionals sought good writing, multimedia production, critical thinking, new technology, computer-assisted reporting and visual production from new hires.[32] Another study reported the five most important skills according to editors were writing/reporting, news judgment, Internet research, knowledge of media law/ethics and a broad liberal arts education.[33]

But researchers found the size of the news organization matters in desired skills of new staff. For example, computer-assisted reporting skills, online reporting skills and online journalism interests were considered more important for larger news organizations.[34]

Some scholars urge caution when deciding to integrate new technologies into the journalism curriculum. Mark Deuze, professor at Indiana University's Department of Telecommunications, said the process of convergence is a challenge between existing and new frameworks and between existing and new tools and practices within the news industry.[35] He said reporters and editors constantly undergo negotiation and evaluation of various influences on daily decision-making and adoption of technologies.[36]

Deuze made the following observations for schools, colleges, programs and courses in multimedia journalism:

1. Think twice about technologies and techniques as the foundational principles for the converged curricula;
2. Focus explicitly on understanding the logic of multimedia;
3. Allow for convergence to be challenged by students, educators, industry partners and other stakeholders within the school, program or course;
4. Think critically about all aspects of teaching and thinking multimedia;
5. Focus more on the quality of interaction between journalists, educators, and journalism students from (formerly) distinct sequences, and attempt to view each other as colleagues.[37]

The skills necessary to practice journalism are rapidly changing along with technological innovations. Educational institutions should take note of such changing media practices as journalism schools help equip the next generation of reporters and editors to present, deliver and share news.

In *Convergent Journalism*, Quinn referred to the Mr. Gadget-type journalists who act as the one-person band and examine and distribute possible stories through cell phones.[38] New tools require new skills but also bring about new and interesting ways to share stories. Quinn believes it is critical for news organizations to move toward a converged model because journalists who have been trained with a multimedia mindset are equipped with better storytelling tools.[39] In essence, new tools help journalists do what they have been doing for centuries: tell stories but in more compelling ways.

Quinn also frequently referred to Newsplex at the University of South Carolina and its efforts to define the future of journalism and encourage news organizations around the world to understand and implement convergence in their newsrooms. Newsplex offers various training opportunities for journalists, helping them understand the changing media market and news consumers. The focus is on changing mindsets rather than on solely training for skills, so that journalists and educators can understand the strengths and weaknesses of each medium and the possibilities of convergence.[40]

Obstacles, Challenges

Many scholars have pointed out that in fact, the most critical obstacle to media convergence is the individualistic nature of journalists and the nature of journalism culture itself.[41] Learning to cooperate and collaborate has not been part of the trade since news organizations have worked separately for so long. The profession is driven by separate media, separate specialties, such as beats, and separation between editorial and marketing functions. Journalists need to understand what practitioners in other media do, to understand the differences and the many shared values. This needs to happen, first, within the journalism profession at the institutional level. This requires a good review of the traditional culture of news production and dissemination and efforts to appreciate each medium's strengths and weaknesses.

Deuze said newspaper journalists need to develop social and communication skills, to understand how to work as a team and to develop flexibility.[42] He argued this shift to team-based, collaborative multimedia journalism will take time, but in the long run it will produce a more meaningful trade.[43]

Another key obstacle is the new understanding and appreciation of the news audience. This requires rethinking the relationship between the news producer (the sender) and the audience (the receiver), where information is produced from a centralized source. New media technologies are changing the fundamental power that the journalism profession has enjoyed. As gatekeepers of information, journalists had the authority to tell the public what is news. However, as technology has developed and the Internet has opened the gates to the individual user, that power has crumbled. Today's media landscape is marked by increased participation from the news audience; the receivers can be senders and sources of information as well. The traditional media can no longer ignore a story if thousands are reading it on websites, or discussions of it are flooding Facebook pages or the Twitter community is spreading it like wildfire. The one-way communication between journalists/news organizations and citizens/communities and between the people and public life[44] is being replaced as newer, interactive digital media allow the news audience to participate in news production in various ways. Jan Schaffer, director of J-Lab, the Institute for Interactive Journalism, called this the convergence of content creators in contrast to the convergence of delivery platforms. And she sees the former having much more significance.[45]

Many have noted that newer information communication technologies have the potential to make news more intimate for the audience. In the interactive digital landscape of news, the audiences may have a newfound role as participants, as information providers contributing to storytelling. Stuart Allen's book *Online News: Journalism and the Internet* provides detailed analyses and observations of how ordinary individuals and communities of news audiences participate in news production.[46] Contributions from news audiences come in the form of fresh perspectives through blogs, online submissions and cell phone images. Often, especially during crises, individuals already on the scene are quicker to provide eyewitness reports and visuals. The social media microblogging tool Twitter was used, for example, during the Mumbai bombings in India in the fall of 2008 to tell others where to get blood transfusions, locations of nearby hospitals and information about the safety of family or friends. Such citizen-produced coverage often brought about a greater sense of connection and community than that offered by the mainstream press.

All in all, journalists must be prepared to have an open, flexible mindset, to challenge previously held conceptions of journalism and the news industry and to fuse them with new media tools along with the cultural climate of participation and engagement.

Strategies from Successfully Converged Newsrooms

Observers of converged newsrooms emphasize that the key to understanding convergence and making it work is having a flexible vision and the willingness to embrace new ideas.[47] Of utmost importance is overcoming barriers—physical barriers of separation within and between newsrooms but also metaphorical barriers of newsroom culture across various media.[48] Creating an environment conducive to convergence is recommended. This can be executed through constant communication among staff members, provision of continuous training opportunities and resources for newsroom staff and development of incentives to keep journalists motivated and dedicated to doing better journalism.[49]

Several media news organizations are repeatedly cited as leaders in developing and maintaining a converged newsroom. Multiple case studies include observations from *The Lawrence Journal-World* in Kansas; *Tampa Tribune* and *Tampa Bay Online*; The Tribune Company in Chicago; *The New York Times*; *The Washington Post*; and *The Los Angeles Times*. Major efforts are under way around the world, such as the BBC in England and the *Maeil Business Newspaper* in South Korea. While convergence is approached in different ways from company to company and culture to culture based on ownership, audience size, resources and skills, similarities can be found in converged newsrooms that succeed.[50]

- Physical proximity: Both physical and metaphorical barriers hinder the convergence process. To overcome those barriers, newsrooms brought staff together into one building for conversation and to observe more easily what other workers do. The goal was to enhance how they learned from each other. They were no longer the competition but colleagues invested in a joint mission.[51]

- Central command desk: Many newsroom personnel voiced the necessity for a central station where editors from different media sat together; it symbolized synergy and collaboration and conveyed the message that collaboration was key to success. These command desks were often stationed at the center of the newsroom with multimedia work desks playing a coordinating role. Multimedia editors act as the liaison among different media platforms.[52]

- Resource sharing: Working together means sharing resources in terms of people, equipment and ideas.[53] While competition among media outlets is familiar territory, in the new model of convergence, resource sharing was key to success in many news organizations.

- Training: Staff and management training is fundamental in an ever-changing newsroom. In the successfully converged newsroom, all members often had specialized responsibilities, but they were also trained to develop basic understandings of the goals, needs and demands of other media and to put the audience before themselves.[54] In addition, incentive policies kept employees' morale high and also offered support for efforts made to meet new expectations.[55]

- Communication: Staff should talk horizontally among themselves and vertically with management. Clear communication across and inside departments was necessary and may have alleviated frustration. Formal communication, such as scheduled meetings, was helpful in coordinating as a team.[56]

- Inclusion: Representatives from all media platforms should be invited to budget meetings. All staff should participate in conversations to better understand what different media platforms can offer. Technical staff also should be included in meetings.

- Leadership: Common leadership is key to a successfully converged newsroom. Convergence and the changing social expectations of news can be approached in many ways. Managers must openly cooperate, sharing resources and staff. Cross-training is also critical for those in leadership positions to better understand the tools and practices needed to put together a solid product. Managers with a vision will learn to capitalize on the opportunities needed for future investment. Examples of leadership included hiring talented individuals, motivating staff and implementing personal supervision.[57]

- Linking with the community: The relationship between the community and the newsroom is core to the idea of convergence. This strategy was most effective in smaller news organizations, but the audience appreciated being invited into the conversation. Allowing news audiences to handle a prominent content section through the help of blogs, for example, showed the audience that the news site was also the community's site.[58]

Future Directions

Traditional news operations have functioned as gatekeepers of information and watchdogs of governments and businesses. Some believe the authority of journalists and their news delivery processes have created a rift between the very audiences they serve, and a long tradition of dissatisfaction with the news industry's practices exists.[59] However, the roles of journalists are in transition. The tools of the trade are constantly being updated, and opportunities for audiences to become more involved as information-seekers and content-contributors are increasing.

The news culture has shifted dramatically, and news organizations must recognize the new culture of participation and use technology wisely. Journalists must reflect on the core values of journalism and reevaluate their roles in the online climate as such interpretations will shape the realities of journalism.

On the surface, convergence appears to be focused on the development and integration of technology. However, as seen throughout this chapter, new tools and skills must be embedded in traditional values and principles. The heart of convergence ultimately leads back to the audience and how best to communicate meaningful stories to them. Janet Kolodzy of Emerson College wrote, "If convergence is a strategy for traditional media to get back to its roots of serving news audiences, then participatory or citizen media is a convergence strategy that news audiences are using to get journalism back to its roots."[60]

Developing and mastering new skills is increasingly valuable as journalists strive to enhance storytelling and to help audiences better understand civic society and function as informed citizens. The craft of storytelling has also evolved into a collaborative activity with the news audience. Kolodzy called this kind of participatory journalism "convergence plus."[61] New tools allow audiences to submit their accounts textually or visually to news sites. A recent study shows that customization features, such as content submissions, letters to the editor and e-mail byline links lead to satisfactory perceptions of newspaper sites.[62]

The key changes happening with the news industry are deeper than skill sets and point to significant foundational shifts in journalism culture. This is an uncomfortable time for some news people, but also an exciting time as the journalism profession is moving toward a model of audience connectivity. Along with opportunities for increased audience agency and participation come responsibilities, and news audiences have a bigger role now—expressing views, reading alternative perspectives and also participating in deliberative democracy—as engaged citizens in society.

Notes

* Deborah S. Chung is an assistant professor in the School of Journalism and Telecommunications at the University of Kentucky. She teaches publications production, media diversity and interactivity. Her doctorate is from Indiana University.

1. Stephen Quinn, *Convergent Journalism: The Fundamentals of Multimedia Reporting* (New York: Peter Lang, 2005).
2. Ibid., 5
3. Janet Kolodzy, *Convergence Journalism: Writing and Reporting Across the News Media* (Lanham, Md.: Rowman & Littlefield Publishers, Inc., 2006), 4.
4. Quinn, *supra* note 1, at 18.
5. Mark Deuze, "What Is Multimedia Journalism?" *Journalism Studies* (2004, Volume 5: 2), 139–152.
6. Jane B. Singer, "Strange Bedfellows? The Diffusion of Convergence in Four News Organizations," *Journalism Studies* (2004, Volume 5:1), 3–18.
7. Ibid.
8. Roy Mathew, "Technology Advances in Journalism." Paper presented at the National Seminar on Emerging Trends in Science and Technology, University of Kerala, Thiruvananthapuram, India, September, 25, 1998. Available at http://cyberjournalist.org.in/advance.html (accessed November 22, 2009).
9. Project for Excellence in Journalism, "The State of the News Media 2005: An Annual Report on American Journalism," *Journalism.org*, available at http://www.stateofthemedia.org/2005/index.asp (accessed November 22, 2009).
10. Katherine Fulton, "A Tour of Our Uncertain Future," *Columbia Journalism Review*, (March/April, 1996 Volume 34: 6), 19–26.
11. Broadband Access Alters Lifestyles, Yahoo! Media Relations, available at http://docs.yahoo.com/docs/pr/release1262.html (accessed November 22, 2009).
12. John B. Horrigan, "Home Broadband Adoption 2009: Broadband Adoption Increases, but Monthly Prices Do Too," The Pew Internet & American Life Project, posted on June 2009, available at http://pewresearch.org/pubs/1254/home-broadband-adoption-2009 (accessed November 22, 2009).
13. Veronis Suhler Stevenson, New York, NY, "Media Usage and Consumer Spending," Communications Industry Forecast, annual, available at http://www.census.gov/compendia/statab/2010/tables/10s1094.xls.
14. Abbey Klaassen, "The Web Is Flat: Why Time Spent Online Is Leveling Off," *Advertising Age*, posted on July 2009, available at *http://adage.com/digital/article?article_id=138159*.
15. Howard I. Finberg, "Our Complex Media Day," Poynter Online, available at http://www.poynter.org/content/content_view.asp?id=89510 (accessed November 22, 2009).

16. Liz Gannes, "Time Spent Watching Video Jumps 40% in One Year, NewTeeVee.com, posted on January 5, 2009, available at http://newteevee.com/2009/01/05/time-spent-watching-video-jumps-40-in-one-year/ (accessed November 22, 2009).
17. Ibid.
18. "Seventy Percent of Media Consumers Use Multiple Forms of Media at the Same Time," American Press Institute, posted on March 24, 2004, available at http://www.americanpressinstitute.org/pages/apinews/api_news_releases/seventy_percent_of_media_consu/ (accessed November 22, 2009).
19. Ibid.
20. Finberg, *supra* note 15.
21. Future Exploration Network. Future of Media Report, July 2008, available at http://www.rossdawsonblog.com/Future_of_Media_Report2008.pdf (accessed November 22, 2009).
22. Michel Dupagne and Bruce Garrison, "The Meaning and Influence of Convergence: A Qualitative Case Study of Newsroom Work at the Tampa News Center," *Journalism Studies*, (2006, Volume 7: 2), 237–255.
23. Ibid.
24. Stephen Quinn, "Media Convergence: Implications for Journalism Education," *Australian Studies in Journalism* (2001–2002, Volume 10–11), 85–105.
25. Ibid.
26. Lee B. Becker, Tudor Vlad, Megan Vogel, Stephanie Hanisak and Donna Wilcox, "Annual Survey of Journalism and Mass Communication Graduates," (2007), available at http://www.grady.uga.edu/annualsurveys/Graduate_Survey/Graduate_2007/Grdrpt2007_merged_June2009_Colorv2.pdf (accessed November 22, 2009).
27. Ibid.
28. Jennifer Wood Adams, Brigitta R. Brunner and Margaret Fitch-Hauser, "A Major Decision: Students' Perceptions of Their Print Journalism Education and Career Preparation," *Studies in Media & Information Literacy Education*, (2008, Volume 8:1), 1–11.
29. Lee. B. Becker, Tudor Vlad and Joel D. McLean, "Enrollments Level Off; Online Instruction Now Routine," *Journalism & Mass Communication Educator* (2007, Volume 62:3), 263–288.
30. Tamyra Pierce and Tommy Miller, "Basic Journalism Skills Remain Important in Hiring," *Newspaper Research Journal*, (Fall 2007, Volume 28), 51–61.
31. Ibid.
32. Edgar Huang, Karen Dvison, Stephanie Shreve, Twila Davis, Elizabeth Bettendorf and Anita Nair, "Bridging Newsrooms and Classrooms: Preparing the Next Generation of Journalists for Converged Media," *Journalism & Communication Monographs*, (2006, Volume 8: 3), 221–262.
33. C. Kraeplin and C. A. Criado, "Building a Case for Convergence Journalism Curriculum," *Journalism & Mass Communication Educator* (2005, Volume 60: 1), 47–56.
34. Pierce and Miller, *supra* note 30.
35. Deuze, *supra* note 5.
36. Ibid., 148.
37. Ibid., 149.
38. Quinn, *supra* note 1.
39. Ibid.
40. Ibid.
41. Singer, *supra* note 6; Deuze, *supra* note 5.

42. Mark Deuze, "Global Journalism Education," in A. S. de Beer and J. C. Merrill eds., *Global Journalism: Survey of International CommunicationTopical Issues and Media Systems* (New York: Longman, 2003, 4th ed). 145–158.

43. Mark Deuze, Axel Bruns and Christoph Neuberger, "Preparing for an Age of Participatory News," *Journalism Practice* (2007, Volume 1: 3): 322–338.

44. Joyce Y. M. Nip, "Exploring the Second Phase of Public Journalism," *Journalism Studies* (2006, Volume 7: 2), 212–236.

45. Kolodzy, *supra* note 3.

46. Stuart Allan, *Online News: Journalism and the Internet* (Berkshire, UK: Open University Press, 2006).

47. Quinn, *supra* note 1; Singer, *supra* note 6; Kolodzy, *supra* note 3; Deuze, *supra* note 5; Maria Ines Miro-Quesada, "Online Technology, Convergence and Organizational Transformation Process in the LJWorld.com: A Case Study," MA thesis, University of Missouri–Columbia, August 2007.

48. Quinn, *supra* note 1.

49. Ibid.

50. Ibid.

51. Ibid.; Dupagne and Garrison, *supra* note 22.

52. Quinn, *supra* note 1; Miro-Quesada, *supra* note 47.

53. Dupagne and Garrison, *supra* note 22.

54. Quinn, *supra* note 1.

55. Miro-Quesada, *supra* note 47.

56. Ibid.; Dupagne and Garrison, *supra* note 22.

57. Miro-Quesada, *supra* note 47; Quinn, *supra* note 1.

58. Quinn, *supra* note 1.

59. Jurgen Habermas, *The Structural Transformation of the Public Sphere: An Inquiry into a Category of Bourgeois Society* (Cambridge, Mass.: The MIT Press, 1962); Tanjev Schultz, "Interactive Options in Online Journalism: A Content Analysis of 100 U.S. Newspapers," *Journal of Computer-Mediated Communication* (1999, Volume 5:1), available at *http://jcmc.indiana.edu/vol5/issue1/schultz.html.* (accessed March 2007).

60. Kolodzy, *supra* note 3, at 217.

61. Ibid.

62. Deborah S. Chung and Seungahn Nah, "The Effects of Interactive News Presentation on Perceived User Satisfaction of Online Community Newspapers," *Journal of Computer-Mediated Communication* (2009, Volume 14: 4), 855–874.

11

The Future (Because There Will Be One)

Angry Iranians took to the streets in June 2009, protesting because they believed the election for their country's president had been rigged. Some were clubbed and shot. Neda Agha-Soltan, twenty-six, was one. Her death likely would have gone unnoticed except that another person—not a reporter, because the government had barred professional journalists—captured her last moments on a cellphone camera and posted the video to the Internet.

Writing about Neda's death later, Pulitzer Prize-winning columnist Leonard Pitts mused about the power of social media as a reporting tool: "This moment recognized that each of us has become a medium unto ourself, that each of us can now reach the rest of us. The death of Neda represents a new promise: Henceforth, you are not alone. We all stand witness, one for another."[1]

Pitts' analysis is true. Yet, if technology allows anybody to "stand witness," or be a reporter, what does that mean for journalism in the future?

A massive technological and business upheaval is changing the profession. Yet we believe that while the changes may be profound, journalism's core principles will endure. As newspapers closed and journalists were laid off, the first decade of the twenty-first century became a terrifying time for many in the newspaper industry. But it also was an exciting time. Digital technology gave reporters new tools to tell stories. Interactive programs enabled readers to discuss news stories with the reporters and with each other, offer news tips and ideas to shape the news, and even post their own reports. News could travel the world in an instant, a staggering advancement from the days when news traveled to America at the speed of a ship bobbing across the Atlantic Ocean from Europe.

As a result of these transformations, newspapers inevitably will also change. Newspapers of the future will be smaller—with fewer pages and employees—than they are now, except perhaps for a few national papers, such as *The New York Times, Wall Street Journal* and *USA Today*. Some big-city newspapers will disappear. Smaller newspapers will focus on local news, even neighborhood news. Many newspapers probably will not print an issue every day, and they will post most of their breaking news online. They will charge you to read at least some of the news they post on the Internet because it takes money to produce news, in the same way it takes money to produce shoes and food. Using digital technology, more reporters will probably become freelancers, not employees of a formal news organization. Newspaper companies will still exist and will still make money, but they will not make nearly the amount they once did. They will respect readers more, asking people for their comments and corrections and taking their tips for news stories to pursue. Some of the newspapers that survive in paper form will probably remain mass media; some will focus on a smaller geographic area; many of the online ones will probably serve niche markets and smaller communities.

In a nutshell, that is how the authors of this book view the future of newspapers at this date in history. As some newspapers were working through bankruptcy protection while others were closing, as readership declined, as ad sales tanked and as journalists lost their jobs in droves, the doomsayers have been strutting around with their handwritten picket signs: The end is near. Some even have added "hooray" to their gloom-and-doom predictions. But we believe their glee is premature. As Robert Niles of the *Online Journalism Review* told the participants at a Knight Digital Media Center News Entrepreneur Boot Camp.

> When the Internet brought unprecedented competition into the news business, and Chicken Little's sky really did fall, the industry amplified its toxic narrative: "No one can make money online." "Journalism is doomed!" But it isn't. All that is doomed is the reactionary management philosophy of monopolists who could not adapt to a world where people, not papers, controlled the narratives of their lives. Good riddance, I say. Journalism is not doomed; people can make money publishing online. All that needs to change to make that happen is journalists' toxic attitudes toward themselves and the value of their work.[2]

We share Niles' view. Still, it might be easier to predict the winner of the Kentucky Derby four years before those graceful thoroughbreds are even born than to understand what newspapers will look like once the seismic upheavals in technology, democracy and economics end…assuming they will.

We have one final prediction, perhaps the most important one: While the "paper" may disappear from many newspapers in the future, journalism itself won't.

What is Journalism?

The Internet has enabled everybody to be a publisher, but not everyone is a journalist. As journalists, the authors of this book believe that journalism is essential for a democratic society to function. Without access to the news of the day, citizens cannot properly decide how to choose their leaders. To be sure, sports news, one of the main topics of today's journalism, is not essential for anyone's life. And the country will not crumble if suddenly we are not told whom the most recent American Idol is dating. Some journalism will remain merely light entertainment, and some of it will continue to more closely resemble gossip than news.

But other journalism will carry on as serious coverage of important issues that affect readers' lives and their livelihoods. In addition to the investigative journalism that reveals how people abuse power, even mundane daily journalism provides a crucial service to readers. By attending meetings of their local city councils, listening to many hours of debate, following up with questions and fact checking, and then summarizing what happened in stories for citizens who did not attend, journalists enable people to understand how authorities are wielding the power of their offices. By reporting on trends in crime, journalists allow citizens to not only protect themselves, but also to monitor how the police serve them. By covering stories of local business activity, journalists not only inform consumers of opportunities to spend money, but they also give residents the information they need to protest if they disagree with a business transaction that will affect the community. All of these are examples of journalism's traditional watchdog role, which we believe will persevere—and indeed must persevere. Because corruption exists even under the watchful eye of journalists, it is not possible to imagine how dishonesty would multiply without such monitors reporting to the public.

Journalism does not work like a bulletin board, where anybody can post items he finds interesting. Journalism does not work like public relations; its stories should not promote a cause or an advertiser. Journalism is neither reporting everything that a powerful person says, like a stenographer, nor is it picking and choosing facts to support a predetermined point of view. American newspaper journalists, by and large, are trained to follow a code of ethical behavior summarized by four major principles:

- Seek truth and report it.
- Minimize harm.
- Act independently.
- Be accountable.[3]

Those principles are idealistic, as all worthy goals should be. They do have a practical effect: They motivate good journalists to create fine news stories. If journalists do not keep them in mind, journalism will lose its value. As the former president of the American Society of Newspaper Editors, Edward Seaton, put it in 1999, "Without ethics there is no quality. Without quality there is no credibility. Without credibility there is no future."[4]

Interlocking Coverage

Newspapers are in the influence business, Philip Meyer, professor emeritus of the University of North Carolina at Chapel Hill, has often said, citing the ideas of Hal Jurgensmeyer, who worked with Meyer at the Knight Ridder newspaper chain. Influence comes in two parts: the commercial influence on people's purchasing decisions, which is for sale in the form of advertisements; and societal influence, which affects what people think about and do in the public sphere—and which is not for sale.[5] This type of influence is why many journalists *become* journalists; they hope to make a difference in their community by shining the newspaper's light on injustices and abuse, and then reporting on efforts to right the wrongs. When the tiny *Point Reyes Light* in California exposed the Synanon drug treatment program for its beatings, weapons purchases and finances, the editor expected to influence government regulators to act. But little was done.[6] This lack of influence frustrated and depressed the paper's editor, who considered dropping the story before the paper won the Pulitzer Prize for its reporting.[7]

The news media's influence is compounded when they build on each other's reporting. Reporters in the Knight Ridder Washington bureau wrote stories that questioned the validity of President Bush's arguments for the war in Iraq in 2003, stories that were ignored by national television stations and by most other print media in the nation's big cities. A single voice often has little range; its influence on the course of events is small. Even *The Washington Post's* coverage of Watergate might have not have had much influence on the course of Richard Nixon's presidency had not other news media elected to report it. *The New York Times'* Frank Rich explained:

> Though CBS News had little fresh reporting of its own, it repackaged *The Post's* to make it compelling TV. *The Post's* logo and headlines often served as the visuals. The piece clocked in at an unprecedented 14 minutes—two-thirds of a news program running 22 minutes without commercials—and was broadcast just days before the election. As Katharine Graham, then the paper's publisher, wrote in *Personal History*, her 1997

memoir, "CBS had taken *The Post* national," giving its Watergate reporting the credibility and mass circulation that would ultimately allow it to affect the course of history.[8]

The Internet Effect

The Internet can and will assist journalists in this kind of interlacing coverage. In one sense, the Internet added to the splintering of the mass medium of newspapers, so that newspapers' power to tell people what to think *about* will probably diminish. Newspapers' monopolies in many cities dissolved and their mass audiences splintered into niches online. Millions of websites offered information about a panoply of topics for a variety of audiences. The Internet has devastated the profits that large newspapers could make, as advertising of all sorts migrated to *www* addresses. This "demassification" process accelerated because of the Internet, but it actually had been happening since the introduction of radio in the first part of the twentieth century. It continued when improvements in printing and computer technology enabled niche publications for individuals and allowed advertisers to send slick mail advertisements directly to people's houses without needing newspapers at all, and when television and cable appeared. This happened long before most readers knew what the Internet was.[9]

However, in another sense, the Internet can help generate a regional or national topic of conversation. When news stories "go viral" on the Internet, it is because many individuals recognize them as valuable and share them with others. Thus, news stories online can reach huge audiences, more massive than the readership of any single newspaper. The story of Neda Agha-Soltan is a case in point. The story of President Clinton's affair with Monica Lewinsky is another. This power is a great strength of the Internet and could confer upon journalists—and their readers and commentators— more, not less, influence on the course of events.

The Internet's system of communication is really no different from how many good newspapers have operated for years. Writing in 1967 about smaller community newspapers in Illinois, sociologist Morris Janowitz's description of these papers as a communication system is an apt depiction of a good Internet news site as well:

> The community press, like any other form of mass communication, can be seen as an operating system. To consider the community press as a system involves linking the characteristics of the producers of the papers to their content, and the content to the impact it has on readership (and to the lack of impact on non-readers). But it means more. It requires investigation of the range of communication—direct and indirect—by which the readers contact and influence the controllers and producers of the community press. The publisher creates a communication intended for

an audience that not only reacts to the communication but which, in one form or another, itself initiates communication back to the original communicator.[10]

Substitute the word "Internet" for "community press" above, and it remains a valid depiction. However, with newspapers, the interaction between news purveyors and news readers was lost as many newspapers grew larger. They grew apart from their readers, becoming more one-way communicators, with messages sent to readers but with little opportunity for the receivers of those messages to react to and communicate back to the paper. The Internet made that feedback loop simpler.

News as a Collaborative Venture

Some newspapers have embraced a "news as a conversation" approach, creating interactive stories and inviting readers to post their own content on newspapers' websites. But we believe news is not a conversation. It is a topic of conversation, and, while others can report, it is the job, the career and the vocation of professional journalists to try to find the truth so that the conversation is rooted in a rational basis.

Consider again the story of Neda Agha-Soltan. Bill Mitchell, blogging for Poynter Online, deconstructed the story of the Iranian woman's on-camera death to reveal seven elements of "Next Step" storytelling, "some more in need of professional journalism skills and values than others." These steps were documentation, context, transmission and distribution, verification, analysis, correction and sense-making.[11] If these are the steps for covering breaking news online, which seems reasonable, we would assert that the Internet allows anyone to document an event and transmit and distribute it. But journalists, trained to seek the truth and report it, are best able to provide context, verification, analysis and correction. Reporters are also skilled at interviewing experts who can provide help with sense-making. And readers, commenting on stories and adding to them, can aid in most of these functions. Thus, online news becomes more collaboration than conversation.

Consider the horror of September 11, 2001. By their reporting through interviews with experts, journalists were able to make sense of what was happening in a matter of hours. The work of journalists that day helped Americans understand that the country was under attack but that the government was responding. Fear was rampant, but widespread panic and chaos were not. Sense-making is one of the biggest jobs facing journalists, a job that must involve the public and experts. Ordinary people have used the instantaneous texting system Twitter to report accidents that they witness. And then, professional journalists have stepped in to guide the sense-making, along with more help from witnesses and experts, online.

In fact, because of the overwhelming amount of information available online, people will need journalists as much as journalists need readers. Journalists are trained to summarize a lot of data and translate it into understandable, interesting stories. True, readers could go to multiple sites to read the transcript of a meeting and analyze budget documents, but how many have the time, the background or even the inclination?

New Media Institutions

The institution of the newspaper may well lose power in the future, but other journalism institutions will take its place. Several new models have already emerged, which we believe will persist.

ProPublica

The purpose of this site, which started operating in June 2008, is to produce investigative reporting that others then publish. One of the links on its home page even dared readers, "Steal our stories." ProPublica was launched to fill the need online for original, fact-based reporting. The non-profit organization was funded by the Sandler Foundation, which had been formed by billionaires in the financial industry.

ProPublica is not the first non-profit news agency to sponsor investigative reporting. The Center for Investigative Reporting began investigative reporting on social justice, environment and international reporting in 1977.[12] The Center for Public Integrity is a non-profit investigative news agency with a broader range of interests.[13] But ProPublica gained a lot of attention when it launched, and it has faced questions about the integrity of its reports since it took money from the fortune made by Herbert and Marion Sandler, who also had donated much to Democratic and politically liberal causes. Could ProPublica be an augury of a return to the partisan press of early America?[14] ProPublica's editors noted that they had written assurances that it would be able to produce news independently, and in mid-2009, the John S. and James L. Knight Foundation gave it a three-year grant to find a sustainable model of funding to diminish its reliance on the Sandlers' fortune.[15]

Independence is crucial if the site is to produce the type of journalism espoused on ProPublica's "About us" page:

> Our work focuses exclusively on truly important stories, stories with "moral force." We do this by producing journalism that shines a light on exploitation of the weak by the strong and on the failures of those with power to vindicate the trust placed in them....In the best traditions of American journalism in the public service, we seek to stimulate positive change. We uncover unsavory practices in order to stimulate reform. We do this in an entirely non-partisan and non-ideological manner, adhering to the strictest standards of journalistic impartiality.[16]

In July 2009, ProPublica's newsroom consisted of thirty-two professional journalists. It also offered news "assignments" to citizen journalists in its ProPublica Reporting Network. In its "Adopt a Stimulus Project," for example, it published official documents online about the money the federal government had given to states to stimulate the economy. It asked readers to choose a project and report to ProPublica about how well it was working.[17] The news stories this generated were to be published under a Creative Commons license, which allowed others to reprint them without cost. ProPublica's editor of distributed reporting, Amanda Michel, said that a core group of contributors included accountants, managers, "policy wonks" and others nationwide who participate "because they genuinely care about holding those in power accountable."[18] She noted that it was important that news organizations wishing to try this same approach have someone on its staff to oversee such collaborative systems to guide the reporting.[19] Michel had experience with such "pro-am" reporting before working at ProPublica; she had overseen a similar project for another online media company, The Huffington Post.[20]

The Huffington Post

HuffPo, as some followers called the site, started online in 2005, co-founded by former America Online executive Kenneth Lerer and Arianna Huffington, its editor-in-chief, who was a book author and former candidate for California governor. It began as a liberal site covering political news, with Huffington's posts complemented by those of celebrity commentators.[21] Its audience grew, and the company hired reporters and opened bureaus to cover local news outside of its New York base,[22] starting in Chicago and Los Angeles. By 2009 its website looked like a mainstream medium's, with tabs for politics, media, living, entertainment, "green" (ecological reporting), business, international and style surrounded by lots of advertising. Reporting on sports and books was planned.[23] Huffington has said that she wanted the site to be a community where people could come to comment and read commentary as well as news—a model that perfectly describes how many other newspapers are trying to position themselves online.

The Non-Newspaper News Site

Website owners recognize that keeping information fresh on their sites is mandatory, and some sites that had nothing to do with newspapers hired journalists to create content. An example is AOL, America Online. This company, which began as one of the earliest Internet service providers in America, by 2009 had owned seventy-five advertising-supported websites such as Engadget.com, which focuses on technology, TheBoomBox.com about hip-hop music and PoliticsDaily. Through its separate unit, MediaGlow, AOL employed about 1,500 staff and freelance reporters, many of them professional journalists who had left newspapers and magazines.[24] *The New York Times* called AOL's approach "akin to a magazine model of niche titles for fragmented audiences interested in specific subjects."[25] To us, it also seems like the old-fashioned trade press—newspapers and magazines that focus in-depth reporting on narrow interests and professions. The Internet allows expansion into as many topics as there are interests. And professional journalists provide the content.

The No-NewsPAPER Town

The number of communities without a daily newspaper may grow. But the Internet offers immense opportunities for relatively inexpensive coverage (the costs would be mostly for salaries for non-volunteers). Entrepreneurs who figure out how to raise enough money to pay the bills will create many online newsrooms of the future.

The *Seattle Post-Intelligencer* became the largest newspaper to switch entirely from paper to online in March 2009, one of several dailies to do so.[26] The online site of the *Post-Intelligencer*, SeattlePI.com, operated with a staff of twenty as opposed to the 165 that the newspaper had employed. The site focused on only a few topics, including the aerospace industry, transportation and crime. After a few months, it appeared to be holding onto its initial readership with the help of about 200 unpaid bloggers. And several former *Post-Intelligencer* reporters had started their own online sites, "expanding Seattle's already-vibrant range of alternative news choices and turning the city into something of an online news laboratory."[27] Meanwhile, the competing newspaper, *The Seattle Times*, absorbed readers of its competitor and began again to make a profit by July 2009.[28]

After the 150-year-old *Rocky Mountain News* closed in Denver in February 2009, thirty of its journalists garnered the support of entrepreneurial investors to start the online INDenverTimes.com. The site had asked people to subscribe for $5 a month for "premium content,"[29] hoping for 50,000 subscriptions by April 23, 2009, what would have been the newspaper's 150th birthday. It got about 3,000.[30] That partnership failed, and a group of fourteen journalists tried again. They started the Rocky Mountain Independent, another online-only news site. That failed too. On October 1, 2009, the site announced its revenues could not pay for the work it took to produce the content.[31] Yet, online journalism continued in the Denver region, with more than 40 sites covering news and information, including the *Rocky Mountain Independent, TheDenverDailyNews.com and DenverPost.com* (operated by the competing daily newspaper).[32]

Future Content

Steve Outing, a journalist who analyzes the effect of the Internet on news, predicted that in online newsrooms, the reporters who keep their jobs in future news organizations would be popular columnists and the stars, the ones who do the best watchdog reporting.[33] We hope so, but we doubt it. From non-scientific conversations with others and simply watching the "most read" stories on news sites, we note that quite possibly news of the weird and news about crime will remain incredibly popular, and reporters who can find it will keep their jobs. We hope that they help to build an audience for the other, more substantive journalism as well.

Paying for News

Journalism needs money to survive. Reporters and editors, historically underpaid, should not be expected to toil for free. We believe that the advertising model that sustained journalism for more than a century will continue because advertisers will still need to reach the audience that newspapers gather. But advertising will not be the mainstay that it once was. In the year 2000, advertising accounted for 82 percent of newspaper revenue, with paid circulation accounting for the rest.[34] In 2009, however, money that *The New York Times* raised from subscriptions was expected to exceed the money it took in from advertisers for the first time. Ad revenue had been twice as high as subscriptions just three years before at *The Times*.[35] This 50:50 split between ad revenues and subscription revenues marked an unambiguous shift in how the newspaper business made money.

Ryan Chittum, a former *Wall Street Journal* reporter writing in *Columbia Journalism Review*, called this shift "stunning." Yet, he added that it indicated that people would pay for news online. He questioned why newspapers would offer free content on their unprofitable products (their websites), thus giving readers an incentive to stop subscribing to their profitable products (their newspapers).[36] Other newspaper futurists argued that information on the Internet should be free, and that if a newspaper charges for news, more people will abandon the product.

But no other business can survive giving away its product, and it is ludicrous to think that journalists should be encouraged to do so. If journalism were strictly a stenographic report—for example, "Councilwoman Smith moved that City Ordinance 37–09 be amended to increase the fine for littering on Main Street to $200. That motion was seconded by Councilman Brown. Councilman Jones said he felt the fine was too steep and police never enforce it anyway. Mayor White asked if anyone else wished to comment. When she heard none, she called for a vote, and the ordinance was amended by a vote of 4–1."—then perhaps it would "belong" to everyone and everyone could draw his own conclusions. But those who believe that kind of stenography is journalism obviously do not understand what is involved in producing a newspaper story.

The move to recognize that journalism is a work product of value is under way. In May 2009, the Associated Press announced it would develop a system to track how its stories were used, who used them and who paid for them. The system would allow the 1,400 member newspapers of the AP to set permission levels for use of their stories.[37] Tom Curley, president and CEO of the AP, told *The Wall Street Journal* that "we are prepared to demand appropriate compensation."[38] Yet journalists and technology buffs were not sure how the AP's new plans would work, since it already had been working with another company that could locate copies of its stories online and request payment. Some observers saw the new plan as signaling that the AP was willing to work with people who used its content if they gave the AP credit for producing it.[39]

Still, newspapers, in paper and online, will have to find new ways of paying for journalism. News websites of the future likely will use multiple models to pay their bills, both online and in print. Here are some ideas that we believe have merit:

Pay per View

In 2005 *The New York Times* started charging readers $7.95 a month for content from its most popular columnists and other popular content. Then, two years later, *The Times* made this content free again. *Times* officials said the experiment was successful, earning $10 million in revenue. But the pay wall stopped readers from coming to *The Times'* news site from search engines, and making it free again presumably helped drive readers searching for news to *The Times* once again, increasing its growth and attracting advertising.[40]

A few years later, Alan Mutter, a veteran newspaper editor and Silicon Valley CEO, and Ridgely Evers, whom Mutter called "a technology wizard and fellow serial CEO in Silicon Valley," developed the idea for an industry-owned ViewPass system.[41] Mutter explained the concept in his "Reflections of a Newsosaur" blog and presented it to industry leaders in mid-2009. Readers would register once for a ViewPass, which they would need to access content from all participating publishers. ViewPass would work behind the scenes, controlling access to content and authorizing readers' payments for individual articles, subscriptions or "bundles of content." If readers rebelled against a pay wall, they could "pay" for viewing content by giving more of their personal information.[42] This system would track what people viewed and keep demographic information about them for marketing purposes. That is its real value to newspapers "because the data would enable publishers to sell their advertising inventory at premium rates to advertisers seeking to target their messages to the most likely consumers," Mutter noted. Consumers' privacy would be protected, and no personally identifying information would be given to advertisers. Publishers who paid for its development would get preferred shares in the profits of the ViewPass system.[43]

James Fallows suggested a similar model in *The Atlantic*, calling it the "E-Z pass model"—named after the card that some big cities' drivers purchase so they do not have to stop to pay every time they pass a tollbooth. The Internet phone company Skype offers a similar program, where people purchase a certain amount of minutes in advance to make calls to landlines. Such a pre-payment system surmounts one difficulty with asking people to pay for content: While some people would be willing to pay for individual stories, Fallows argued, asking readers to decide to pay every single time they clicked a link would likely drive them away.[44]

Still other variants of this idea include Kachingle, which started in 2009 as a company that asked online visitors to pay at least $5 a month. If they wished, donors' names would appear on whatever member news site or blog they supported. The news still would be available free to others, but in this model, a donation acts as a digital vote of confidence in the site and a proclamation about what donors value. Kachingle would get $1 of every $5 donated, and publishers would get a percentage of the rest, depending upon how often readers visited their sites and clicked on a Kachingle medallion.[45] Other "micro-patronage" models included Payyattention, BeneVote, Contenture, in-a-moon and EmanciPay.[46] Their business models varied. They might ask readers to click a link to deposit money, and the total accumulated would help rank the site for others. They might offer patrons the ability to disable ads or view "premium" content. Or they might not ask for money but would instead show an advertisement when a reader clicked to denote his approval of a news story. Some of these payment systems were meant to help all businesses, not just newspapers, make money online. One system may rise to the top, or multiple systems might survive, but we believe newspapers will have to ask people for money to support journalism online in the future.

Some newspapers required online subscriptions before they allowed people to read their reporting, notably the *Wall Street Journal*. In August 2009, Rupert Murdoch, whose News Corp. owned the *Journal*, the cable television network Fox News and many other media companies worldwide, announced that the company would require readers to pay before they could visit any of its newspaper or television sites. How the payment system would work was unclear, and even the *Journal's* content was accessible if readers arrived at the site by clicking a link to a story found by a search engine. Nonetheless, Murdoch predicted of his ideas about charging for news, "If we're successful, we'll be followed by all media."[47]

As long as most news on the Web is free, it is unlikely that asking people to pay will generate much money for the industry. Yet public radio operates on a similar system, allowing people who do not donate to listen free.

Member-Supported News

National Public Radio pays for its high quality news with a mixture of membership fees from radio stations, sponsorships, sales of merchandise and government funding. The fund-raising appeals on the radio annoy many listeners, but thirty-one percent of the funding for NPR member stations came from listeners who valued the organization's professional news reports so much that they wrote checks to support it. Only eleven percent came from the Corporation for Public Broadcasting, which was federally funded with tax dollars, and another five percent came from state and local government funds. The remainder came from many other sources.[48] Raising money from multiple sources frees any news organization from being beholden to any one. Thus, independence is preserved.

The NPR model is mentioned in a book about newspapers because we believe the distinctions between different forms of news media have blurred and will eventually disappear. In fact, NPR revamped and relaunched its website in July 2009 to emphasize that it is no longer just a news radio organization but a multimedia news site, according to Vivian Schiller, NPR's CEO. The website, she told *Newsweek*, was the linchpin of "a strategy to transform NPR into the No. 1 destination for free news on and beyond the radio."[49] Not radio news, just news. Schiller noted the "scary" decline in local reporting in many communities by other media, saying that local NPR affiliates could help fill that void with new tools, resources, knowledge and infrastructure.[50] Critics of the NPR system have said that it should require its member stations to produce more local news coverage as newspapers cut back.

Foundations also support the news. Non-profit news sites, such as *MinnPost* and *Voice of San Diego*, had accepted foundation funds as well as individual memberships to produce news reports for their communities.[51] In fact, J-Lab, the institute for interactive journalism, published a database of organizations that donated more than $128 million to fund 127 news and information projects around the country.[52] Much as this model has worked for the non-profit NPR, and while some foundations have funded reporting projects at profit-making newspapers, we do not believe such foundation support should be diverted to for-profit news organizations at all.

Freelance Fund-Raising

In 2009 *The New York Times* told freelancer Lindsey Hoshaw that it might be interested in publishing her story about a huge mass of garbage floating in mid-ocean, but it could not fund a $10,000 trip on a research ship.[53] So the freelancer went to the website Spot.Us to ask donors for money. The site helps journalists finance their projects by collecting tax-deductible donations from multiple individuals. It also limits the amount of money any one individual may give, except for news organizations. If a news organization donates more than half the cost, it would get first publication rights to the story. Otherwise, the stories would be available for anyone to publish through a Creative Commons copyright license.[54] This model allows individuals to directly "commission" news about topics of interest.

Government Intervention

Newspaper publishers asked a Senate Commerce Committee in May 2009 to give newspapers a limited exemption from antitrust laws. The newspaper industry told legislators that publishers needed to collaborate to come up with innovative ideas to save the industry because if one newspaper site tried to, for example, block access to its information until readers paid, readers could easily go to another newspaper site for that information.[55] Recognizing that "we need a strong news industry for our democracy to thrive," the chairman of the Federal Trade Commission announced that he would convene a series of meetings later in the year titled, "Can News Media Survive the Internet Age? Competition, Consumer Protection, and First Amendment Perspectives." The plan was to invite stakeholders to discuss the possibility of an exemption, as well as consumer protection and First Amendment protection, in new business models for newspapers.[56]

While the newspaper industry is undeniably suffering, we believe government intervention is unnecessary. Discussing alternatives may be helpful, but such discussions were actively taking place countrywide without the government's help. What's more, newspapers already had had an exemption from the antitrust laws through the Newspaper Preservation Act of 1970, which the industry had argued was needed to preserve newspapers from dying. It had no such effect. Nor would anti-competitive laws help the industry in the future. Innovation must take place in the existing marketplace to make sure new business models can survive in that marketplace.

The New Journalist

We were fortunate to have worked in newspapers at a time when specialization was possible: Reporters investigated and wrote stories. Photographers took pictures. Editors laid out pages and edited. But journalists of the future will need multiple skills. They will need to feed the online market with words, sound, pictures, both still and moving, and interaction. Journalists will need to know some computer programming. They will belong to multiple social networks and will express opinion as well as write dispassionate reports (we do hope that the ethic of reporting the truth, without bias, persists). Journalists will still have long hours and low pay. Fewer people will be able to gain competence in all these skills, and they will be competing for fewer jobs than existed at the turn of the twenty-first century.

We believe Steve Outing's prediction that reporters will become online personalities, where the audience gets to know them and interact with them. This new news system means reporters will build micro-communities around topics and themselves,[57] extending the television news model, where reporters became as much a celebrity as their sources were.

We also believe that professional journalists do something different from what non-professionals online do. Professional journalists take seriously their obligation to find facts and tell the truth. They attempt to meet high standards of readability and story-telling. Journalists for years have resisted any form of licensing or examinations to prove competence, arguing that it trampled their First Amendment rights, and that any attempt to enforce standards would be unworkable. Instead, newspaper companies enforced their own standards. Janet Cooke and Jayson Blair are only two of a long list of "truth inventors" who were fired for misusing their opportunity to report at one of the nation's large newspapers.

As journalism decentralizes from newspaper chain ownership to websites, credibility will become an even more critical issue. Seventy years after Orson Welles deceived at least some of the radio audience with his description of an alien invasion on his War of the Worlds broadcast, the opportunity to prosper through dishonesty has risen anew with the Internet. This places responsibility on readers, who also will need to be savvy about the source and credibility of what they are reading. Their contributions to collaborative journalism will help keep it accurate.

Journalism organizations—the Society of Professional Journalists, the Radio Television Digital News Association,[58] the Associated Press Managing Editors, the National Press Photographers Association—all have codes of ethics. While they are voluntary, they nonetheless serve as measuring sticks for the conduct of those who call themselves journalists. Many journalists have steadfastly opposed institutions such as news councils that render opinions on the performance of journalists. One reason for their opposition is that members of a council may not fully understand journalism. That is at least in part because the most important story journalists have failed to tell clearly over the years is how and why journalists do what they do.

Philip Meyer has argued that "when nonprofessional behavior comes to public attention, somebody needs to speak for the profession and say, in effect, 'This is outside the bounds of our normal and approved behavior; this person's actions do not define us.'" That would not, however, guarantee the behavior would stop. For example, while the New York Times made very public its findings on its investigation into the plagiarism and ethical violations of Jayson Blair, the episode did not serve as a warning to every journalist because other cases of plagiarism have been reported. Episodes like this show that the old Latin adage, caveat emptor– let the buyer beware – has an Internet and news application as well. Media consumers must critically examine what they read and hear.

Meyer also proposed certifying journalists who achieve competence, another controversial idea in the profession, which resists efforts by anyone telling it anything, citing freedom of the press. Because the authors both teach journalism at universities, we believe that a journalism degree could serve as one such certificate. Lacking the degree or certificate would not prevent someone from working in the profession, but having it would mean they had been taught at least a standard level of competence. On the whole, though, Meyer's idea is probably unworkable. Perhaps the bottom line is that this new journalism will require a greater commitment from readers to examine carefully what and whom they believe. It will also mandate that people who call themselves journalists practice the profession honestly and remember their duty to inform citizens about important issues. They also should do what previous journalists largely did not: They should promote the profession as a fascinating and honorable career.

In the past, newspapers punished errant behavior by firing unscrupulous reporters. In the future, the power of the newspaper probably will be diminished. Some newspaper owners already have diluted the quality of their editions to the point where they appear to devalue the entire profession. Individual journalists, the reporters and editors and photographers who for years have gathered and reported the news to the best of their ability are positioned to assume that authority to monitor their own. This could go a long way toward preserving a profession that is frustrating, difficult and exhausting—and profoundly important and rewarding.

We end where we began. The future of journalism is about more than money, jobs and power. It is about the preservation of democracy.

Being a citizen of a democracy is demanding; individuals must take responsibility for their own self-governance. Citizens must inform themselves to be active members of their communities. The truth is that the people in power in government listen to citizens who are informed because they want to be re-elected. And for more than 300 years now, newspapers have been informing citizens of what the responsible and the corrupt were doing in city halls, statehouses and Washington, in business, social services and the military. That must continue, or dictators and widespread corruption are just around the corner. A free press cannot exist without a democracy, and a democracy cannot exist without a free press.

To those journalism students who read this text, we would impart what we consider the most important lesson of Journalism 101: Journalism is a calling. It is not for everyone. It is hard work, and every word you write, every picture you take, could be criticized by editors and readers. But the modern world offers few opportunities to make the difference journalists can make when they shine the light on what is really going on. To you we say, go forth and do good work. Your fellow citizens probably don't understand it, but they will be depending on you.

Notes

1. Leonard Pitts, "'Neda Moment' Shows Promise of New Media," originally published in *The Miami Herald*, republished in *The Cincinnati Enquirer*, June 24, 2009, A13.

2. Robert Niles, "Journalists Must Emerge from a Culture of Failure in Order to Survive," *Online Journalism Review*, posted on May 25, 2009, available at http http://www.ojr.org/ojr/people/robert/200905/1735/ (accessed August 2, 2009).

3. "Code of Ethics," Society of Professional Journalists, available at http://www.spj.org/ethicscode.asp (accessed July 23, 2009).

4. Blake Fleetwood, "The Broken Wall," *Washington Monthly* (September 1999), 40–45.

5. Philip Meyer, *The Vanishing Newspaper* (Columbia, Mo.: University of Missouri Press, 2004), 6–7.

6. Dave Mitchell, Cathy Mitchell and Richard Ofshe, *The Light on Synanon* (New York: Seaview Books, 1980), 173–174.

7. Ibid., 154–155.

8. Frank Rich, "And That's Not the Way It Is," *The New York Times*, published on July 25, 2009, available at http://www.nytimes.com/2009/07/26/opinion/26rich.html?_r=1&em (accessed August 21, 2009).

9. Meyer, *supra* note 5, at 8.

10. Morris Janowitz, *Community Press in an Urban Setting* (Chicago, Ill.: University of Chicago Press, 1967), 9.

11. Bill Mitchell, "The Story of Neda's Death Reveals 7 Elements of Next-Step Journalism," PoynterOnline, posted on June 24, 2009, available at http://www.poynter.org/column.asp?id=131&aid=165662 (accessed July 24, 2009).

12. "About CIR," Center for Investigative Reporting (2009), available at http://centerforinvestigativereporting.org/about (accessed August 8, 2009).

13. "About the Center for Public Integrity," Center for Public Integrity (2009), available at http://www.publicintegrity.org/about/our_organization/faq/ (accessed August 8, 2009).

14. Jack Shafer, "What Do Herbert and Marion Sandler Want?" *Slate*, posted on October 15, 2007, available at http://www.slate.com/id/2175942/ (accessed August 8, 2009).

15. Clark Hoyt, "One Newspaper, Many Checkbooks," *The New York Times*, posted on July 18, 2009, available at http://www.nytimes.com/2009/07/19/opinion/19pubed.html?_r=1 (accessed July 30, 2009).

16. "About Us," *ProPublica*, available at http://www.propublica.org/about/ (accessed July 30, 2009).

17. Amanda Michel, "Adopt a Stimulus Project," *ProPublica*, posted on May 20, 2009, available at http://www.propublica.org/feature/adopt-a-stimulus-project-520 (accessed July 30, 2009).

18. Steve Myers, "ProPublica Reporting Network Adds 1,000 Members; Starts with Stimulus," Poynter Online, posted on July 6, 2009, available at http://www.poynter.org/column.asp?id=101&aid=165980 (accessed July 23, 2009).

19. Ibid.

20. Ibid.

21. Brian Stelter, "The Huffington Post Is being Reborn as an 'Internet Newspaper,'" *The New York Times*, posted on March 31, 2008, available at http://

www.nytimes.com/2008/03/31/technology/31iht-huffington.1.11545354.html (accessed June 1, 2009).

22. Caroline McCarthy, "Huffington Post's Next Expansion: Local News, More Venture Funding," CNET, posted on June 19, 2008, available at http://news.cnet .com/8301–13577_3–9973053–36.html (accessed July 26, 2009).

23. Stelter, *supra* note 21.

24. Michael Arrington, "AOL Newsroom Now Has (Wow) 1,500 Writers," TechCrunch.com, posted on July 29, 2009, available at http:// www.techcrunch.com/2009/07/29/aol-newsroom-now-has-wow-1500-writers/ (accessed July 30, 2009).

25. Brian Stelter, "Quietly, AOL Becomes an Overseer of Niche Sites," *The New York Times*, January 12, 2009, B4.

26. Dan Richman and Andrea James, "Seattle P-I to Publish Last Edition Tuesday," posted on March 17, 2009, available at http://www.seattlepi.com/busi-ness/403793_piclosure17.html (accessed July 30, 2009).

27. Richard Perez-Pena, "Seattle Paper Is Resurgent as a Solo Act," *The New York Times*, posted on August 9, 2009, available at http://www.nytimes.com/ 2009/08/10/business/media/10seattle.html?_r=2&hp (accessed August 9, 2009).

28. Ibid.

29. Aaron Harber, "Is It Too Late to Save (Newspaper) Journalism?" INDenverTimes.com, posted on June 24, 2009, available at http://www.inden-vertimes.com/2009/06/24/is-it-too-late-to-save-newspaper-journalism/ (accessed August 8, 2009).

30. "Meet Our Staff and Contributors," INDenverTimes.com (2009), available at http://www.indenvertimes.com/meet-our-staff-and-contributors/.

31. Ed Sealover, "Rocky Mountain Independent, ex-Rocky Staffers' News Website, to Cease New Content," *Denver Business Journal*, posted on October 2, 2009, available   at http://denver.bizjournals.com/denver/stories/2009/09/28/daily78.html (accessed December 1, 2009).

32. "ABYZ News Links: Denver Colorado Newspapers and News Media Guide," ABYZ Web Links Inc., posted on August 2009, available at http:// www.abyznewslinks.com/unitecodn.htm (accessed August 7, 2009).

33. Steve Outing, "The All-Digital Newsroom of the Not-So-Distant Future," *Editor & Publisher*, posted on January 28, 2009, available at http://www.edi-torandpublisher.com/eandp/columns/stopthepresses_display.jsp?vnu_con-tent_id=1003936131 (accessed July 30, 2009).

34. Meyer, *supra* note 5, at 37.

35. Ryan Chittum, "*NYT* Now Gets as Much Money from Circulation as from Ads," *Columbia Journalism Review*, posted on July 23, 2009, available at http://www.cjr.org/the_audit/nyt_now_gets_as_much_money_fro.php (accessed July 30, 2009).

36. Ibid.

37. Joe Strupp, "AP to Create Registry to Track and Protect Online Content," *Editor & Publisher*, posted on July 23, 2009, available at http://www.editorand-publisher.com/eandp/news/article_display.jsp?vnu_content_id=1003996916 (accessed July 21, 2009).

38. Russell Adams and Shira Ovide, "AP Creates Registry to Monitor Use of Stories Online, *Wall Street Journal* online, available at http://online.wsj.com/article/ SB124839020548977423 (accessed July 31, 2009).

39. Megan Taylor, "How AP's News Registry Will (and Won't) Work," Poynter Online, posted on August 7, 2009, available at http://www.poynter.org/con-

tent/content_view.asp?id=167852 (accessed August 8, 2009).

40. Suzanne M. Kirchhoff, "The U.S. Newspaper Industry in Transition," Congressional Research Service, posted on July 8, 2009, available at http://www.fas.org/sgp/crs/misc/R40700.pdf (accessed July 31, 2009).

41. Alan D. Mutter, "What I Recommended to Publishers in Chicago," posted on June 4, 2009, available at http://newsosaur.blogspot.com/2009/06/what-i-recommended-to-publishers-in.html (accessed July 10, 2009).

42. Alan D. Mutter and Ridgely C. Evers, "Viewpass," (2009), available at http://www.niemanlab.org/pdfs/ViewPass.pdf (accessed July 25, 2009).

43. Ibid.

44. James Fallows, "An E-Z Pass Model for Web Content," *The Atlantic*, posted on June 23, 2009, available at http://ideas.theatlantic.com/2009/06/charge_for_online_news.php (accessed July 26, 2009).

45. "The Economy of Social Signals—A Source for a Viable Business Model?," SavetheNews.us (2009), available at http://savethenews.us/?p=37 (accessed July 28, 2009).

46. Ibid.

47. Kenneth Li and Andrew Edgecliffe-Johnson, "Murdoch Vows to Charge for All Online Content," *Financial Times*, posted on August 6, 2009, available at http://www.ft.com/cms/s/0/7f6edc2c-821f-11de-9c5e-00144feabdc0.html (accessed August 8, 2009).

48. "Annual Reports, Audited Financial Statements, and Form 990s," NPR, available at *http://www.npr.org/about/privatesupport.html* (accessed November 29, 2009).

49. Johnnie L. Roberts, "NPR's Digital Makeover," *Newsweek Web Exclusive*, posted on July 27, 2009, available at http://www.newsweek.com/id/208703/page/1 (accessed July 27, 2009).

50. Ibid.

51. Tom Price, "The Future of Journalism," *CQ Researcher*, posted on March 27, 2009, available at http://www.cqresearchers.com (accessed July 31, 2009).

52. "Meet the New Media Makers—and the Foundations that Make Their News Sites Possible," available at http://www.kcnn.org/toolkit/funding_database (accessed August 8, 2009).

53. Hoyt, *supra* note 15.

54. "What Is Spot.Us About?" Spot.Us (2009), available http://spot.us/pages/about (accessed July 25, 2009).

55. Kirchhoff, *supra* note 40.

56. "Extra! Extra! FTC Announces Workshop: 'Can News Media Survive the Internet Age? Competition, Consumer Protection, and First Amendment Perspectives,'" Federal Trade Commission, posted on May 19, 2009, available at http://www.ftc.gov/opa/2009/05/news2009.shtm (accessed July 31, 2009).

57. Steve Outing, "The All-Digital Newsroom of the Not-So-Distant Future," *Editor & Publisher*, posted on January 28, 2009, available at http://www.editorandpublisher.com/eandp/columns/stopthepresses_display.jsp?vnu_content_id=1003936131 (access July 28, 2009).

58. In October 2009, the Radio-Television News Directors Association changed its name to the Radio Television Digital News Association, reflecting the changing media world.

59. Meyer, *supra* note 5, at 237.

Index

Media Industries

General Editor
David Sumner

The Media Industries series offers comprehensive, classroom friendly textbooks designed to meet the needs of instructors teaching introductory media courses. Each book provides a concise, practical guide to all aspects of a major industry. These volumes are an ideal reference source for anyone contemplating a career in the media.

To order other books in this series, please contact our Customer Service Department:

(800) 770-LANG (within the U.S.)
(212) 647-7706 (outside the U.S.)
(212) 647-7707 FAX

Or order online at www.peterlang.com